THE TEACHER-STUDENT RELATIONSHIP

THE TEACHER-STUDENT RELATIONSHIP

A Translation of

*"The Explanation of the Master and Student Relationship,
How to Follow the Master, and How to
Teach and Listen to the Dharma"*

Jamgön Kongtrul Lodrö Thayé

Foreword by Lama Tharchin Rinpoche
Introduction by Gyatrul Rinpoche
Translated and Introduced by Ron Garry

Snow Lion Publications
Ithaca, New York

Snow Lion Publications
P.O. Box 6483
Ithaca, New York 14850 USA
607-273-8519

Printed in the Canada

ISBN   1-55939-096-4

Library of Congress Cataloging-in-Publication Data

Koṅ-sprul Blo-gros-mtha'-yas, 1813-1899.
  [Śes bya kun khyab. English]
  The teacher-student relationship: a translation of the explanation of the
master and student relationship, how to follow the master, and how to teach
and listen to the dharma / Jamgön Kongtrul Lodrö Thayé; foreword by Lama
Tharchin Rinpoche; introduction by Gyatrul Rinpoche; translated and intro-
duced by Ron Garry.
       p.   cm.
  Includes bibliographical references.
  ISBN 1-55939-096-4 (alk. paper)
  1. Teacher-student relationships—Religious aspects—Buddhism.
2. Spiritual life—Buddhism. 3. Buddhism—China—Tibet—Doctrines. I. Garry,
Ron, 1955-   . II. Title.
BQ7756.K6513 1997
294.3'61—dc21   98-35834
                                                              CIP

Table of Contents

Foreword

by Lama Tharchin Rinpoche

I am very pleased with this work of Yeshe Nyima (Ron Garry) because it fulfills a need of Western students for a comprehensive manual explaining all aspects of the relationship between the wisdom teacher and the student. During these degenerate times, and especially in the West, we do not even have the concept of how to develop our buddha-nature because due to our point of view we focus all of our energy and abilities upon material things. The end result of this approach is that our precious buddha-nature never gets touched, resulting in suffering, especially mental suffering, that never seems to end.

I highly recommend this book because it shows us in a clear and concise way how to create and nurture this relationship—including the necessity of having a wisdom teacher, the qualities needed by both the wisdom teacher and the student, and how we can relate properly and effectively with our wisdom teacher. The wisdom teacher and student relationship is the only method that aids us in awakening our own buddha-nature, which is the main point of all spiritual practice. Without this relationship there is no way to attain buddhahood. So for people like us who have not as yet realized buddhahood, attempting to do so without a wisdom teacher who has fully developed wisdom and a compassionate mind is entirely futile and will leave us utterly lost.

My lama has said that in ancient times all people concentrated on practicing the dharma and in conversations spoke often of the life stories of sublime beings. But now the signs of degenerating times abound.

People no longer speak of their wisdom teacher in their conversations, but instead all they talk about is "my horse, my dog, my cat," etc. This is a clear sign that the methods for developing wisdom mind are in decline.

We are very fortunate that due to the efforts of Yeshe Nyima a detailed elucidation of the relationship between the wisdom teacher and the student is now available. This current translation of Kongtrul Rinpoche's work, along with the commentary drawn from some of the great masters of the Vajrayana tradition, is a manual on the wisdom teacher and student relationship for the dharma practitioner; and because this relationship is the foundation for all Vajrayana practice, I wish that its timely release will be of great benefit to all practitioners in the West.

Offered by the tenth lineage holder of the Kyang Lung Wona Tsang, in Repkong, eastern Tibet, who has taken the form of the ngagpa yogi, at Pema Osel Ling, Santa Cruz Mountains, California

All the siddhis of the profound secret mantra arise from following the lama, and not from anywhere else.

H.H. Dudjom Rinpoche

There is no mention in any of the sutras, tantras, or commentaries of anyone accomplishing buddhahood without following a lama. It can be seen that no one has attained the noble qualities of the levels and paths by their own creation and conjecture. Similarly, all sentient beings, including ourselves, are very good at following the wrong path.

Patrul Rinpoche

Homage to Guru Padmasambhava

བླ་མ་པདྨ་སཾ་བྷ་ཝ་ལ་ཕྱག་འཚལ་ལོ།

Lama Padmasambhava-la chag tsal lo

Introduction

by Gyatrul Rinpoche

Tibetan Buddhism has taken root in Western countries due to the contributions of Western spiritual seekers as well as their Tibetan teachers. Twenty-five to thirty years ago, the seeds were sown when many Western college graduates and others journeyed to the East, in search of life's inner meaning. Arriving in India, Nepal, China, and other bordering countries, these Western pilgrims made contact with some of the greatest teachers of the East, many of whom are no longer with us in the flesh. These spiritual quests coincided with the arrival of Tibetan refugees on Indian and Nepalese soil, so that the opportunity to spend time with masters as great as H.H. the Dalai Lama, Konjur Rinpoche, the Karmapa, Kunnu Lama, and so many others was at hand. As the Western students met with these great masters of all four lineages (Nyingma, Kagyu, Sakya, and Gelug), they posed many questions, received answers, and began to develop the three wisdoms of hearing, contemplating, and meditating.

During these important transitional years the wealth of the Buddhist canon as preserved in Tibet was reprinted in New Delhi and distributed to important libraries and institutions worldwide. In this way, the complete collected works of the *kama* (*bka'-ma*), *terma* (*gter-ma*), and other important lineages became available in university libraries around the United States. Many Western scholars had the opportunity to invite prominent Tibetan scholars and meditation masters to the West, providing the opportunity to study and learn the contents of these invaluable manuscripts. All of this was possible because of those original pioneers of the dharma and the opportunity provided by the educational systems in the West. Soon after, several important teachers came to the West to live, foremost of whom were Chogyam Trungpa and Tarthang Tulku. This paved the way for their teachers, H.H. the Karmapa and H.H. Dudjom Rinpoche, to come to America. Many great and highly realized teachers followed, including H.H. the Dalai Lama.

The students who extended invitations to these teachers did not do so out of worldly concern. Their interests, although varied, were in all cases to learn from the vast knowledge preserved within the Tibetan civilization. From 1972 until now, hundreds and thousands of volumes of literature containing the wisdom of Tibet, including Buddhism, have been translated into Western languages by these students who took the time to develop the three levels of wisdom.

In the beginning years there was very little opposition to the propagation of this culture and spiritual tradition. Yet, opposition should not be unexpected. This arises due to the karma of sentient beings. Beings observe objective appearances according to their own karmic predispositions. Take, for example, the substance "water." Water is, for the *devas, amṛita* or nectar; for hell beings, lava; for the *pretas*, pus; for animals, liquid to drink, and so forth. The substance itself does not change. The change occurs in the minds of those who perceive it. This is neither good nor bad; it is merely the karmic condition. Perhaps it is better to meet with opposition, so that our own shortcomings and faults can be easily identified. Then genuine improvement occurs through mindfulness, conscientiousness, and acting in accordance with the path of virtue.

A student who is a follower of the authentic path of truth is doing precisely that. Such a person would not find or express faults in his or her spiritual teacher or in the dharma. However, if a student's intention was impure, then the situation would be entirely different. If we trace the history of the tradition and the difficulties that occurred not only in India but especially in Tibet, it becomes very clear. For example, in Tibet the tradition of debate was popular because it allowed committed students to improve their knowledge and recognize their faults. In debate, students would be grateful to each other for the exchange of views and opinions. There was no reason to react to adversity nor was there any reason to follow it. It was simply a process of self-improvement. Likewise, with a substance as pure as gold, you can fire it, pound it down and so forth, and its quality will improve.

In dharma, because ordinary people are the practitioners, they must approach the path gradually. There will be mistakes. If an individual has merit equal to that of the great realized beings of the past, then it is a different story. Such beings have amassed vast amounts of merit from countless past lifetimes. In the case of most ordinary people, the path will go very gradually. These days the Buddhist tradition and other sciences of the Tibetan heritage are widespread. There are dharma centers virtually everywhere, and they are increasing. Yet, due to the karma of beings, there will always be ups and downs. This is not even worth paying attention to. Furthermore, this condition is not necessarily the fault of any Westerner or any spiritual teacher. It is the karma of sentient beings. If a teacher has a fault, he or she should point the finger towards himself or herself. That is fairly reasonable.

We have to bear in mind that everything which occurs is due to the karma of sentient beings. When the time arrives for the wisdom of the tradition to decline, even if every person in the world were offering his or her assistance, the tradition would still decline. On the other hand, if the time for decline has not come and the time for propagation is ripe, then even if sentient beings of the three galaxies were in opposition, the tradition would slowly increase. Consider the extent to which the Communist Chinese attempted to destroy Buddhism in Tibet. They certainly did their very best. Ironically, in the end, their opposition assisted in the propagation of Buddhism. Through their "kindness," Buddhism has spread around the world to countries where even the name of the Buddha may have been previously unknown. This is an example of the enemy becoming the companion.

Whether Buddhism is truly practiced or not is entirely up to each individual. It has been over twenty years since I came here to America. There is not a single day that has gone by when I thought that Buddhism was declining. There is not a single day that passed when I thought the students here had specific faults. I have not thought that the teachers here have any specific shortcomings either. Of course, there are many things that one sees. I already explained that this is because our minds are affected by the five delusions. Since we individuals have yet to abandon our delusions, the display of our own delusion will be what we ignorantly pursue to be true. However, I personally feel that there is great progress being made here in America. This is due to the openness of the general population as well as the government. The same holds true for many other countries worldwide where dharma is spreading rapidly.

Now, I want to specifically address the topic of the manner in which teachers and students rely upon one another. According to the four great lineages of Tibetan Buddhism, from the beginning of all lineages down to the present time, countless lineage-holding teachers and their students have relied on the many teachings and texts that deal with the subject commonly referred to as "relying upon the spiritual teacher." Most of these teachings have been translated into the English language. The main point of these teachings is to teach the student to regard the teacher not as an ordinary human being but as an enlightened one, as a Buddha. At least, students must regard the mentor to be a pure and qualified spiritual friend. The teacher should not become involved with a student who has incorrect views concerning this. The teacher should be able to clearly see the motivation of the student. Whether a student has a pure motivation or not may involve a process of examination that takes the teacher some three years or more to determine. If there is time to examine one another, this is very useful. At least, one should try to avoid jumping headlong into a teacher-student relationship without taking care. These days, teachers don't necessarily take the time to examine students, perhaps because of their pure view. Of course, if this is so, that is good.

All too often, because of looking only externally, the student fails to check the inner qualities of the teacher. Becoming attracted to the outer appearance and charisma of the teacher, excitement arises and a sudden relationship begins. This is called "jumping in." Reliance upon a spiritual teacher is not merely physical by any means. If attachment to the external appearance of the teacher becomes the focus of the relationship then, since Lord Buddha Shakyamuni passed into nirvana some two thousand five hundred years ago, that would mean that, with his physical passing, the object of refuge was lost. Intelligent people would laugh at the thought of this. More than that, if care is taken to practice what the teacher advises, then true progress occurs.

All teachers must eventually leave this world, just as did the Buddha himself. Yet, the lineage that we still receive, the legacy of their enlightened awareness, is passed on from generation to generation through the teachings that remain. Since that is inevitable, what we have to call a lineage in their physical absence is the blessing of their unbroken lineage of teachings. This is what we, in turn, are expected to pass on to our and future generations. If we were to depend solely upon the physical presence of the teacher, then the lineages would have been lost long ago. The Buddha said, "I shall reveal the path that leads to liberation. You must practice the path in order to reach liberation." Accordingly, students should understand that the path to enlightenment is not a push-button affair. Have there ever been any realized beings in the past who snapped their fingers and suddenly became enlightened?

Initially, it is essential to come to know the basic nature of cyclic existence to be that of suffering. This comes about by practicing the teachings given on the Four Noble Truths and the Four Thoughts that Turn the Mind. Understanding the cause of cyclic existence, the manner in which to abandon the cause, and the methods through which one discerns what should be accepted and what should be rejected determines whether one will be free from the bondage of samsara or not. One must know whether or not liberation from suffering is possible and, if so, then how to accomplish it. By gradually becoming familiar with the Four Thoughts and the Four Truths, these questions are answered.

If true renunciation is developed, then wrong view towards the spiritual teacher and the dharma will never arise. The taste of dharma will do nothing but improve as a deep sense of satisfaction with the path permeates your being. The essential meaning of dharma will become clearer and clearer. Otherwise, not having this recognition towards the teacher, not having renunciation for the round of existence, and thinking that the teacher can give you the magical push-button technique to suddenly attain buddhahood means that the time to even begin to approach the path that leads to enlightenment is still far away. If faith in the teacher is great, then the blessings received will be great. If your faith in the teacher is mediocre, then the blessings will be mediocre. If faith is weak, the blessings will be weak. And, if there is no faith, there will be no blessings. If incorrect, perverted views are developed, then rebirth will be taken in the lower realms.

Since the spiritual teacher is the one who bestows the gift of the dharma and the dharma is the path leading all beings from the three realms of cyclic existence to the state of permanent freedom, accomplishing the purposes of self and all other sentient beings, the importance of this relationship should be obvious. Since Western practitioners are educated, intelligent people, this point should be easily understood. If, when first embarking upon the path, you are already thinking yourself to be someone very special, how can you expect to receive true benefit from your relationship with the teacher and the dharma? If you are feeling hungry and your mouth is hanging open, then at least you should take the food that you receive into your mouth, chew it, and digest it. In this way, you can avoid hunger, indigestion, and poor health. Otherwise, ingesting food into your mouth, failing to chew it properly, and digesting it poorly so that it contributes to ill health, is similar to the way that many Westerners approach the dharma. Taking too much food into the mouth is also going to produce similar results. Many Western students, although unprepared and under-qualified to receive spiritual transmissions on certain levels, force themselves into the teaching situation. Without a strong foundation, not only are they utterly unequipped to help others, they actually bring harm upon themselves. Children who eat like this will vomit their food, and adults who act like this will end up confused.

In the Buddhist tradition, one is meant to gradually proceed from the lower vehicles to the higher. This tradition does not take one from the higher to the lower. From the relative point of view, you must build a house from the ground up, not from the roof down. When you go to the top of a house, you approach from the bottom. Perhaps a helicopter can land directly on the roof, but even the helicopter has to take off from the ground. The dharma path begins by developing the wisdom of hearing the teachings, contemplating, and meditating. The dharma path requires you to examine your own faults by constantly observing the nature of cyclic existence. In this way, the dharma will truly be of benefit to your mind-stream, and the relationship you develop with the teacher will be invaluable.

These days, many students choose to receive spiritual teachings from just about every direction they are available. It may be useful to consider the need to have a strong trunk that can support the many branches that are meant to beautify the tree. If the trunk of one's developed qualities is strong, then it is excellent to improve upon that basis. Generally, whenever students see faults in the teacher and when teachers see faults in the students, it is a sign of the individual's own shortcomings. In particular, if someone has formally entered the path of Buddhism and has developed a strong relationship with a spiritual teacher from whom vows and instructions have been received, and then turns on the teacher and actually sees and expresses faults of the teacher, it is very negative. Forget about expressing a fault of the teacher; to even express a fault of one of the sangha members causes one to break the vows of refuge. This accumulates the karma of abandoning the dharma.

Expressing the faults of the root teacher is the same as finding fault with the Buddha. When you take the vows of refuge you repeat, "I take refuge in the teacher; I take refuge in the Buddha; I take refuge in the dharma; I take refuge in the sangha." To express fault in the sublime objects of refuge only serves to blatantly demonstrate your own shortcomings. If care is taken from the very beginning, then there should be no problem; but unfortunately these days most people like to excitedly jump in and make a big splash that is noisy so that others can take note of it. If someone is a true follower of the Buddha, whether teacher or student, then their delusions should be decreasing and it should be obvious that a true effort is being made to do so. If the antidotes for desire, anger, pride, jealousy, and so forth are being applied, it will be apparent in the outer mannerisms of the practitioner. Such a person should have less delusion and self-cherishing than ordinary people. If so, then it is good. Whether that person is male, female, ugly, old, poor, or rich, the authentic presence of a true practitioner will be apparent, if you know how to look for it. Check for yourself to see if this is true or not. You are the one who should be intelligent enough to know if the food can fit in your mouth and be digested or not. Even if someone is world-renowned for their scholarship, if they verbally abuse and look down upon others, especially their own spiritual teachers and practitioners of the same tradition, then who will really respect them in the end? Any time you express the faults of others, you automatically express your own. It is important to be careful from the very beginning. At least, don't try to hide your own faults, like a cat who covers his own excrement, and intentionally expose the faults of others. Try to practice the opposite.

I offer the prayer that the aspirations of all sincere practitioners may be accomplished in accordance with the dharma, bringing a shower of blessings that descend to nourish all beings who seek the path to true freedom.

Preface

This book consists of three sections:
  I. Translator's Introduction
  II. Translation of Jamgön Kongtrul Lodrö Thayé's ('Jam-mgon kong-sprul blo-gros mtha'-yas) root verses found in "The Chapter on the Explanation of the Characteristics of the Master and Student [Relationship], How to Follow [the Master], and How to Teach and Listen [to the Dharma],"[1] located in *The Treasury of Knowledge (Shes-bya kun-khyab)*[2]
  III. The Auto-commentary on the preceding root verses

The purpose of my introduction is to clarify and enhance Jamgön Kongtrul's work, so as to make it clearer and more accessible to a Western audience. I have undertaken it for the following reasons: To date, no full commentary to *The Treasury of Knowledge* exists in English; Kongtrul Rinpoche's work is terse and often difficult to understand; his work is encyclopedic, drawing from many sources and borrowing large sections from Gampopa's *The Wishfulfilling Jewel-like Sacred Dharma Which Is an Ornament to Precious Liberation (Dam-chos yid-bzhin nor-bu thar-pa rin-po-che'i rgyan)* and Buton's *The Jewelry of Scripture (Chos' byung)*. He omits important material from these sources that he assumes his audience is familiar with. Omitted material will be furnished from the original Tibetan of *An Ornament to Precious Liberation*, from *The Jewelry of Scripture*, and from the *Sutra Arranged Like a Tree (sDong-po bkod-pa'i mdo; Gaṇḍavyūha-sūtra)*. I have drawn upon sutras, writings, and oral instructions of accomplished lamas in an effort to weave together a net of commentary that supports and embellishes Jamgön Kongtrul's priceless teachings.

Authors and wisdom teachers I have referred to extensively are:

Buton (Bu-ston rin-chen grub-pa, 1290-1364), a scholar famous for compiling a history of Buddhism[3] and for editing and arranging the Kangyur (*bKa'-'gyur*) and Tangyur (*bsTan-'gyur*) into their present form. (Material is drawn from *The Jewelry of Scripture*, translated by Obermiller.)

Je Gampopa (sGam-po-pa, 1079-1153), heart disciple of Milarepa. Gampopa integrated the Kadampa (*bKa'-gdams-pa*) lineage of Atisha (Atiśa) with that of the Mahamudra (*Mahāmudrā*) and Six Yogas of Naropa (*Na-ro chos-drug*) lineage of the Marpa Kagyu. Gampopa established monasticism as part of the Kagyu tradition. Dusum Khyenpa, the first Karmapa, was one of Gampopa's heart disciples. (Material is drawn from *The Wishfulfilling Jewel-like Sacred Dharma Which Is an Ornament to Precious Liberation*, translated from the original Tibetan, *Dam-chos yid-bzhin nor-bu thar-pa rin-po-che'i rgyan*.)[4]

H.E. Kalu Rinpoche (1903-1989). One of the foremost enlightened masters of the twentieth century, H. E. Kalu Rinpoche was lineage holder of both the Karma and Shangpa Kagyu lineages. He is considered to be the activity emanation of Jamgön Kongtrul Lodrö Thayé. (Material is drawn from *The Dharma: That Illuminates All Beings Impartially Like the Light of the Sun and the Moon* and *The Gem Ornament of Liberation*).[5]

Khenpo Tsultrim Gyamtso Rinpoche, an eminent Kagyu scholar and renowned accomplished yogi. Early in his life he was a renunciate who practiced the Six Yogas of Naropa and Mahamudra while wandering in mountains and living in caves and cemeteries. Later in life he mastered the philosophy pertaining to the three vehicles (*yānas*) and became an esteemed abbot at Nalanda University, located at Rumtek Monastery, the seat in exile of H.H. the Sixteenth Karmapa. Khenpo Tsultrim Rinpoche is founder of Marpa House in Nepal, where he currently resides. (Material is taken from interviews granted in the autumn of 1990 and 1991.)

Kun Khyen Longchenpa (kLong-chen rab-'byams-pa, 1308-1364), Dzogchen master and prolific writer (with over two hundred titles) who brought together the two *nyingtig* lineages, those of *Padmasambhava and Vimalamitra*. (Material is drawn from *Resting in the Nature of Mind*, translated from the original Tibetan, *Sems-nyid ngal-gso*.)[6]

Patrul Rinpoche (dPal-sprul o-rgyan 'jigs-med chos-kyi dbang-po, 1808-1887), a great master of the Nyingma lineage who is the speech emanation of Jigme Lingpa. He played an important role, along with Kongtrul, in the nonsectarian (*ris-med*) movement of the nineteenth century in Tibet. (Material is drawn from *The Oral Instructions of My Excellent Lama*, translated from the original Tibetan, *Kun-bzang bla-ma'i zhal-lung*.)[7]

CONSIDERATIONS OF STYLE

Terminology

Difficulties arise when referring to the sections of Kongtrul's text because it is itself a chapter and not a book. It consists of ten sections, and each section consists of numerous parts and points. In my commentary I refer to Kongtrul's chapter on the teacher-student relationship as *the work*, consisting of ten *chapters*. Each chapter contains numerous *points*.

It is important to keep in mind the use of the following terms:

> *Auto-commentary*: This always refers to Jamgön Kongtrul's commentary to his root verses on the teacher-student relationship. This comprises the bulk of the material translated in this book.

> *Commentary*: This always refers to my own introduction to the text, which follows below, and is a treatment of Kongtrul's auto-commentary.

In Kongtrul's auto-commentary, the root verses appear in bold type.

Chapter Headings

Chapters three through twelve of my introduction correspond to the ten chapters of Kongtrul's text; however, chapter headings in my introduction are not exactly the same as the chapter headings given by Kongtrul. Instead, they are paraphrases intending to communicate the meaning of the chapter in question. For instance, Kongtrul entitles chapter four, "The Way in Which One Enters into and Goes Astray." In my introduction chapter six is called, "How to Choose a Teacher," because this is primarily what the chapter is about.

Transliteration

I have used the Wylie system of transliteration. Titles of texts have been translated into English, with the Tibetan and Sanskrit (where applicable) transliterated in parentheses at the first citation; occasionally, when the

Tibetan or Sanskrit title is well known, the text is cited in a phonetic transcription of the original language. Names of people are cited in phonetic Tibetan or Sanskrit with a transliteration in parentheses at the first appearance.

Gender

In order to meet the need for fairness and clarity, I have alternated between the use of the pronouns "he" and "she," and avoided the cumbersome "s/he" and the impersonal "one."

ACKNOWLEDGMENTS

There were numerous people whose expertise and support made this book possible. I would like to extend my deep gratitude to Khenpo Tsultrim Gyamtso Rinpoche, who elucidated the difficult sections of the text and also graciously gave commentary from his vast knowledge and realization. I want to express my gratitude to Tulku Thubten Rinpoche, who is the sole reason for any positive qualities I have as a translator, for his assistance in reviewing the final draft of this translation. And I especially thank my dear, precious teacher, Lama Tharchin Rinpoche, who naturally embodies the perfect teacher in all his actions, and particularly in his inconceivably vast view, humility, humor, and tireless compassion for all sentient beings. I am deeply indebted to my friend Maude Honneman for her excellent work editing my original manuscript, making my disgraceful use of the English language lucid and clear. Also, I thank Jeff Cox for publishing this work, Sidney Piburn and Jesse Townsley for the beautiful cover, David Patt for his diligent work on the preliminary editing, Susan Kyser for her expertise on editing the final manuscript, along with the entire staff at Snow Lion. I also wish to thank Michelle Martin and Susanna Schefczyk for their help with colloquial Tibetan; Dr. Mark Tatz, my first Tibetan language instructor; and all my vajra brothers and sisters residing at Pema Osel Ling, for the purity of their dharma practice. Finally, I thank my wife, Sonam, for her technical support—editing, proofreading, and computer expertise—and for her loving support and patience with my late hours working on this translation. If this book is of any benefit it is due to the brilliance of Kongtrul Rinpoche's writings and the blessings and contributions of the lamas, and also all the support I received from my friends mentioned above. Any mistakes or omissions the reader may find are entirely mine and I regretfully apologize.

This book is dedicated to the long life of the Jewel of Activity. May his boundless enlightened activity liberate limitless sentient beings. May all our wisdom teachers live long and continuously turn the wheel of the unsurpassable dharma. Whatever merit may arise from this work I dedicate to my loving mother, dharma friends, and all parent sentient beings without exception: may they swiftly and joyfully realize fully awakened buddhahood.

Ron Garry (Yeshe Nyima)
Pharping, Nepal

PART I
Translator's Introduction

1 The Importance of Having a Wisdom Teacher

From the Buddhist perspective, it is considered essential for a person to have a teacher in order to make progress on the path to full awakening. In Mahayana Buddhism it is said that without relying on a spiritual friend it is not possible to attain full buddhahood. It is said in *The Sutra Arranged Like a Tree*:

> What is the reason [for not tiring to seek spiritual friends]? It is from spiritual friends that bodhisattvas learn the practice of bodhisattvas; it is through spiritual friends that all bodhisattvas' virtues are perfected; spiritual friends are the source of the stream of all bodhisattva vows; the roots of goodness of all bodhisattvas are produced by spiritual friends; the provisions for enlightenment are produced by spiritual friends; the purification of all ways to enlightenment derives from spiritual friends; the accomplishment of all studies of bodhisattvas are based on spiritual friends....[8]

Also, Gampopa states:

> The condition [for attaining enlightenment] is wisdom teachers.[9]

From the Vajrayana perspective, the guru is considered to be inseparable from the Buddha. Ashvaghosha (Aśvaghoṣa) writes:

> Therefore, a disciple with the noble qualities of compassion, generosity, moral self-control, and patience should never regard as different the guru and Buddha Vajradhara.[10]

According to the Vajrayana, the guru is the source of all blessings, thus the student's relationship to him is crucial. Ashvaghosha writes:

> It is from your guru that powerful attainments (*siddhi*), higher
> rebirth, and happiness come. Therefore, make a wholehearted ef-
> fort never to transgress your guru's advice.[11]

It has also been said throughout the scriptures and oral instructions
that if enlightenment could be attained solely by one's own effort, then
we would already be enlightened. Instead, according to tradition, sentient beings are seen to have wandered in the ocean of samsara for
countless lives. H.H. the Fourteenth Dalai Lama, in his commentary
to *The Essence of Refined Gold*, writes that a spiritual teacher is a necessary condition for the attainment of enlightenment:

> The reason why we have been wandering unceasingly in cyclic
> existence (*saṃsāra*) since time immemorial is because we have not
> met a spiritual master before; or even if we have met one we did
> not cultivate an effective relationship with him. We should deter-
> mine to take the opportunities afforded by our present human
> situation and cultivate a spiritual practice under the guidance of
> a master.[12]

In the sutras and in the pith instructions of the great wisdom teachers, it is also said that not only is it necessary for us to rely upon a
wisdom teacher, but that all the Buddhas of the past, present, and future attained enlightenment by relying on a teacher. Patrul Rinpoche
writes:

> There is no mention in any of the sutras, tantras, or commentaries
> of anyone accomplishing buddhahood without following a lama.
> It can be seen that no one has attained the noble qualities of the
> levels and paths by their own creation and conjecture. Similarly,
> all sentient beings, including ourselves, are very good at follow-
> ing the wrong path.[13]

Gampopa supports this point with the following quotation from *The
Life Story of Paljung (dPal-byung-gi rnam-thar; Śrīsaṃbhava)*:

> The enlightenment of a Buddha is obtained by serving spiritual
> friends.[14]

And in *The Fifty Stanzas on Guru Devotion (bLa-ma nga-bcu-pa)* Ashvaghosha writes:

> All the Buddhas of the past, present and future, residing in every
> land in the ten directions, have paid homage to the tantric mas-
> ters from whom they received the highest empowerments [which
> led to their enlightenment].[15]

The importance of relying upon a wisdom teacher in order to attain
enlightenment is stated unambiguously in *The Sutra Arranged Like a Tree*:

> In sum, all practices of bodhisattvas, all transcendent ways of bodhisattvas, all stages of bodhisattvas, all concentrations of bodhisattvas, all mystic knowledges and spiritual powers of bodhisattvas, all manifestations of mental command and intellectual power of bodhisattvas, all knowledge of dedication and infinity of super-knowledge of bodhisattvas, all accomplishment of vows of bodhisattvas, and all perfections of attainments of all aspects of Buddhahood, derive from spiritual benefactors, are rooted in spiritual benefactors, are born of spiritual benefactors, are fostered by spiritual benefactors, are based on spiritual benefactors, are caused by spiritual benefactors, are produced by spiritual benefactors.[16]

From another perspective, it might be said that it is necessary to have a wisdom teacher in order to attain enlightenment, in the same way that it is necessary in our culture to receive training in order to become a professional, or learn a trade. We go to teachers in order to become expert in carpentry, plumbing, medicine, law, accounting, music, and so forth. In fact, even a child prodigy of the violin is sent to the finest teacher available so her full potential will be realized. In the European tradition, the master-apprentice relationship is designed to facilitate the learning of a trade. The master possesses the knowledge, techniques, and tricks of the trade which she teaches to her apprentice. In this way the apprentice inherits the knowledge and experience of the trade.

In a similar way, it is believed to be necessary for a practitioner on the Buddhist path to work with a teacher in order to realize her true nature. In the Buddhist context, one's true nature is that of a Buddha, and it is considered to be present within us from the beginningless beginning.[17] As it is said in *The Changeless Nature* (*Theg pa chen po'i rgyud bla ma'i bstan bcos; Mahāyāna-uttaratantra-śāstra*):[18]

> The Buddha has said that all beings possess the essence of buddhahood because the *buddha-jñāna* has always been present in all beings, the immaculate nature is nondual, and the buddha-potential (buddha-nature) is named after its result.

The tenets of Buddhism hold that we are not enlightened now because our inherent buddha-nature (*tathāgatagarbha*) is covered over by defilements.[19] Again it is said in *The Changeless Nature*:

> This Buddha-nature abides within all sentient beings but is obscured by the stains of fleeting passions.[20]

Thus a wisdom teacher is needed in order to help train us in how to remove these defilements. Patrul Rinpoche writes:

> Each one of us who have come together here to listen to the dharma
> has, as our foundation, buddha-nature (*bde-gshegs snying-po;
> sugata-garbha*), as our support, the precious human birth, and as
> the condition, the wisdom teacher, who embraces us with his in-
> structions as the method. Thereby, we are future buddhas.[21]

There remains the question of how we unfold our buddha-nature
and attain enlightenment. For Buddhists, the answer is to practice the
dharma, the teachings of the Buddha. These teachings include not only
meditation techniques but an entire way of life which facilitates the
transformative process. Generally speaking, the dharma teachings
address discipline (*tshul-khrims*), meditative techniques, and the attainment of wisdom. These are called the three higher trainings (*bslab-
gsum*): training in higher discipline (*lhag-pa tshul-khrims kyi bslab-pa*);
training in higher meditative concentration (*lhag-pa ting-nge-'dzin gyi
bslab-pa*); and training in higher wisdom (*lhag-pa shes-rab kyi bslab-pa*).

Training in discipline refers to the way one conducts oneself both
outwardly and inwardly. It encompasses reliance on the teacher as
well as the three vows: pratimoksha (*prātimokṣa*), bodhisattva, and
mantrayana (*mantrayāna*).[22] Teachings on meditative concentration
refer to any number of practices in which one's mind focuses on an
"impure" object such as the breath, or on a "pure" object such as a
yidam or Buddha. The training in wisdom refers to wisdom gained
through listening, reflecting, and meditating.[23]

From the perspective of a bodhisattva's training, the three higher
trainings encompass the six perfections. Gampopa writes:

> 1) Training in higher discipline consists of the triad of generos-
>   ity, discipline, and patience.
> 2) Training in higher meditative concentration involves medi-
>   tative concentration.
> 3) Training in higher wisdom is wisdom (*shes-rab; prajñā*).[24]

Buddha gave thousands of teachings and techniques to his students
to guide them to enlightenment; traditionally it is said that Buddha
gave eighty-four thousand teachings. These teachings are contained
in the Kangyur, comprising eighty volumes of sutras consisting of 317
treatises, and twenty-four volumes of tantras consisting of 729 treatises.[25] The Tangyur contains 185 volumes comprising 3,786 treatises
written by the Indian masters. In addition, there are a vast number of
teachings and methods contained within the oral instructions passed
down from the Buddha to present-day masters in an unbroken lineage.

From the Buddhist perspective, this vast amount of scripture does not substitute for the guidance and oral instructions of the wisdom teacher. In the *Rain of Wisdom*, the oral instructions of the wisdom teacher are described as follows:

> In Vajrayāna, the guru personally communicates the essence of meditation practice to his students. In this manner, both the literal instructions and their intuitive sense are conveyed to the student. Even if the student came across the instructions in written form, it would still be necessary for him to receive them directly from the mouth of the teacher.[26]

In order to attain full awakening it is not sufficient to merely read books, which lack the compassionate intention that only another conscious being can have. The sutras, tantras, and *shastras* are without a doubt extremely beneficial, but alone they do not have the power to stimulate actual experience in the student's mind. The wisdom teacher is necessary because he has the knowledge that has been transmitted from teacher to disciple through an unbroken lineage originating with the Buddha. The wisdom teacher has verified these teachings through his own experience and, motivated by compassion, speaks to the student from the realization he has in his heart.

To obtain the full blessings of the instruction, the student should view the teacher as Vajradhara, the primordial Buddha, or as Padmasambhava, transmitting the teachings of the lineage that led numerous practitioners to complete awakening. The student should also view this opportunity to receive teachings as rare and precious, and should have uncontrived devotion to the wisdom teacher. Thus, teachings from the lama can eventually lead to enlightenment, whereas merely reading books cannot.

The type of relationship the teacher and student engage in depends on the level of development of both the teacher and the student. Generally, the relationship fuctions in one of two ways:[27] in accordance with the general Mahayana training in which the teacher functions as a spiritual friend (*dge-ba'i bshes-gnyen*) to the student; or, in accordance with the Vajrayana training in which the wisdom teacher functions as a spiritual master (*bla-ma*) connected to the disciple by the tantric vows (*dam-tshig; samaya*).

On the Mahayana level of training, the spiritual friend gives teachings, guidance, and advice to the students, and by her actions sets an example of how a bodhisattva lives a virtuous life. Jamgön Kongtrul III explains:

> In the Mahayana tradition, the spiritual friend is more than a
> guide. It is most important to see our spiritual teacher as a special
> realized individual who does not only convey Lord Buddha's
> words and meanings but who truly lives by the Buddha's instruc-
> tions. He is a bodhisattva, a representative, and is the personifica-
> tion of the Buddhadharma in every respect.[28]

At the Vajrayana level of practice the relationship between the guru
and disciple becomes more powerful than the relationship between
the spiritual friend and the student, with devotion playing a prominent role. Jamgön Kongtrul III continues:

> In the Vajrayana tradition, the spiritual friend is vital and utterly
> significant. He is actually seen as a Buddha. Seeing one's lama as
> a Buddha isn't a mental construct or contrivance but a vivid ex-
> perience. It is only possible to recognize him as a Buddha after
> having developed serene confidence and devotion. Vajrayana
> practice depends upon the inspiration and blessings the lama be-
> stows.[29]

This is not a relationship which a qualified guru allows a person to
enter into easily, because of the dangers involved. On the contrary, a
qualified teacher encourages the beginning student to reflect upon
the teachings and ask questions, and does not permit a student to enter into a relationship based on total surrender. Actually, a student
who approaches an authentic wisdom teacher with the desire to give
everything away and obey any and all commands is considered very
immature. This is a sign that it is necessary to begin with foundational
trainings in Mahayana practices and the preliminary practices of the
Vajrayana.

Therefore, when a person desires to set out upon the path which
liberates from suffering and leads to full awakening, and then realizes
the necessity of having a wisdom teacher, the next step is to find a
wisdom teacher and begin practicing his instruction. Jamgön Kongtrul
Lodrö Thayé dedicates most of his writing on this topic to instructing
the student on how to recognize a qualified teacher and then how to
train with this teacher. Kongtrul Rinpoche spends very little time dis-
cussing the need to have a teacher on the spiritual path because this
was taken for granted by practitioners in Tibet.

2   Jamgön Kongtrul

Jamgön Kongtrul (1813-1899) was a prolific writer, and was one of the guiding forces of the nonsectarian *rimay* (*ris-med*) movement, which took place in the nineteenth century in Tibet.[30] Kongtrul Rinpoche was born in Kham, in eastern Tibet, and was raised by his father, Sonam Pel, a Bonpo teacher.[31] Kongtrul firmly believed that his genetic father was the Khyungpo Lama Yungdrung Tendzin, connecting him with the distinguished lineage of the Khyungpos. This lineage produced many famous lamas, among them the great poet-yogi Milarepa, and Khyungpo Naljor, the founder of the Shangpa Kagyu. Gene Smith describes the origins of the Khyungpo lineage as follows:

> The Khyungpo lineage (*rus*) traced its origins to a legendary ancestor, the Great Eagle (*Khyung-chen*), an emanation of a mythical Buddha of the Upper Realm, Kunzang rig nang. This gigantic eagle (*garuḍa*) descended from the heavens at the six-peaked mountain of Gyim-shod. When the great bird flew back into the heavens, he left behind four eggs, white, black, yellow, and green. When these eggs opened, four youths emerged. From the first three originated the Khyungpo tribes of Kar-ru, Nag-ru, and Ser-tsha. The fourth youth, Khyung-chag Tra-mo, mounted a turquoise dragon and rode off to the Gyal-rong. There he became the ancestor of all the Khyung lineages of those states.[32]

Until the age of fourteen Kongtrul Rinpoche received a thorough Bonpo education, and his principal teacher was Yung-drung phun-tshog, the realized one (*rtogs-ldan*) of the Liberation-Bliss hermitage (*Thar-bde ri-khrod*). In 1827 Kongtrul's father was imprisoned by the Derge authorities for participating in a local feud. This changed the course of the young Kongtrul's life, because it led to his study with the Nyingma lama Jamgön Gyurme Tutob Namgyal of Zhechen, culminating in his taking the final vows as a Nyingma monk in 1832.

In 1833 at the behest of his mentor, Kongtrul moved to the Karma Kagyu monastery of Palpung, headed by Situ Padma Nyinje. From Situ Rinpoche he took the Vinaya vows for the second time. Situ Rinpoche also recognized Kongtrul Rinpoche as an incarnate lama, the rebirth of the servant of the previous Situpa. Kongtrul Rinpoche studied with great lamas from all the lineages of Tibet, and was also knowledgeable in the traditional Buddhist arts and sciences. Smith states that:

> The list of Kongtrul's teachers is an amazing one; a referential petition to his gurus written in 1843 [at the age of thirty] contains over sixty names. He studied with teachers representing all of the sects and esoteric lineages. His interests covered the entire field of traditional Tibetan scholarship.[33]

The latter half of the nineteenth century brought a cultural and spiritual renaissance to eastern Tibet. There is no question Jamgön Kongtrul was a key participant, along with the other great teachers of the nonsectarian "*rimay* movement," such as Jamyang Khyentse Wangpo (1820-1892), Mipam Jamyang Namgyal Gyatso (1846-1912), and Chogyur Lingpa (1829-1870).

3   Our Precious Human Life

Jamgön Kongtrul explains that to fully use our precious human existence a person should practice the dharma, and in order to practice the
dharma fully a qualified wisdom teacher must be found and followed
(*bsten*). Kongtrul Rinpoche writes:

> Intelligent people who enter [the teaching] in the beginning seek
> the wisdom teacher who has the characteristics [of a qualified
> wisdom teacher]. They do this so as not to let go to waste, and for
> the purpose of making worthwhile, their attainment of the hu-
> man body, which is like a wishfulfilling jewel, endowed with the
> qualities of leisure and opportunity (*dal-'byor*). Then, on finding
> him, one should properly follow him.

According to Buddhist teaching, the human body is considered rare
and precious when it is free from the eight unfortunate conditions
and possesses the ten endowments. Je Gampopa, in *An Ornament to
Precious Liberation*, lists the eight unfortunate conditions as found in
The Sutra of the True Dharma of Clear Recollection (*mDo dran-pa nyer-
bzhag; Saddharma-smṛtyupasthāna*):

1) Hell beings (*dmyal-ba*)
2) Hungry ghosts (*yi-dwags*)
3) Animals (*dud-'gro*)
4) Barbarians (*kla-klo*)
5) Long-lived gods (*tshe-ring lha*)
6) Those with wrong views (*log-lta*)

7) [An age] without a Buddha (*sangs-rgyas kyi stong*)

8) Mutes (*lkugs-pa*)

These are the eight unfavorable conditions.[34]

The ten endowments are divided into five circumstances which are dependent on oneself (*rang-'byor lnga*) and five circumstances dependent on others (*gzhan-'byor lnga*). Gampopa lists the five endowments dependent on oneself as:

1) To be a human being

2) To be born in a central country

3) To have perfect faculties

4) To be engaged in right livelihood

5) Having faith in [the holy dharma which is] the basis[35]

The five endowments dependent on others as given by Gampopa are:[36]

1) The Buddha appears in this world

2) He teaches the dharma

3) The dharma remains

4) The dharma is followed

5) [One enjoys] the kindness and compassion of others[37]

A person who possesses these eighteen elements should practice the dharma, because this is the source for everything beneficial: it ends suffering and is the cause of lasting happiness. It is best to practice now, because our future is uncertain, and the opportunities that present themselves to us today may not be available to us later on.

For those of us who wish to journey on the path that will eventually lead to our full awakening, a qualified guide, a wisdom teacher, must be found.

4 Why a Wisdom Teacher Is Necessary

Jamgön Kongtrul explains the necessity of following the wisdom teacher. He does this by citing scripture (*lung*), using reasoning (*rigs*), and giving examples (*dpe*). This is the traditional way of proving a point among Buddhists. Kongtrul begins by invoking the words of the Buddha, by drawing upon *The Perfection of Wisdom Sutra* (*Phags-pa sdud-pa; Prajñāpāramitā-saṃcaya*) and *The Sutra Arranged Like a Tree*, to show that the source of all good qualities (*yon-tan*) and virtuous qualities (*dge-ba'i chos*) is the spiritual friend. He concludes by stating that this point is made countless times throughout the scriptures. In fact, "The Justification for Following a Wisdom Teacher" is the shortest of the ten chapters from this work, because for Tibetan Buddhists the necessity of a wisdom teacher was beyond doubt.

Next, Kongtrul Rinpoche uses reasoning to prove his point. The syllogism[38] is that a person who desires to attain enlightenment must rely upon a wisdom teacher, because the person does not know how to gather the accumulations of merit and wisdom, nor how to purify the obscuration of the passions and the obscuration of that which can be known. This is shown by the example of all the Buddhas, who attained enlightenment only through reliance on a wisdom teacher. The counter example is given as the *pratyekabuddhas*, who do not attain full enlightenment on their own.

5 Categories and Qualifications of the Master Who Should Be Followed

Once the desire for awakening is burning in our heart, and we understand the need to have a guide, how do we recognize a qualified wisdom teacher? Fortunately, precise qualifications are given that can guide us in our search. Jamgön Kongtrul describes the different types of wisdom teachers and the qualities and characteristics they should possess, citing the four traditional classifications:

1) An ordinary person
2) A bodhisattva
3) The nirmanakaya (*nirmāṇakāya*) of the Buddha
4) The sambhogakaya (*sambhogakāya*) of the Buddha

This is taken from Gampopa's *An Ornament to Precious Liberation*, the standard Kagyu text for teachings that cover the stages of the path (*lam-rim*).

Kongtrul Rinpoche explains that the type of wisdom teacher a student takes as her wisdom teacher is dependent upon the student's level of development. For a bodhisattva who is in the tenth and final stage (*bhūmi*) before attaining enlightenment, the appropriate wisdom teacher is one in the sambhogakaya form of the Buddha. For a bodhisattva who has attained the level of being on the greater path of accumulation, the appropriate teacher is one who has taken the form of the nirmanakaya of the Buddha. Someone who has almost completely eliminated karmic obscurations (*las-kyi sgrib-pa*) can take a high level bodhisattva as a teacher.

The majority of us, however, fall into the "beginner" category, and are described as sitting "in the dungeon of karma and passions." In this situation, one is not able to take the previous three types of spiritual friends as a wisdom teacher. In fact, Kongtrul Rinpoche states that such beginners "do not even have a glimpse of the face of those wisdom teachers." Thus the beginner should take a wisdom teacher who is in the form of an ordinary person.

It is important for the beginner to be discriminating when choosing a teacher. Kongtrul refers to three standard lists of qualities that a spiritual friend should possess. Again, he takes these lists from Gampopa's *An Ornament to Precious Liberation*.[39] Gampopa's sources for the three lists are as follows: The list of eight qualities is from *The Stages of the Bodhisattva* (*Byang-chub sems-dpa'i sa; Bodhisattva-bhūmi*) of Asanga (Thogs-med; Asaṅga). The list of four qualities is from *The Ornament of the Mahayana Sutras* (*mDo-sde rgyan; Mahāyāna-sūtrālaṅkāra*) ascribed to Maitreya-Asanga. The list of two qualities is from *The Bodhisattva's Way of Life* (*Byang-chub sems-dpa'i spyod-pa la 'jug-pa; Bodhisattva-caryāvatāra*) of Shantideva.

When investigating whether to take a particular lama as a teacher, Kongtrul recommends that the student first examine the teacher, using criteria described in *The Stages of the Bodhisattva*. The teacher should lead a moral life and uphold the bodhisattva vows.[40] He should be knowledgeable in the Mahayana sutras and shastras, and this knowledge should be accompanied by personal realization attained through the practice of meditation.

It is essential that the teacher deeply care about the well-being and happiness of all sentient beings—in fact, this is said to be one of the most indispensable qualities of a wisdom teacher. If the teacher in question cares more for his own benefit than the benefit of others, he is not a qualified teacher.

Jamgön Kongtrul next gives Gampopa's summary of the qualities that the teacher who is an ordinary person should possess:

> Accordingly, [the wisdom teacher who is an ordinary person] is learned [in the meaning of the Mahayana] and possesses the [bodhisattva] vow.

The bodhisattva vow can be practiced with three different levels of intent. The first is "king-like bodhicitta": the intention to attain enlightenment and then to bring all sentient beings to enlightenment is compared to that of a benevolent king, who first gains power and then brings his subjects to prosperity. Second is "boatman-like bodhicitta," the intention to attain enlightenment together with all sentient beings, as a boatman reaches the other shore along with his passengers. Finally there is "shepherd-like bodhicitta," the highest intention, which is to defer complete enlightenment until all sentient beings have attained it; this is compared to that of a shepherd who, when leading his sheep safely home, first takes care of their food and shelter, and then looks to his own needs.

A more detailed explanation of the spiritual friend can be given when classifying them according to the particular vow associated with the relationship. From this perspective the wisdom teacher is classified as a pratimoksha master (*so-sor-thar-pa'i slob-dpon; prātimokṣa-ācārya*), a bodhisattva master (*byang-chub-kyi slob-dpon*), or a mantra master (*sngags-kyi slob-dpon*). Kongtrul describes the specific qualifications of each type of master.

Pratimoksha Vow Master
There are five types of pratimoksha master:

1) *Khenpo (mkhan-po; upādhyāya)*
2) Ritual master (*las-byed-pa slob-dpon; karma-kāraka-ācārya*)
3) Private instructor (*gsang-ste ston-pa; rahas-nuśāsaka*)
4) Reliance or reading master (*gnas-sam klog-pa'i slob-dpon*)
5) Novice monk master (*dge-tshul-gyi slob-dpon*)

Kongtrul Rinpoche only briefly summarizes the functions, qualities, and characteristics of these masters, because the information is only pertinent to—and therefore only taught to—those who hold monastic vows. In an interview with Khenpo Tsultrim Gyamtso Rinpoche I asked him to elaborate on this section. His response was that this information is only pertinent to those in the monastic order and is not appropriate or necessary for laymen and laywomen.[41]

In general, the characteristics of the pratimoksha master fall within three sections:

Steadfastness (*brtan-pa*) refers to moral discipline. The pratimoksha master is considered to truly possess discipline only if he has kept unimpaired vows for at least ten years since taking the higher ordination (*bsnyen-par rdzogs; bhikṣu*).

Learning (*shes-pa mkhas-pa*). The section on learning encompasses the knowledge of all the Vinaya (*'Dul-ba*) rituals that the pratimoksha master must know.

Doing benefit (*phan-'dogs-pa*). The pratimoksha master must act in a way that is of benefit to all sentient beings in general,

and to his students in particular, which includes having compassion for his disciples. He must benefit all sentient beings
by teaching the dharma and providing material things.

Each type of pratimoksha master has its own function within the monastery, though they all share the same fundamental characteristics
mentioned above.

Kongtrul writes that the qualities of a *khenpo* regarding steadfastness and learning total 105, and are expounded in the commentary to
The Three Hundred, and in the writings of Pema Karpo (Pad-ma dkar-
po). He mentions twelve attributes that are needed for the khenpo to
benefit sentient beings. In addition to the general qualities possessed
by all pratimoksha masters as stated above—compassion and the giving of dharma and material things—the khenpo must be patient while
working with his students, and should have students who uphold the
pratimoksha vows. The khenpo must have the qualities necessary for
a pratimoksha master, and he must also have the "correct view." In
addition, he must understand the meaning of the teaching and be capable of articulating this meaning to his students. The khenpo must
have a stable personality, and only manifests in the human form within
the human realm; the khenpo doesn't emanate bodies in different
realms, as do the bodhisattvas, because the pratimoksha vow is only
possible for human beings.

Jamgön Kongtrul writes that the ritual master is the one who has:

1) The completely pure full monk vow (*dge-slong*)
2) The corresponding characteristics
3) The corresponding view
4) Possesses the three conventions
5) Inhabits an ordinary body
6) Resides naturally on the earth

On top of these six qualities, he is learned in imparting the
[pratimoksha] vow.

As Kongtrul relates, the special function of the ritual master is imparting the pratimoksha vow to the student. It is written in the
Mahavyutpatti (*Mahāvyutpatti*) that the ritual master oversees "the
proper conduct of the ritual, and presents the formal motion to the
sangha for granting ordination."

Kongtrul states that the private instructor must have the same six
qualities mentioned above, and that his special area of knowledge is
in the interrogation of the prospective student for any hindrances that

may prevent him from taking the pratimoksha vow. In the *Maha-vyutpatti* it states that the function of the private instructor is "to inquire privately during the ordination ritual about the novice's freedom from the physical impediments," which would make him ineligible to take monastic ordination. In many texts the example given is that the candidate would be ineligible if he were a hermaphrodite.[42]

Kongtrul writes that the reliance master possesses the same qualities as the khenpo, and he is responsible for giving the transmission of advice concerning what types of behaviors are to be engaged in and what are to be avoided, thus enabling the student to purify himself of negative karma.

Finally, the reading master's job is to help the student understand the teachings and reading assignments given by the dharma master.

Bodhisattva Vow Master

A student who wishes to enter into a relationship with a wisdom teacher for training in the Mahayana must find a guide possessing suitable qualities. The master of the bodhisattva vow should have attained ten qualities as given in *The Ornament of the Mahayana Sutras* (*mDo-sde rgyan; Mahāyāna-sūtrālaṃkāra*),[43] and twelve qualities as given by Nagarjuna (kLu-sgrub; Nāgārjuna). Kongtrul briefly glosses the ten qualities or accomplishments found in the *Ornament of the Mahayana Sutras*:

> 1) Training in discipline (*tshul-khrims kyi bslab-pa*). Discipline functions to tame (*dul-ba*) the mind, not only to discipline the body.[44]
>
> 2) Training in samadhi (*ting-nge-'dzin gyi bslab-pa*), thereby attaining calm abiding (*zhi-gnas*).
>
> 3) Training in the wisdom of analytic meditation (*so-sor dpyod-pa'i shes-rab kyi bslab-pa*). Through the preceding samadhi practice wisdom arises which dissipates delusion.

These first three qualities refer to the "higher" trainings (*bslab gsum*)—those that address higher discipline, higher concentration, and higher wisdom. All of the Mahayana practices can be condensed into these three trainings. Nagarjuna, in *A Letter to a Friend* (*bShes-springs; Suhṛllekha*) writes:[45]

> Always train yourself in morality, concentration, and wisdom.
> Even the one hundred and fifty-one trainings are truly subsumed
> under these three.

Kongtrul Rinpoche continues with the list of qualifications of the bodhisattva vow master:

4) The wisdom teacher must be more advanced than the student.

5) The wisdom teacher benefits others: The Mahayana teacher actively helps people.

6) He knows the scriptures: He is knowledgeable in the Mahayana Tripitaka—Vinaya, Sutras, and Abhidharma.[46]

7) She realizes the emptiness of phenomena. Through studying, reflecting, and meditating, the wisdom teacher should realize the emptiness of all phenomena. At the Hinayana level of training, the practitioner realizes the emptiness of self. In this case, the master of the bodhisattva vow is also expected to have experience of the emptiness of all phenomena.

8) She skillfully teaches the dharma: by guiding the student along the graduated path to enlightenment according to disposition, personality, and capability.

9) The wisdom teacher has the pure motivation of compassion. Her motivation to teach the dharma is to help all sentient beings attain enlightenment, and not for selfish reasons such as acquiring wealth and fame.

10) She does not get "burnt out." She does not get worn out when having to explain the dharma over and over. She also must have forbearance when people direct their anger at her.

Jamgön Kongtrul then cites a list of twelve qualities given by Nagarjuna which are essentially the same as those in *The Ornament of the Mahayana Sutras*, mentioning compassion, wisdom, bodhicitta motivation, and the ability to teach as qualities essential in the wisdom teacher.

Vajrayana Vow Master

Kongtrul Rinpoche categorizes the characteristics needed by a master of the Vajrayana into five sets of ten characteristics.

The five sets are:

1) Summary of common characteristics as given in *The Fifty Stanzas on Guru Devotion*

2) Ten essential points which are requirements (*nye-bar mkho-ba'i de-nyid bcu*) for the vajra master

3) Ten essential points of the ritual (*cho-ga'i de-nyid bcu*)

4) Ten essential points of suchness (*de-kho-na-nyid bcu*)

5) Ten secret essential points (*gsang-ba'i de-nyid bcu*)

Jamgön Kongtrul also includes the qualities deemed necessary as given by the Nyingma school. He concludes this section with a brief discussion of whether a lama who is a layman (one who has not reached the bodhisattva bhumis), a novice monk, or a fully ordained monk is best to take as a wisdom teacher. Kongtrul states that from among these three types of lamas, the fully ordained monk is best, but the best of all lamas is the "glorious lama" (*dpal-ldan bla-ma*), that is, one who has reached the first bodhisattva bhumi, irrespective of whether he is a monastic or layman.

Jamgön Kongtrul writes that on top of the qualities required for the pratimoksha master and bodhisattva master, the mantra master must have particular qualities that pertain to the Vajrayana. To illustrate the general qualifications needed, Kongtrul comments upon verses seven to nine of *The Fifty Stanzas on Guru Devotion*.[47] Kongtrul writes that the first six qualities are held in common with that of the bodhisattva master:

1) The Vajrayana master is in full command of his action, speech, thoughts, and feelings.

2) He has thoroughly tamed his mind through meditation practice.

3) He is wise.

4) He is patient so he does not become angry with his students.

5) The Vajrayana teacher must be honest. He does not hide his faults from himself.

6) Nor does he try to mislead his students.

7) He knows the practices of the Vajrayana.

8) He also knows the tantras and how to distinguish between the provisional meanings, definitive meanings, hidden meanings, etc.

9) He must have compassion and love towards all sentient beings.

10) In addition to knowing the tantras, he must also be familiar with the sutras and shastras.

Finally, Kongtrul comments that the mantra master must be familiar with and skilled in the practices and rituals of the Vajrayana. He must also have skill in imparting the teachings of the Mantrayana according to the particular abilities of each disciple. This ends Kongtrul's commentary to *The Fifty Stanzas on Guru Devotion*.

There are also specific qualifications of the Vajrayana master eluci- dated in four categories of ten essential points. These four sets of ten characteristics list, respectively, the qualities needed from an outer, inner, suchness, and very secret perspective.

Jamgön Kongtrul states that according to the *Consecration Tantra* (*Rab-tu gnas-pa mdor-bsdus-pa'i rgyud; Supratiṣṭha-tantra-saṃgraha*) the ten essential points required for the vajra master from an outer per- spective are:[48]

1) Mandala (*maṇḍala*): He must be able to construct and visual- ize the mandalas of the various deities.

2) Samadhi (*samādhi*): He must have attained one-pointed con- centration.

3) Mudras (*mudrā*): He must know the appropriate mudras for the various rituals.

4) Ritual dances: He must be familiar with all appropriate dances.

5) Sitting posture: During meditation practice he sits in the va- jra posture, sometimes referred to as the "seven-point pos- ture of Vairocana."

6) Recitation: He knows and recites the appropriate mantras dur- ing the ritual.

7) Fire offering: He knows how to perform the fire offering ritual.

8) Torma (*gtor ma*): He knows how to construct and offer tormas.

9) Performing the activities: This refers to conducting rituals based upon the four activities—peaceful, expanding, mag- netizing, and wrathful.

10) Reabsorption stage: He must know how to dissolve the sum- moned deities back into himself.

Kongtrul Rinpoche next lists the ten essential points needed by a Vajrayana master in order to perform tantric rituals (*cho-ga*) as given in Dombipa's *Ten Verses on the Essentials of the Sphere of Wisdom Mind* (*Gur-gyi dgongs-pa Dom-bi-pa'i de-nyid bcu*). These are the characteris- tics of the Vajrayana master from an inner perspective:

1) Protection: He must be capable of creating protection circles which eliminate obstacles during the empowerment.

2) He must be qualified to give tantric empowerments.

    3) Torma: He knows how to make and use tormas during the ritual.

He is also skilled in:

    4) Mantra recitation

    5) Meditation

    6) Diverting obstacles

    7) Mandala

    8) *Siddhi*: He has attained various accomplishments due to his meditation practice

    9) Purifying misdeeds

    10) Requesting the deities to depart: Due to his realization he is capable of invoking and dismissing the deities

The two remaining sets—the ten essential points of suchness, and the ten secret essential points—refer to qualities needed by the Vajrayana master in order to teach the highest levels of tantra, and are therefore beyond the scope of Kongtrul's discussion of the teacher-student relationship. Therefore there are not any accessible commentaries.

The ten essential points of suchness are:

    1) Vajra

    2) Bell

    3) Primordial Wisdom

    4) Deity

    5) Mandala

    6) Fire offering

    7) Mantra

    8) Colored sand used for making mandalas

    9) Torma

    10) Giving empowerments

The ten secret principles are:

    1, 2) Ritual of the two reversals

    3) Secret initiation

    4) *Shes-rab yeshe* initiation

    5) Ritual of unifying and dividing

    6) Torma

    7) Vajra recitation

    8) Ritual of the wrathful accomplishment

9) Consecration of images

10) Accomplishment in the mandala

Another general description of the characteristics expected in the master of the Vajrayana is given by the great Nyingma master Patrul Rinpoche, in his work *The Oral Instructions of My Excellent Lama*:

> Especially, as it is explained in the precious tantras, the lama who reveals the vital points of the profound special oral instructions of the secret mantra Vajrayana has been brought to fruition through the uninterrupted stream of ripening empowerments. He does not transgress the *samayas* and vows taken at the time of the empowerment. His mind-stream is peaceful and tamed because his passions and discursive thoughts are few. He completely understands the entire meaning of the ground, path, and fruition tantras of the secret mantra Vajrayana. He has attained the signs of completion of the approach and accomplishment [stages of practice] such as directly seeing the face of the wisdom deity and so forth. His mind-stream is liberated by having realized the nature of reality. Because his heart is filled with compassion, he cares only for the benefit of others. He has given up attachment to worldly life so he is involved with few activities and he vigorously contemplates the dharma because he believes in future lives. He sees samsara as suffering, thereby feels great revulsion, and also encourages others to feel this great revulsion. He is skillful in the methods of taking care of his disciples through training each according to their needs. He has fulfilled the commands of his lama, therefore he has the blessings of the lineage. You should follow such a lama.[49]

Next, Kongtrul Rinpoche describes the qualifications of the master of the Vajrayana as delineated in the Nyingma tradition. He describes two alternative sets of accomplishments that the master must have. The first set relates to view, meditation, and action:

> View: The master must have the realization of the inseparability of the relative and absolute truths.
>
> Meditation: The master must have attained an advanced level of meditation practice in which she has realized the generation and completion stages of tantric practice.
>
> Samaya:[50] The master must have kept the root and secondary commitments unimpaired.

According to Kalu Rinpoche in *The Gem Ornament of Manifold Instructions*, the samaya number as follows:

> In the traditional literature we find reference to the fourteen root downfalls, and, in some classifications, the twenty-one aspects of

body, speech, and mind commitment. Some texts speak of such a detailed classification that they enumerate 1,100,000 vows which are part of this tantric samaya.[51]

A summary of the fourteen root downfalls as told by Kalu Rinpoche are as follows:

1) Contradicting one's lama
2) Contradicting or refuting the teachings of the Buddha or the personal teachings that we receive from our guru
3) Creating disharmony within the sangha
4) Breaking one's bodhisattva vow
5) Impairing the white and red *bindu*
6) Denigrating or abusing *any* spiritual system, regardless of whether it is Buddhist or non-Buddhist
7) Revealing secret teachings to those unfit to receive them
8) Regarding our physical bodies, or the *skandhas*—which are the aggregates of our pyscho-physical makeup—as impure and base
9) Having doubts or hesitations about one's involvement in tantric practice
10) For an advanced tantric practitioner, not bringing a halt to a being doing terrible harm
11) Falling into the extreme view of either eternalism or nihilism
12) Refusing to teach a sincere student
13) During the *ganachakra* (*gaṇacakra*), abstaining from the ritual use of alcohol or meat because it is impure or against our beliefs
14) Disparaging women, either by a mental attitude of considering women to be lower than men, or by verbalizing these opinions

The master of the Vajrayana must be knowledgeable in an alternative set of three requirements, classified in the context of levels of tantra:

Mahayoga: The master must be knowledgeable in the generation stage of practice, which corresponds to the Mahayoga level of tantra.

Anuyoga: The master must be knowledgeable in the completion stage of practice which corresponds to the Anuyoga level of tantra.

Atiyoga: The master must have experience of the view which is related with the highest level of tantra, Atiyoga—Dzogchen, the Great Perfection.

The great Nyingma master, the omniscient Kun Khyen Longchenpa, in his text *Resting in the Nature of Mind*, elaborates on the qualifications of the secret mantra lama (*gsang-sngag bla-ma*):

> He holds the empowerments, keeps pure the vows and samaya, and has reached the other shore of the special oral instructions on the meaning of the tantras. He has mastered the enlightened activities of approach, accomplishment, and activity, and has attained the signs of experience of fruition in view, meditation, and action. He has great love and places his disciples on the path of ripening and liberation with skillful means. He is an undiminishing cloud of lineage blessings, so you should follow the wise and accomplished glorious lama.[52]

In summary, Kongtrul Rinpoche condenses all the requirements of the Vajrayana master previously discussed into six:

Unbroken lineage: It is very important for the Vajra master to maintain the unbroken lineage which originated with Dorje Chang and has been passed down from teacher to disciple to the present lama. Lineage plays an important role in the practice of Vajrayana Buddhism, with the special oral instructions and blessings of a teacher being indispensable.

Samaya is unimpaired: Unimpaired samaya is essential for the Vajrayana practitioner because this commitment is the receptacle for the attainment of all siddhi.

Conduct in accord with the vows: The vajra master must live his life according to the dharma—he must practice what he teaches. Specifically, the teacher must act in accordance with his pratimoksha and bodhisattva vows, and his samaya must be pure.

Pith instructions: The wisdom teacher must possess the special oral instructions which have been passed down through the lineage and received from his wisdom teacher.

Scriptural knowledge: It is expected that the master is knowledgeable in the sutras, shastras, and tantras.

Compassion: All the characteristics required of the Vajrayana master are condensed into one quality: having compassion for all sentient beings.

The order in which Kongtrul delineated the six characteristics of the vajra master shows us the emphasis on practice over mere scholasticism which is found in the Kagyu, Nyingma, and nonsectarian (*ris-med*) masters. Kongtrul began his enumeration of the necessary characteristics with "the importance of the unbroken lineage" and ended with "knowledge of the scriptures." He displays the importance of the Mahayana teachings as a foundation for Vajrayana practice when he writes that all the qualifications required for the vajra master are contained within the single characteristic of "having compassion for all sentient beings." Just like the bodhisattva master, the vajra master's motivation in all activities is to help guide sentient beings to full enlightenment—the realization of their true nature as a Buddha.

Patrul Rinpoche places a similar emphasis on the above qualifications in *The Oral Instructions of My Excellent Lama,* where he describes the minimum qualifications of the lama as follows:

> Nowadays, during this degenerate time, although it is difficult to find a lama completely endowed with the qualities described in the precious tantras, whatever lama is followed must definitely have these qualities: He holds a pure lineage since he has not contradicted the commitments and prohibitions of the three vows— the outer vows of pratimoksha, the inner vows of the bodhisattva, and the secret vows of the secret mantrayana. He should be very learned, which means not to be unclear about the sutras, tantras, and shastras. His mind-stream should be so saturated with compassion that he loves all the limitless sentient beings as his only child. He should be expert in the outer *tripitakas* and on the inner level he should be expert in the ritual of the four classes of tantras of the secret mantra. He should have manifested the outstanding noble qualities of abandonment and realization in his mind-stream by having relied upon practicing the meaning of this. He gathers fortunate disciples by the four ways of attracting: generosity, pleasant speech, his conduct should benefit others, and he should act in accord with the dharma. These qualities he must have.[53]

Kongtrul Rinpoche concludes the section on the characteristics of the vajra master with a discussion of the "support" that is best for the lama to have. "Support" here refers to the type of vows that are held, layman (*dge-bsnyan*), novice monk (*dge-tshul*), or fully ordained monk (*dge-slong*). Kongtrul writes that out of these three it is best to take a fully ordained monk as your teacher. This advice does not include a lama who has reached at least the first bodhisattva bhumi,[54] because this type of lama is considered a superior teacher regardless of whether he is fully ordained or lay. A lama on or above the first bhumi is called a *"palden"* or "glorious" lama (*dpal-ldan bla-ma*). Kongtrul writes:

> The lama who has attained the first bhumi is the palden lama who distinctly becomes even greater than the other types of lamas.

He concludes by explaining that the palden lama is the highest type of master because he is able to bestow the blessings of Mahamudra and the fourth empowerment on the disciple.[55]

6 How to Choose a Wisdom Teacher

After familiarizing yourself with the necessary qualifications, it is very important for a student to fully examine the qualifications of the wisdom teacher and not be misled by outer appearances. Kongtrul Rinpoche writes:

> However great a lama's social status, fame, reputation, and so forth may be, those [students] who possess discernment examine [the wisdom teacher carefully].

We need to be careful in choosing a wisdom teacher because the consequences of working with an unqualified teacher are detrimental to spiritual growth; some students, after being "burnt" once, recoil from all teachers and even dharma practice itself. An unqualified teacher is one who lacks most of the characteristics previously described, or one who teaches or behaves in ways contrary to the dharma. Kongtrul advises students to stay away from teachers who are unqualified in order to avoid dire consequences. He quotes from the *Kalachakra-tantra* (*Kālacakra-tantra*):

> [The lamas who] cling to enjoyments, are careless, use harsh words, and are endowed with desiring the objects of the sense faculties, those people should be rejected by intelligent disciples, as if rejecting hell as a cause for complete awakening.

Patrul Rinpoche, in *The Oral Instructions of My Excellent Lama*, affirms that the student should not get involved with an unqualified lama:[56]

> Those [lamas who are] like brahmins defending their caste, or who live in a pool of fear for the survival of their monastery, bathe

themselves in the inappropriate results of their study and contemplation.

These guides are like a millstone made of wood,[57] and although their nature is not distinct from that of ordinary people, they acquire a superficial position due to the idiot faith of people.

Becoming arrogant through the offerings of wealth and respect, such a friend is like a frog in a well,[58] has little learning, and disregards his vows and samaya.

Although the level of their mind is low, their conduct has gone high above the earth. Cutting the lifeline of love and compassion, these crazy guides increase negative actions.

Especially, if they do not have greater noble qualities than yourself, or if they are without bodhicitta, but you still follow them because of the magnetism of their fame, then following such a blind captain as this is a big mistake. Through associating with such a charlatan you will wander into dense darkness.

Patrul Rinpoche also helps us understand the dangers of not properly examining the wisdom teacher:

The lama is the one on whom you place your trust, life after life. He is the one who shows you what should be accepted and what should be rejected. So if you encounter a false teacher through not having examined him properly, then all the virtues you accumulated as a faithful disciple throughout your entire life will be squandered, and the human body with its freedoms and endowments that you have now obtained will be wasted. For example, it is like mistaking a snake coiled beneath a tree for the tree's shadow, and upon approaching it, being killed by the snake.[59]

Sometimes a student examines the characteristics of the lama *after* taking him as a teacher. Kongtrul suggests that in the case of subsequently discovering that the lama is not qualified, the student should quietly distance himself from that lama. This should be done without criticism or generating negativity in any way. Obviously it is preferable for the student to examine the lama before taking him as a teacher, based upon the qualifications previously listed.

As we have seen, although it is important to find a lama who has the qualifications previously described, and to avoid a lama who lacks them, it is difficult to find someone who possesses all these qualities. Therefore, one must discern wisely when selecting a wisdom teacher. Kongtrul relates a few minimum essential characteristics which the lama should possess:

It is very rare for all the excellent characteristics (*legs-pa'i mtshan-nyid*) to be complete; therefore, even if you have not found a wisdom

teacher like that, because time is short, you should take as a lama
one who has few faults and more noble qualities.

Although the student familiarizes herself with the qualifications
previously mentioned, it is still difficult to recognize an authentic
teacher, because these qualities are internal. We can not depend upon
external factors, but external factors are what we see. It is very difficult to see the inner qualities of another person. A businessman might
be friendlier to us than our best friend, while his unseen motivation is
merely to make a sale. Likewise, if a "teacher" acts in a very kind and
loving manner towards us it does not necessarily mean that he is compassionate and selfless, because we cannot see his motivation. We also
cannot determine a teacher's qualifications based upon her fame, or
whether she has thousands of students. So the seeker is left with this
paradox.

There is no simple solution, but there are things we can do. First, it
is important that we familiarize ourselves with the characteristics discussed by Kongtrul Rinpoche. Second, we must maintain awareness
of our own motivation during the process of finding a teacher. Am I
seeking a teacher in order to attain enlightenment for the benefit of all
sentient beings, or am I seeking to fulfill my need to acquire the prestige
associated with a famous teacher, or am I merely attracted to a lama's
beautiful retreat land or the social scene of a hip sangha, and so on.

These motivations need to be acknowledged if we are to recognize
an authentic wisdom teacher, because the teacher you find is related
to your karma, and your karma is intimately connected to your motivation. Fortunately, there are methods that help us purify our motivation and create the proper conditions for finding a wisdom teacher,
such as bringing our awareness to our motivations as much as possible, doing daily meditation practice, and praying to the Triple Gem
that we will meet and recognize an authentic wisdom teacher.

7   The Qualifications of the Student

It is also necessary for the student to possess certain positive qualities and be free of certain negative ones. The qualifications of the student are dependent upon the level of the vow and training he will engage in: pratimoksha, bodhisattva, or, mantrayana.

The necessary qualifications become more stringent as one moves from the pratimoksha vow to the bodhisattva vow, and then to the tantric samaya. Each higher vow necessitates the qualities required by the lower; in the case of a contradiction between the vows, the higher would always override the lower.[60]

PRATIMOKSHA VOW: QUALIFICATIONS OF THE STUDENT

Jamgön Kongtrul states that a student suitable to take pratimoksha vows and practice accordingly must not do the four things which destroy the pratimoksha vow:[61] sexual intercourse, theft, murder of a human being, and false claim to spiritual achievement. In other words, the student must not commit acts that will completely sever the vow, nor acts that will create obstacles to the fulfillment of the pratimoksha vow. For instance, if one has killed someone, enjoys stealing, or even is merely undisciplined, one would not be considered a suitable candidate for the pratimoksha vows.

For the pratimoksha vow to become a support for one's spiritual practice, certain qualities should be present. The suitable candidate for the pratimoksha vows should have the following :

> Devotion: The student must have respect for his wisdom teachers. Only with the development of respect and devotion is a

student able to learn. Respect and devotion is also a sign of maturity and the loosening of the ego's tight grip.

Capacity to correctly take the vow: For the student to correctly take and follow the moral code, he must totally reject the four causes for its downfall (*ltung-ba*), as described above.

Meditation: It is important for the student to practice meditation, and for his concentration (*bsam-gtan*) to have reached a level that enables him to begin eliminating negative habitual tendencies.

Diligence in his studies: This includes the ability to recite the appropriate texts by heart.

Discipline: Both his mind and body must be under control.

Patience: The student must be mature enough to work with a teacher, and also mature enough to handle any altercations with others with patience.

Thus, Jamgön Kongtrul clearly shows that the pratimoksha vow is not appropriate for someone motivated by a desire to escape daily responsibilities or flee emotional problems. Kongtrul describes the student who is qualified to take and practice the pratimoksha vow as one who is well-balanced, ethical, and has stabilized his mind and behavior to some degree.

BODHISATTVA VOW: QUALIFICATIONS OF THE STUDENT

The student who is qualified for the bodhisattva training must have had bodhicitta awakened. Kongtrul Rinpoche quotes from *The Sutra of the Ten Noble Dharmas* (*Chos-bcu-pa'i mdo; Daśadharmaka-sūtra*):

> One knows the family (*rigs; gotra*) of the intelligent bodhisattva from the pure characteristics he possesses, just as from smoke one knows fire, and from a riverbank one knows there is water.

In order to undertake the bodhisattva vow training, Kongtrul states that the student must possess several important characteristics in addition to those of the pratimoksha vow:

Faith: The student must have faith in the Mahayana sutras, shastras, and the wisdom teacher.

Compassion: The student must not merely be concerned about her extrication from the suffering of samsara, but her concern must encompass all sentient beings without exception. According to Mahayana teachings, seeing the suffering of beings in the six realms of samsara, who have all been the student's mothers in past lives, arouses deep compassion in the student.

Intelligence: The student must have a sharp intellect, capable of understanding emptiness and of assimilating the extensive teachings of the Mahayana level of practice.

Acceptance of the extensive bodhisattva path: The Mahayana practices, such as the six paramitas, are very rigorous and require a complete commitment by the student, from moment to moment, in order to be fulfilled. According to tradition, through the Mahayana training the student becomes enlightened after being on the path for many eons or *kalpas*. Therefore, although her task is formidable, it is repeatedly stated by the Tibetan and Indian masters that the student should apply herself joyfully to the accomplishment of her aim. After attaining enlightenment, the bodhisattva continues to work towards liberating all sentient beings. Kongtrul states that in the face of this monumental task, the student needs to have an inner strength developed through her practice.

Enjoys bringing beings to liberation: Kongtrul explains that taking the bodhisattva vow means that the student rejects liberation for herself alone, and is committed to attaining enlightenment for the sole purpose of helping all other sentient beings attain enlightenment.

Diligence: Uninterrupted effort focused upon the practice and goal of the bodhisattva.

Inspired by teachings on emptiness: Kongtrul Rinpoche explains the importance for the student who is preparing to embark on the Mahayana training of having an understanding that is advanced enough that the teachings on emptiness inspire rather than frighten or discourage her.

Kongtrul also refers to three characteristics found in Aryadeva's *The Four Hundred* that the student should possess to enable him to maintain the relationship with a wisdom teacher:

Nonsectarian: The student must be mature enough to not denigrate other lineages, schools of Buddhism, or religions.

Discriminating: The student must also have the intelligence to discriminate between the numerous paths, and choose the one that will lead him and others to liberation.

Eagerness: The student should have enthusiasm for practicing the Mahayana path.[62]

Kongtrul states that a student who has those three qualities will have the correct view of the wisdom teacher:

> If the disciple is endowed with those three, then, on the one hand, he will see the good qualities of the wisdom teacher as good qualities [and therefore engage in a proper relationship with the spiritual friend]. If the disciple is not endowed with those three qualities, then on the other hand, the great number of good qualities of the wisdom teacher will be seen as faults [and a proper relationship will not develop].

VAJRAYANA VOW: QUALIFICATIONS OF THE STUDENT

Kongtrul Rinpoche writes that to be a qualified disciple for tantric training, the student must have all the characteristics previously described for the pratimoksha and bodhisattva trainings, plus additional qualities:

> Those who are suitable vessels, who are given the ripening [empowerments] and liberating [instructions] of secret mantra, are summed up by these kinds of qualities in addition to those just explained [for the pratimoksha and bodhisattva vows]: [The disciple should] be very devoted to the lama; tantrically capable in the profound view and practice, and so forth; have a vast intellect, which is without doubt in the aim of the secret mantra, and which realizes reality (*de-nyid*); be capable of diligence in [keeping] the samaya and in the practice (*sgrub-pa*) of [what needs to be] rejected and accepted.

As Jamgön Kongtrul indicates, first and foremost, the disciple must have deep devotion toward his root lama, which goes beyond the appreciation and respect he has for the wisdom teacher in the pratimoksha and bodhisattva trainings. Although Kongtrul does not elaborate on the role of devotion, it is important for us to briefly look at the role devotion to the lama plays on the Vajrayana path.

Devotion

In the Vajrayana tradition it is held that at this level of training devotion is equal in importance to compassion. The student must have devotion for all the enlightened beings and compassion for all sentient beings.

The Vajrayana disciple, like all Buddhists, cultivates devotion towards the Triple Gem: the Buddha, the dharma, and the sangha. In addition, she must also cultivate strong devotion to the three roots: the lama, who is the root of blessings; the *yidams*, who are the root of accomplishment; and the dharma protectors, who are the root of activity. At the Vajrayana level of practice the lama takes on supreme importance because she embodies the Triple Gem and the three roots, and transmits the teachings of the Buddha to the disciple. H.E. Kalu Rinpoche explains:

> The importance of the Lama is characteristic of the Vajrayana, and is not found in the Hinayana or Mahayana. It is true that praying to the Buddhas and bodhisattvas and taking refuge in them is an effective way to attain enlightenment, but it is more gradual than the Vajrayana way of establishing a working relationship with a Lama. The Vajrayana contains teachings that can take one to the experience of complete enlightenment in this lifetime. The Lama is the one who bestows those teachings. That is why the Lama is so crucial in tantric practice, and why Mahamudra teachings, which are part of tantric practice, place such emphasis on the student's relationship with the Lama.[63]

Patrul Rinpoche, in *The Oral Instructions of My Excellent Lama*, commenting on the importance of the lama, states:

> The essence of what is to be accomplished in all practices, such as the two stages of creation and completion, is embodied in the lama. That is why it is said in all the sutras and tantras that the lama is the actual Buddha.[64]

The lama is the root of all blessings for the disciples because it is through the lama that we receive the teachings and guidance which liberate us from all suffering. The lama bestows his blessings upon the disciple in three ways:[65] through teachings, symbols, and action. It is through teachings that students most often receive blessings. Blessings are received through symbols during an empowerment ritual. Receiving blessings through action does not occur in a formal way but rather during the ordinary activities of the day. The stories of the great tantric masters and *mahasiddhas*, such as Naropa and Milarepa, are full of examples of this third type of blessing.

As the disciple slowly begins to experience, through practice, the futility of samsaric living, he begins to develop appreciation for the dharma teachings as practical tools for living a meaningful life. He then naturally begins to develop respect and gratitude towards the lama, who devotes his time and energy to the sole purpose of helping the student realize his true nature.

Devotion is a prerequisite to receiving the lama's blessings; and the lama's blessings are needed to attain enlightenment (the supreme siddhi) or the worldly benefits (common siddhi) that will support practice. Kongtrul, in his commentary on *guru yoga* practice emphasizes this point:

> It is said that a disciple who is intensely devoted and reverent towards a fully qualified Vajrayana master with whom he has formed a sacred bond (*samaya*) will achieve supreme and worldly siddhi without doing anything else. But a person who lacks devotion and reverence for the guru, even if he performs a great many *nyendrub* practices for the yidams of the four tantras, will obtain no supreme siddhi whatsoever.[66]

Kongtrul Rinpoche first states that supreme siddhi, in other words complete awakening, has never been attained without the blessings of the guru. All tantric practitioners, such as Tilopa, Naropa, Marpa, and Milarepa, have attained enlightenment through receiving the blessings of their gurus. These blessings are not material but occur through the compassion of the guru and the devotion of the disciple. The disciple can see whether blessings have been received by specific signs, such as the disciple's body, speech, and mind becoming soft gentle, and nonaggressive; a natural disdain developing for activities which bring negative consequences for self and others; and concurrently, the disciple naturally becoming involved with activities that benefit self and others. Another sign that blessings have been received is that the disciple develops a strong interest in the spiritual biographies of the enlightened masters, and a strong desire grows to follow that path.

As the blessings alter the conduct of the disciple, indicated by the above signs, uncontrived devotion arises. When this occurs, the lama's enlightened mind dissolves into the disciple's buddha-nature, both becoming inseparable. This is the supreme siddhi, which cannot be received without the guru's blessing.

Ability to understand the profound view

Second, Jamgön Kongtrul states that the disciple must also have the ability to understand the profound view of the Vajrayana. The view that Kongtrul is referring to is called "pure vision" (*dag-snang*), or seeing all appearances as pure. In this view, particular to the Vajrayana, the practitioner sees herself and all sentient beings as the deity, all sounds as mantra, and the external world as the pure land of the deity. Thus, all forms are the form of the deity—the union of form and emptiness; all sounds are the mantra of the deity—the union of speech and emptiness; all thoughts and feelings are inseparable from primordial awareness (*ye-shes*)—the union of clarity and emptiness. The disciple must then be able to put this view into the practice of the development stage (*bskyed-rim; utpattikrama*) and completion stage (*rdzogs-rim; sampannakrama*).

Confidence in the efficacy of tantric practice

Third, Kongtrul writes that it is also important for the practitioner to be without doubt in the efficacy of tantric practice. In Vajrayana practice intention is considered very important, and the practitioner must have full confidence in the Vajrayana methods in order for them to be effective. For instance, if one is meditating on Guru Rinpoche while doubting that he is real or the method effective, then no results will occur. On the other hand, a disciple who meditates with full confidence will receive results and obtain the blessings of the enlightened mind of Guru Rinpoche.

Ability to keep samaya unimpaired

The fourth important quality a disciple should have is the ability to keep the samaya with her lama and yidam. Keeping samaya means that the disciple does not commit the fourteen root downfalls or the eight secondary downfalls.[67]

THE TYPE OF STUDENT: WHO IS REFUSED AND WHO IS ACCEPTED

Kongtrul Rinpoche next describes the type of person the lama should refuse as a disciple. At the Vajrayana level of training, the lama should not take as a disciple someone who exhibits selfishness, develops arrogance through dharma study, lacks faith in the Triple Gem, is dishonest, aggressive, has contempt or belittles the empowerments, and so forth.

Kun Khyen Longchenpa, in his work *Resting in the Nature of Mind*, describes the unworthy disciple as follows:

> Otherwise, the foundation of everything that goes wrong is the unfortunate disciple. Without shame or modesty, and having little compassion, their type (*rigs*), nature, behavior, and opportunity are unworthy. In their mind and actions the passions' five poisons are obvious. They are confused in their training of what is dharma and what is not dharma, what is virtuous and what is unvirtuous. They do not protect their vows and samaya, and are without any remedy. They are ignorant, with little intelligence, and difficult to satisfy. Their anger and harsh words increase more and more.[68]

Jamgön Kongtrul indicates that usually the situation is not so clear-cut—a disciple rarely possesses either all the good qualities or all the negative qualities previously described. Most prospective practitioners of the Vajrayana teachings have a mixture of good qualities and faults. Under such circumstances, the lama should take on as a disciple one who is genuinely eager to practice the Vajrayana teachings of the Buddha.

Kongtrul also suggests intelligence as a minimum criterion for accepting a disciple, as is expressed in *The General Tantra (sPyi-gyud)*:

> A disciple who is physically intact, has exceptional noble qualities, is free from illness, is from a respectable family, has faith, and possesses vows is rare. In summary, these are great sentient beings who have faith in the three jewels, delight in the system of the Mahayana, and who possess merit. Therefore, the disciple who is eager and strives to practice the Sugata's secret mantra, although possessing an inferior form and not possessing noble qualities, because of being intelligent, should be brought onto the path.

Thus, Kongtrul advises the wisdom teacher to accept as a disciple someone with the minimum requirements of eagerness as well as intelligence.

8 How to Follow the Wisdom Teacher

Jamgön Kongtrul states that the teacher-student relationship is created and nurtured in two steps. First there should be a careful, mutual examination by the wisdom teacher and the student, then they should enter into a relationship. Through it, the student attains enlightenment and the teacher fulfills his commitment to guide sentient beings to enlightenment; thus it is very important for the relationship to be pure, uncontaminated with negativity, and unbroken.

He explains that examining the relationship is important, because if a relationship is begun with an unqualified teacher or student, both will break their samaya and they will have many problems. Kongtrul quotes from the *Fifty Stanzas on Guru Devotion* to emphasize the importance of a good relationship between the wisdom teacher and the student:

> Because the lama and student will fail together in the samaya, in the beginning, the warrior should examine the relationship of the master and the student.

Kongtrul writes that if a lama gives empowerments to a student who cannot keep the tantric commitments (*samaya*), the lama will experience problems such as taking progressively worse rebirths, the attainment of siddhis will be postponed for a long time, and numerous problems and obstacles will occur.

He also enumerates the many problems the student will encounter if he receives empowerments from an unqualified lama: the student will be led down the wrong path; he will not be able keep his samaya; he will not be able to attain the siddhis; his precious human rebirth will be squandered.

Thus, Jamgön Kongtrul emphasizes that it is necessary for both the teacher and the student to examine each other before committing to a relationship. Many of us in the West, practicing on various spiritual paths, leap into the teacher-student relationship, *then* begin examining our teacher and find faults. Often the student becomes angry and leaves the relationship, feeling hurt and speaking negatively about the teacher. Had the student examined the teacher initially, this problematic situation might not have arisen. This tendency is not confined to Western students. In fourteenth-century Tibet Kun Khyen Longchenpa wrote:

> First, when the relationship is new, they recklessly get involved without examination. They speak of each of the lama's noble qualities, but later on there is only recrimination. For some, whatever they do is mixed with deception and backbiting, and they dishearten the close circle [of disciples] around the lama; for them the result is the lowest hell itself.[69]

Thus, it is necessary for a Buddhist student in the Tibetan tradition to be familiar with the traditional lists given by Kongtrul of the qualities which characterize the qualified wisdom teacher. After examining a teacher, the student may choose not to enter into a relationship for two primary reasons: the teacher is unqualified, as Kongtrul previously described; or, although he is qualified, his style or personality may not be suitable for that particular student. To determine whether or not the wisdom teacher is qualified, the student should refer to chapters three and four of the auto-commentary, in which Kongtrul describes the authentic teacher.

On the second point, although in the present work Kongtrul does not refer to the style or personality of the lama, it is frequently mentioned in the oral instructions given by lamas. Khenpo Tsultrim Gyamtso Rinpoche illustrated this point with the example of an inharmonious match between a wisdom teacher who likes to focus upon logic and philosophy, and a student who prefers meditation practice.

Kongtrul Rinpoche states that after the student has examined the wisdom teacher and has decided he is both qualified and suitable, he should then fully rely upon that teacher as the necessary condition (*rkyen*) for attaining enlightenment. Gampopa, in *An Ornament to Precious Liberation*, writes:

> ...although you may possess the most perfect support [*rten*, the precious human body], but are not urged on by spiritual friends as a condition [for attaining enlightenment], it is difficult to set

out on the path towards enlightenment, because of the power of habitual tendencies (*bag-chags*) due to bad deeds committed repeatedly in former times.[70]

In order to correctly rely upon the teacher, the student must have the proper attitude and then apply herself towards following the teacher. Kongtrul states that the proper attitude is to rely upon the spiritual friend in order to attain complete enlightenment. It is important that the student not be motivated to enter a relationship with a lama by the desire for personal gain, for example, the desire to gain respect by being associated with a great teacher.

Kongtrul writes that after having established the proper attitude, the student then follows the lama through action. He enumerates three principle methods for following the lama: giving material things and honor; paying respect; and following the lama by means of practicing his teachings. He explains that the student should be willing to offer the lama all his material possessions. The traditional texts state that an advanced disciple, such as Naropa, Marpa, or Milarepa, would offer everything to the lama, including wife, children, or his own body, speech, and mind. For most students today, however, these types of offerings are not only not expected, but strongly discouraged.

Honoring the lama means that the disciple is respectful. When the lama enters the room the student stands until the lama sits down, and then the student offers three prostrations. Also, upon entering a room where the lama is present the student should prostrate three times. Because the student treats the wisdom teacher as if he is Buddha himself, he will not use the wisdom teacher's utensils, clothing, or seat. In the teacher's presence, it is considered disrespectful for the student to lie down, yawn without covering his mouth, or to sit on the floor with his feet pointing towards the teacher.

Paying respect includes doing the various things a student can do for the teacher. In Tibet, for example, a student might have the opportunity of bathing or massaging the wisdom teacher. In the West, paying respect may include running errands, doing chores, helping carry things for the teacher, and so forth.

Traditionally, the most important way of following the wisdom teacher is to carry out all his instructions and advice concerning dharma practice. To this effect Kongtrul states:

> Cheerfully practicing all the commands (*bsgo-ba*) given by the lama, and assiduously practicing whatever possible in the way of listening (*thos*), contemplating (*bsam*), and meditating (*sgom*) upon

all the dharma teachings, is better worship (*bsnyen-bkur*) than the ways previously mentioned, because the authentic wisdom teacher is pleased by the offering of practice, and not by material things and so forth.

Patrul Rinpoche, in *The Oral Instructions of My Excellent Lama*, reiterates that the best offering is one of practice:

> Although the lama is pleased by three types of service, it is said that the supreme type is the offering of practice. This means persevering in the practice of all the teachings taught by the lama and enduring all hardships. The intermediate way of rendering service is serving your lama by doing whatever he wants you to do with your body, speech, and mind. The lowest way to please your lama is by making generous offerings of material things such as food and wealth.[71]

Therefore, we are shown that although it is important to be generous with offerings and to pay respect to the wisdom teacher, the best offering is to put her teachings into practice and thereby attain enlightenment for the benefit of all sentient beings.

9 The Necessity of Following the Wisdom Teacher

Jamgön Kongtrul explains in two ways the necessity of following a wisdom teacher: "by proof" and by describing the advantages as given in the sutras and tantras. The teacher is proof that the dharma is an effective means for attaining enlightenment, and following the wisdom teacher is the purest activity, itself leading the student to enlightenment. He uses the term *brahmacharya*, which is usually associated with celibacy, but also generally refers to living a life in accordance with the precepts of Buddhism. Kongtrul quotes from Nagarjuna's *A Letter to a Friend:*

> Because the Sage has said: "The pure conduct (*brahmacarya*) of following the wisdom teacher is perfect," follow the wisdom teacher; and after following the wisdom teacher, very many disciples have obtained peace.

Lama Mipham Rinpoche (Mi-pham 'jam-dbyangs rnam-gyal rgya-mtsho) comments on Nagarjuna's verse:

> Furthermore, reliance on a spiritual friend is a pure act. "Pure" means beyond emotional needs and "act" means the path.[72]

Another commentary on this famous verse of Nagarjuna is by Venerable Rendawa Zhonu Lodrö (Re mda'-ba gzhon-nu blo-gros), a great lama of the Sakya school (1349-1412):

> In pursuing the path, one should first rely upon a spiritual teacher (*kalyāṇamitra*). This reliance was said by the *Muni* [Sage] to bring about the fulfillment of a religious way of life (*tshangs-par spyod-*

pa; brahmacarya). As a sutra states: "Ananda, it is thus: spiritual teachers and virtuous companions are the fulfillment of the religious way of life. The reason for this, if you should ask Ananda, is that every good quality that arises does so on the basis of a spiritual teacher—and it is through their arising that one achieves liberation." Therefore, one should always rely upon wise persons, as did the numerous individuals who attained peace through relying on the *Jina* [the Victorious One]. In this instance, a "religious way of life" (*brahmacarya*) is meant as the path to liberation, in the sense that one's conduct (*carya*) in this direction constitutes an endeavor to accomplish the eradication (*bṛdha*, relating to *brahma*) of all the defects of existence—that is, to attain nirvana.[73]

Next, Kongtrul states that the sutras and tantras describe numerous benefits and advantages of following the spiritual friend. Kongtrul refers to some of the benefits, as described in the Mahayana teachings, for a bodhisattva who follows a spiritual friend: He will not take lower rebirths; he will not get involved in negativity; he does not contradict the bodhisattva's training; he completes the accumulation of merit and wisdom; he purifies obscurations; liberation is quickly attained; and provisional and ultimate aims will be achieved.[74]

If the student does not follow, or follows improperly, problems will arise, such as sickness and obstacles in this life, and rebirth in lower realms in future lives.

Kun Khyen Longchenpa, in *Resting in the Nature of Mind*, lists several benefits of following a wisdom teacher:

> You should always follow the sublime virtuous friend. Virtuous actions increase through them, while negative deeds and passions diminish, and all faults are halted. You cross over existence, achieve the higher realms and liberation. In this life you will be happy, in the future you will have the fruition [of your positive actions], and you will become a worthwhile guide of gods and humans. By following a wisdom teacher and virtuous friend your accumulation of virtue increases and you will attain the result of happiness. You will be fearless in the world and experience inexhaustible benefits and exaltation, and you will accomplish the infinite wealth of the two benefits of beings. The wisdom teacher is the emanation of the Victorious Ones; he is the universal guide appearing in this way during degenerate times. Hence, until the heart of enlightenment is attained, you should rely upon these sublime beings.[75]

Kongtrul Rinpoche states that according to the sutras and the tantras the student should follow the wisdom teacher with even greater devotion than that for the Buddhas. He quotes from *The Vajrapani*

Empowerment Tantra (*Lag-na rdo-rje dbang-bskur-ba'i rgyud; Ārya-Vajra-pāṇi-abhiṣeka-mahātantra*):

> O Lord Guhyapati, if you ask, "How should the disciple view the wisdom teacher?" Just as [you would view] the Buddha Bhagavat, [view the wisdom teacher] like that.

Especially in the Vajrayana, the lama is viewed as being even greater than the Buddha, because it is from the lama that we receive teachings, empowerments, and advice. We are not advanced enough to take teachings directly from the Buddha, as Kongtrul explains in chapter three. H.E. Kalu Rinpoche, in *The Gem Ornament of Manifold Instructions*, explains:

> We consider our guru to be equal to the Buddhas and bodhisattvas
> in terms of the qualities and realization that our guru embodies,
> but even more kind than they are from our point of view.[76]

It is the lama who, out of deep compassion, guides us out of the suffering of samsara. It is said that even if the Buddha were to appear before us, he would not give teachings different from those of the lama. Kongtrul makes this point by quoting the famous passage from *The Guhyasamaja-tantra* (*gSang-ba dus-pa; Guhyasamāja-tantra*):

> There is greater merit through offering to a pore of hair of the
> lama, than offering to the Buddhas of the ten directions and three
> times.

Kongtrul Rinpoche concludes this section by reminding the student that any action she does in relation to the wisdom teacher, whether good or bad, will have a very powerful effect, thus implying that the student should cultivate meritorious actions of even the smallest kind, and be very mindful not to commit even the smallest negative action towards the wisdom teacher.

10 How to Avoid a False Teacher and the Wrong Path

In this chapter Jamgön Kongtrul describes the two kinds of obstacles that can hinder the student on the path to enlightenment. The obstacles are taking an unqualified person as your wisdom teacher, and various hindrances that arise after taking a qualified wisdom teacher and embarking on the true path to awakening.

TAKING AN UNQUALIFIED PERSON AS YOUR TEACHER

Kongtrul strongly re-emphasizes the importance of rejecting a teacher who pretends to be a lama but is unqualified and inauthentic. In the scriptures such a person is called a "non-spiritual teacher" (*mi-dge-ba'i bshes-gnyen*) or a "harmful spiritual teacher" (*sdig-pa'i bshes-gnyen*). Kongtrul defines the non-spiritual teacher as:

> ...a lama, teacher, dharma brother [or sister] and so forth, all those who are attached to the phenomena of this life and who get involved in unvirtuous activity.

To be "attached to appearances" means to relate to oneself, others, and the world while being motivated and controlled by the three poisons (*dug-gsum*) of attachment ('*dod-chags; rāga*), aversion (*zhe-sdang; dveṣa*), and stupidity (*gti-mug; moha*). An unqualified teacher's motivation is primarily to benefit himself, contradicting the bodhisattva's vow to benefit others. Some of the additional characteristics listed by Kongtrul to aid the student in recognizing a false teacher are: the teacher is involved in unvirtuous activity; he has a bad temperament, glorifies himself, puts down others, or speaks negatively about authentic teachers.

Kongtrul emphasizes the importance of rejecting such a teacher because, in addition to obstructing the student's progress towards enlightenment, mere association with him causes the development of negative qualities in the student. He emphasizes this point by quoting from the *Sutra of the True Dharma of Clear Recollection:*

> As the chief among the obstructors of all virtuous qualities is the sinful teacher, one should abandon being associated with him, speaking with him, or even being touched by his shadow.

The great Nyingma master Kun Khyen Longchenpa also warns of the danger of becoming associated with an unqualified teacher. In *Resting in the Nature of Mind* he explains:

> Also, harmful friends must be abandoned. To the extent they are your friends, negative deeds will increase, virtue will diminish, and the passions will descend like rain. Going to the higher realms of happiness will be blocked and they will be your stairs down to the lower realms. They will disparage the sacred and hate wholesome dharmas. They praise what is bad and follow after unwholesome dharmas. They glorify those who participate in the same kind of nonvirtuous deeds, and since they always lead you along the wrong path and to the lower realms, a person with the eye of intelligence will keep them far away.[77]

HINDRANCES ENCOUNTERED AFTER TAKING A QUALIFIED WISDOM TEACHER

The types of hindrances that arise after one has formed a relationship with a qualified lama can be generally classified as various types of "mara" (*bdud; māra*). Here Kongtrul quotes from the *Compendium* (*sDud-pa; Ratnaguṇa-saṃcayagāthā*):

> There is continuous damage to the precious dharma and the three jewels. Those sentient beings whose intellectual abilities are low, who have newly entered into the vehicle, some of them do not even find this precious rare one. In order to create obstacles for them, mara will be energetic.

The term "mara" is used throughout the sutras and tantras and is usually translated as "demon." For the Western reader it is important to clarify this term, which does not refer to external beings or entities separate from the mind. Khenpo Tsultrim Gyamtso Rinpoche explained that all obstacles to attaining the ultimate goal of enlightenment are maras. He emphasized that maras are not ghosts or demons, but obstacles, by giving the following example: If a student asks for the concise explanation of a particular subject, but the lama gives an extended one, this may be a hindrance, a mara, for the student. Or, if the teacher's predilection is for extensive study while the student's is for practice, this could also be considered a mara.

Traditionally, there are numerous classifications of mara. Jamgön Kongtrul mentions that the maras can be classified into six outer maras, three inner maras, eighteen secret maras, and so forth. He does not describe these classifications. Khenpo Tsultrim Gyamtso Rinpoche, when asked for his commentary, declined to comment on them, saying that an explanation of the three inner maras, six outer maras, and eighteen secret maras is not relevant for this text.

Instead, Kongtrul describes the four maras that interfere with the practice of dharma, followed by the antidotes with which the practitioner armors himself in order to conquer these maras. These four maras are:

1) Thinking about the faults of the spiritual friend and not desiring to exert oneself in hearing and contemplating.
2) Relying on divisiveness, foolish talk, and so forth, which are the causes of anger.
3) Distractions of food, drink, a [comfortable] bed, business, and so on.
4) Sinking under the influence of sleepiness and laziness.

The first of the above refers to focusing upon the perceived shortcomings of the lama, and, out of laziness, not engaging in study and reflection on the teachings. The antidote for this mara is to develop faith and devotion in the lama and one's dharma brothers and sisters (*mched-grogs*).

The second mara refers to using speech in negative or idle ways. The antidote for this mara is to become fully engaged in studying dharma teachings, reading, reflecting, and practicing meditation.

The third mara personifies the distractions and attachments we encounter daily. Trust (*yid-ches*) in the dharma is the antidote to conquer this mara. Trust here means confidence that the teachings passed down to us from the Buddha through our lama are effective, and that by engaging in them wholeheartedly we will attain full Buddhahood.

The fourth mara refers to the pitfalls of laziness and lethargy. The antidote for this mara is the determination not to be overpowered by discursive thoughts (*rnam-rtog*) and not to have an agitated mind.

11   The Importance of Faith

In chapter nine, Jamgön Kongtrul paraphrases and briefly comments on Je Gampopa's discussion of faith (*dad-pa*) found in *An Ornament to Precious Liberation*.[78] Kongtrul skims over Gampopa's discussion of faith because his readers would already be familiar with the material, since this text is the principal *lam rim* text of the Kagyu tradition.[79] A lam rim text elucidates the stages one traverses on the path. Because Kongtrul's handling of the material is unclear unless the reader is familiar with *An Ornament to Precious Liberation*, the following is based directly on Gampopa's work.

Faith is an important element in Buddhism. In *An Ornament to Precious Liberation* Gampopa discusses faith in the context of the preciousness of human birth,[80] and as a foundation for the discussion of the wisdom teacher.[81] He first describes the reasons why human birth is precious—because it is difficult to obtain, easily lost, and is the vehicle that brings us to enlightenment. Gampopa quotes from *The Guide to the Bodhisattva's Way of Life* (*Bodhisattva-caryāvatāra*):

> Relying on the boat of the human body, save yourself from the great waters of samsara. Since later this boat will be difficult to find, do not sleep in ignorance![82]

In order to make use of this precious human birth and set out on the path to full awakening, faith is a requisite because faith is the cause of the attainment of all positive qualities. Kongtrul writes:

> In general, faith is the preliminary of all positive qualities, and in particular, generating the three aspects of faith is very important at the beginning of both following the wisdom teacher and being diligent on the path.

Positive qualities allow the accumulation of merit, which, in addition to wisdom, is needed on the path to full awakening. Gampopa writes:

> For one who does so [aims for enlightenment], faith is necessary.
> It is said that if one lacks faith, the positive qualities will not arise
> in one's mind-stream. This is affirmed in *The Sutra of the Ten Noble
> Dharmas*:
>
>> Positive qualities do not grow in people without faith, just as a
>> green sprout does not grow from a burnt seed.
>
> And it is also said in the *Buddha-Avatamsaka Sutra* (*Sangs-rgyas
> phal-po-che'i mdo; Buddhāvataṃsaka Sūtra*):
>
>> Worldly people with little faith are unable to understand the
>> enlightenment of the Buddha.
>
> Therefore, faith has to be cultivated, as is stated in *The Sutra of
> Vast Display* (*Phags-pa rgya-che rol-pa; Lalitavistara*):
>
>> The Buddha said, "Ananda, you must adhere to faith."[83]

In the Buddhist context, faith does not represent a blind acceptance of doctrinal truths, but rather, faith refers to the confidence the student develops as he begins to experience these truths for himself. Gampopa describes three types of faith: trusting faith (*yid-ches-pa'i dad-pa*), longing faith (*'dod-pa'i dad-pa*), and clear-minded faith (*dang-ba'i dad-pa*).

Gampopa describes trusting faith as having confidence in karma, cause and result; in the truth of suffering (the first noble truth); and in the truth of the origination of suffering (the second noble truth). It is important for the beginning student to understand the workings of karma, because positive actions will lead to worldly happiness in this and future lives, as well as favorable conditions for progress on the path. Negative actions will lead to suffering in this and future lives, and will create many obstacles on the path to awakening. The results of karma are infallible. Gampopa quotes from the *Sutra of the True Dharma of Clear Recollection*:

> Although it may be possible for fire to turn cold; and it may even
> be possible that the wind may be caught with a lasso; and it may
> yet be possible that the sun and moon fall down; still the results
> of karma are infallible.[84]

The student, by observing his experience, can develop faith rooted in this experience. For instance, we can notice that after drinking sour milk our stomach gets upset. If we eat honey, it tastes sweet, not salty. This is knowledge based upon experience. We can also make the same type of connection with regard to our emotions. If we are very angry with someone and express this anger, we will create suffering for ourself and the other person. If we are aware while feeling this anger, we will see that we feel terrible inside. Even after the situation is over, a very unpleasant feeling may linger. Also, in retrospect, we may regret having hurt the person who was the object of our anger. We can also see the suffering inflicted on the other person—he or she may feel sad, hurt, or in turn respond with anger.

Therefore, by being mindful of his experience, the student begins to develop faith in the truth of karma. It is said that a very angry person may be born in the hell realm. This is difficult for us to confirm through our own experience, but based upon our faith in karma, rooted in our experience, we can trust that this is also true. So, the faith of trust is trusting that positive actions lead to happiness and negative actions lead to suffering. In some situations we will be certain that this is true, and in other situations we will trust that it is true.

One must have trust concerning the truth of suffering and the truth of the origination of suffering. In this context, Gampopa states that one must have trust that the source of suffering, the second noble truth, is caused by the passions (nyon-mongs; kleśa), namely ignorance (ma-rig-pa), desire ('dod-chags), anger (khong-khro), pride (nga-rgyal), doubt (the-tshom), and wrong views (log-lta). One must also have trust that the result of these actions is the generation of the five aggregates (phung-po; skandha), namely form, feeling, perception, karmic formation, and consciousness. The aggregates are inherently suffering and correspond to the first noble truth.

The second type of faith is longing faith. This means that the student recognizes enlightenment as the most valuable goal in life. Then she desires to attain enlightenment, and begins to engage upon the path itself.

The third type of faith is called clear-minded faith. This refers to someone whose mind is clear with regard to relying with devotion and without doubt on the three jewels and the lama. Gampopa states:

> Clear faith is relying on the three excellent and rare objects, then giving rise to them. It is a clear mind having respect and devotion for the excellent rare objects: the jewel of the Buddha who shows the path; the jewel of the dharma as being the path; and the jewel of the sangha as being the [spiritual] friends who accomplish the path.[85]

Next, Gampopa describes the qualities needed in order to be considered a person who has faith. He states that a student who has faith will not abandon the dharma due to desire, anger, fear, or delusion.

Every day situations arise in which we experience the above afflictions, and by surrendering to them we abandon the dharma and are shown to be without faith. For example, Gampopa says that a student with faith in the dharma will not abandon it due to desire. Even if the student is offered wealth, fame, and prestige under the condition he drop dharma practice, the student with faith in the dharma won't do it. This is because he has faith that through the dharma he will attain his aim in life—enlightenment for the benefit of all sentient beings. The same is true regarding delusion. Gampopa gives the following example:

> Not passing over the dharma because of delusion (rmongs-pa), means to not give up the dharma from the perspective of not knowing (mi-shes). For example, if someone says, "Karma is not true, effect is not true, the three jewels are not true. What is the use of practicing the dharma? Leave the dharma!" Still you should not give up the dharma.[86]

Gampopa next writes that a person with faith experiences inconceivable benefits, and this person is considered the perfect vessel for dharma teachings. He describes some of the benefits as follows:

> The mind of the supreme person (skyes-bu mchog) arises; [the eight] unfavorable conditions are abandoned; the senses are sharp and clear; discipline is unimpaired; afflictions are removed; mara's sphere of activity is passed beyond; the path of liberation is found; extensive virtues are accumulated; many Buddhas are seen; and so forth.[87]

From the above benefits we can see the tremendous importance Buddhism places on faith. There may seem to be a tension between the Buddhist emphasis on one's own experience and the importance placed on faith, but they are not mutually exclusive. In Buddhism, faith is grounded in one's experience and is not blind faith. It is because experience is emphasized that real faith or confidence is possible. Buddhism emphasizes listening to and studying the dharma, then experiencing whatever was discussed by putting it into practice. After having experienced the truth of a previous teaching, when the student is confronted with a new teaching which she has not yet confirmed in her experience, it is easier to have faith that it is so.

For instance, after hearing that from the ultimate view there is no self to be found (bdag-med; nairātmya), the student can study this. There is not the expectation by the wisdom teacher that this must be accepted at face value. Instead, the student will be encouraged to study the five aggregates—that they comprise the apparent self, and so forth.

Through this process the student might intellectually grasp the teaching that there is no permanent self, or he still may have some doubts. In either case, the student would then go and meditate on this. Step by step, investigating each aggregate, he would look at his own body and mind and search for a permanent self. At the end of the process the student would have some experience of no-self. Perhaps the next teaching might be on the inseparability of samsara and nirvana, a truth that the student has trouble immediately experiencing for himself. Because he has the previous experience of the concordance between the Buddha's teaching on no-self and his own experience, his faith in the truth of the inseparability of samsara and nirvana is based on intelligence and experience, not blind adherence to doctrine.

Therefore, the more the student tries to practice the dharma teachings, the less tension will be found between self-reliance and faith. Actually, self-reliance, experiencing the truth of the dharma, becomes the foundation for faith in the Buddhist sense.

Gampopa concludes his discussion of faith by stating that only a person who has obtained the precious human body—which includes the eight leisures and ten opportunities—and whose mind has the three types of faith, is considered qualified to attain complete enlightenment. Kongtrul summarizes his paraphrase of Gampopa's discussion of faith as follows:

> To summarize, because faith is the basis of all positive qualities, you should try to rely on the causes and conditions which create and increase faith, eliminate the causes and conditions which decrease faith, and you should strive to stabilize faith.

12 How to Teach and Listen to the Dharma

Kongtrul divides the discussion of how the wisdom teacher and student should participate in teaching and learning the dharma into four sections:

1) What the wisdom teacher and student need to do in order to prepare for the teachings
2) What they should do during the teachings
3) What they should do at the conclusion of the teachings
4) A discussion of the benefits obtained by teaching and learning the dharma

This chapter summarizes Book I, part 3 of Buton's *The Jewelry of Scripture*.[88]

WHAT THE WISDOM TEACHER AND STUDENT NEED TO DO IN ORDER TO PREPARE FOR THE TEACHINGS

Preparation of the wisdom teacher

Regarding the wisdom teacher's preparation to teach the dharma, Kongtrul writes that the teacher must prepare for giving dharma teachings by making the proper arrangements, removing obstacles, and engaging in proper behavior.

"Proper arrangements" refers to the wisdom teacher's motivation to teach for the benefit of all sentient beings, rather than to gain wealth, fame, prestige, and so forth. He should wear clean and appropriate clothing, and should arrange a throne to sit on. Traditionally, this throne is raised off the ground by resting upon eight sculptured lions, and the seat is adorned with fine silk. When the wisdom teacher sits on the throne his motivation is to teach the dharma out of devotion to the Buddha and dharma, and with compassion for all sentient beings. When the wisdom teacher sits on the throne it becomes an opportunity for the students to accumulate merit and purify their obscurations.

"Removing obstacles" means that after completing the previous arrangements the wisdom teacher must eliminate any obstacles that may arise during the teaching. This is accomplished by reciting the mantra of a "wisdom protector," whose compassion manifests in a wrathful form. Jamgön Kongtrul refers to the *Sutra Requested by Sagaramati the Naga King* (*bLo-'gro rgya-mtshos zhus-pa'i mdo; Sāgaramati-paripṛcchā-sūtra*) to illustrate how to accomplish this. This sutra says that the wisdom teacher should initially:

> Generate the five notions, namely: oneself as the doctor, the dharma as the medicine, the listener [disciple] as the patient, the holy person as the Tathagata; and that the activity of the dharma will reside for a long time; and recite loudly the mantra so that the deities of mara's faction can't come within one hundred miles.[89]

The preparation of the wisdom teacher concludes with a discussion on "proper behavior," which involves the proper ways in which he should comport his body, speech, and mind. Kongtrul says that the wisdom teacher should not lie down, stretch out his legs, or be sloppy with his body in any way during the teachings. Instead, the wisdom teacher sits cross-legged upon the throne.

Preparation of the student

Before the teachings begin, the student should first offer a gift to the wisdom teacher, behave respectfully, and cultivate joyful appreciation for the opportunity to hear the dharma.

The student should first prostrate to the teacher, then offer a gift. This is done out of respect and devotion for both the dharma and the teacher. The dharma is very precious because it contains countless methods which bring the student to full awakening. The student offers a gift to the lama out of a feeling of gratitude for the person who will present the precious teachings to him.

The student should also offer a visualized mandala of the entire universe, because it is considered to be a pure and inexhaustible offering, as opposed to a material gift which is considered impure and by its nature is very limited. Kongtrul, in *The Torch of Certainty*, explains the benefit of offering a mandala:

> However boastful you may be about your generosity, your [ordi-
> nary offerings are by their nature] numerically limited to a hun-
> dred, a thousand, ten thousand, a hundred thousand, etc. When
> you offer a gift with the egoistical thought that "I have offered
> this much," or with desire for recognition, your gift is tainted by
> these [unwholesome] thoughts....The mandala offering is the con-
> summate offering because it includes all the riches of the entire
> universe. It is not susceptible to the taints of proud thoughts, since
> you think, "I am offering a product of the mind." It does not in-
> spire hope or fear about pleasing [or displeasing] the Precious
> Ones. A person who [offers the mandala] and visualizes the ex-
> cellent recipients of the offerings—the Precious Ones in the ten
> directions and four times—the spacious realms, etc., cannot help
> but gather the accumulations [of merit and wisdom] with every
> thought, word, and deed.[90]

The next step in the student's preparation is to comport herself in a
respectful way. The student should enter the meditation hall with respect, and make prostrations to the three jewels in front of the altar. If
the lama is already present, then the prostrations should be directed
to him as the embodiment of the three jewels. She should then sit on
an unraised cushion or on the floor. It is important that the student
not behave in a pompous way. Also, the student should not be sloppy
or lazy. This means that she should not lie down in the shrine room,
put her feet up on the meditation tables, and so forth. Instead, the
student should sit down and wait to listen to the dharma with a one-
pointed mind.

To "cultivate joyful appreciation for the opportunity to hear the
dharma" is the third aspect of the student's preparation, and means to
cultivate a joyous frame of mind. This is done by recalling the preciousness of having the opportunity to hear the buddhadharma taught.
Here Kongtrul quotes from *The Sutra on the Inconceivable Secret* (*gSang-
ba bsam-gyis mi-khyab-pa*):

> Buddha[dharma] very rarely appears in the world. The human
> body is very difficult to acquire. O! Have faith and listen to the
> dharma. Conditions like this are very rare in the world.[91]

It is important for the student to rejoice in having obtained a human body, and in the fact that he has the opportunity to listen to the
dharma, because this situation rarely occurs in samsara. Je Gampopa,
in *An Ornament to Precious Liberation*, explains the precious chance we
have as human beings:

The two aspects of freedom and endowments meet in the precious human body. The latter is called precious because it is similar to the wishfulfilling jewel in being difficult to find. It is also called precious because it is greatly beneficial. As for it being difficult to find, it is said in the *Bodhisattva Collection* (*Byang-chub sems-dpa'i sde-snod*): "It is difficult to become a human being; it is difficult to obtain the noble dharma; and it is difficult for a Buddha to appear [in the world]."[92]

Buton, in *The Jewelry of Scripture*, continues his discussion of the need to cultivate an appreciation of the buddhadharma as one's preparation:

> And *The Sutra of Vast Display* says:
>
>> Human birth and the appearance of a Buddha [in this world] are not easy to be met with, and so are likewise the attainment of faith, avoidance of the eight unfavorable states of existence, and the opportunity to study the Doctrine. At present, the Buddha has appeared, and the favorable states of existence, faith, and the possibility to study the Doctrine are all of them secured. Therefore, do away with all distraction. There may come a time when for millions and millions of aeons, it will not be possible to hear [the word of] the Doctrine. Therefore, since you may obtain it now, give up all distraction.
>
> Moreover, we read in [Vasubandhu's] *Principles of Elucidation* (*rNam-bshad rigs-pa; Vyākhyāyukti*):
>
>> The word of the Buddha, the opportunity to hear it, the desire [to study], wisdom, and the absence of impediment—these four are hard to obtain. Therefore, listen to the word of the Buddha [when it is possible].
>
> And:
>
>> If a living being dies, will he [in his next birth] meet with the Jewel of the doctrine or not, will he come to study the doctrine, and will there be one that explains it to him—no one can tell. Therefore, at present you must zealously listen to the words of the Teacher.
>
> Again [in *The White Lotus of the True Dharma Sutra*, (*Saddarma-puṇḍarīka-sūtra*)]:
>
>> If one exists in the phenomenal world, one is inevitably reborn, but this new life usually passes away in vain, for the perfect word [that shows us the right way] is seldom to be heard here. It is rare as the flower of the *udumbara*.[93]

Jamgön Kongtrul concludes this section on cultivating joy with a one-line summary:

After the conditions have been gathered, listen with joy and cheerfulness that you have the capacity to listen to the dharma.

THE DHARMA TALK

This section is the lengthiest discussion in chapter ten of Kongtrul's text, addressing what the wisdom teacher and student should do during the dharma teaching: the way the teacher should explain the dharma; the way the student should listen to the dharma; how both should put the six perfections into practice.

The way the wisdom teacher should explain the dharma

Jamgön Kongtrul writes that it is necessary that the wisdom teacher have expertise in three areas: in the subject matter (which is related to mind); in teaching skills (which is related to speech); and in his manner (which is related to body).

Regarding the subject matter of the dharma teaching, Kongtrul writes that the wisdom teacher must have knowledge of the appropriate sutras, shastras, and oral instructions. In addition, he must be familiar with all the technical terms related to the subject being discussed. For instance, if the talk is on the precious human existence, the first of the "four thoughts which turn the mind to the dharma," the wisdom teacher needs to know the eight leisures and ten opportunities, and have the ability to quote from supporting scriptures and oral teachings.

To be expert in teaching the dharma, the teacher must be able to explain it clearly to the students. He should speak clearly, bringing in appropriate references from other sources to illustrate and substantiate the teaching. The wisdom teacher should not talk too much or too little. His voice should be pleasant to hear and be free of the eight faults of discourse, cited by both Buton and Kongtrul from *The Ornament of the Mahayana Sutras*:

1) Being lazy while giving a teaching

2) Lacking understanding of the topic

3) Speaking about things that are irrelevant to the subject matter

4) Being uncertain about the subject being taught

It is also considered a shortcoming of speech if the wisdom teacher

5) Is incapable of removing doubts of the student

6) Doesn't confirm the absence of doubts

7) Teaches while being sad or depressed

8) Withholds teachings from students who are qualified to receive them

Jamgön Kongtrul also refers to the classification of the faults of discourse as explained in the *Principles of Elucidation*, but doesn't include it in his summary. Buton does include it in his exposition.[94] In the *Principles of Elucidation* it is explained that there are twenty remedies for eleven types of mistakes related to speech.

1) Teaching at the appropriate time is a remedy against giving dharma teachings to a person who is not ready or qualified to receive them.

2) Teaching precisely and carefully counteracts the mistake of forgetting to include a section of the teaching.

The next three points counteract the mistake of giving a talk that is rambling and not to the point:

3) The teacher needs to describe the topic in sequential order. A teaching on the perfections should begin with generosity and end with wisdom in the correct sequence.

4) It is important to keep the teaching related to the subject matter and not get side-tracked into other topics.

5) The teacher needs to apply the teaching to those in attendance.

The next three points enable the wisdom teacher to avoid the mistake of giving a talk that is incomprehensible or irrelevant to those in attendance. The teacher should speak so that:

6) Those who are already devoted to the dharma are inspired.

7) Those who are hostile to the dharma become interested.

8) Those who are unsure whether the dharma is true or not have their concerns satisfied.

There are two remedies to counteract the mistake of having disregard for the dharma:

9) The teacher should not try to gratify the misguided needs of those who desire dharma teachings for samsaric purposes.

10) The teacher should not miscalculate the mental state of a

person who might become harmfully depressed by the teaching (i.e., emphasizing the impermanence of all beings to someone who is mentally and emotionally unstable.)

11) In order to counteract the fault of speaking incorrectly, the teacher must be able to explain any concept by means of valid reasoning.

12) Next, it is a mistake to teach an unqualified student the higher teachings. To avoid this mistake the teacher must teach the gradual path according to the needs of the student.

13) The remedy against causing students to become distracted is for the teacher to remain focused on the present topic without straying into discourses on other subjects.

14) The remedy against teaching useless theories and doctrines is for the teacher's words to rely solely on the sacred dharma.

15) The remedy against inappropriate teachings is to teach in accordance with the predilections and capacities of the people present. The teacher must also be sure that his own selfish thoughts and impure motivations do not infect the teaching.

The remedy against the pride of considering oneself pure and holy is to

16) Have loving-kindness for all sentient beings.

17) Have the desire to help all beings.

18) Have compassion for all beings.

19) The remedy against desiring honor and praise is simply to be aware of this desire as it arises, and then not be motivated by the desire to seek profit, praise, and honor as a result of teaching the dharma.

20) Finally, the remedy against envy towards others is to take leave of pride in oneself and criticism of others.

Jamgön Kongtrul continues his explanation by drawing on Buton's writings.[95] He says that the wisdom teacher must also know how to conduct herself and know the conduct of the student. Therefore, with regard to herself, the wisdom teacher must act virtuously with her body, speech, and mind. With regard to teaching the student effectively, she must know the student's predilections, personality, habitual tendencies, ability, and so forth.

The appropriate conduct of the teacher towards the students is that of having love and compassion for them.[96] She should teach with the motivation that all sentient beings attain enlightenment through these teachings. If she cannot generate this motivation, then Kongtrul and Buton advise that she should at least teach without any desire for profit or fame. Kongtrul warns that:

> While your own explanation functions as [placing the disciple on] the path, lacking the desire to benefit [all sentient beings] and [instead] having an eye for material things and so forth functions as the fault of selling the dharma.

Buton continues—though Kongtrul omits this—by emphasizing the need for loving-kindness and compassion with this quote from the *Ornament of the Mahayana Sutras:*

> The Powerful Ones, with a joyful heart, ever and anon give away their lives and property, which are hard to obtain and of no real value, for the sake of the suffering living beings, thus practicing the highest form of generosity. How much more will they do so in regard of the High Doctrine, which administers help to all that lives, always and in every way, is easy to obtain, increases the more you grant of it and never becomes exhausted. Now, if the teaching has not such a character, a great sin will be committed.

We read in the *Mañjuśrī-vikurvāṇa-parivarta:*

> If the doctrine is expounded, but compassion with regards to the students is wanting, it will be an action of Mara, and if a teacher, being himself greatly learned, conceals [parts of] the doctrine for fear that others should come to know them, this will be likewise an action of Mara.

The *Saṁdhinirmocana* says:

> Those who teach the Highest Doctrine out of desire [of gain], having got their wishes fulfilled, take birth again and again. These infatuated beings, though they are in possession of the invaluable jewel of the Doctrine, roam about, as if they were beggars.[97]

Kongtrul Rinpoche continues to refer to Buton's handling of the topic,[98] saying that the teacher must also have three types of patience: patience in maintaining endurance during a long and perhaps difficult teaching session; patience in dealing with the student's questions and behavior; and patience in responding to someone who is being argumentative. Kongtrul leaves the discussion here, while Buton continues:

> It is said likewise, that tolerance with regard to the faults made
> by the students is needed. This may be fulfilled if one is possessed
> of that supernatural insight through which one comes to know
> the amount of help that is to be administered to others [usually
> only possessed by teachers who have higher realizations]. If [this
> insight] is wanting, one must abstain from teaching to those that
> are not devoted to the doctrine, and to those that wear insignia,
> and to the following five [categories of person, teaching to whom
> is prohibited by the Vinaya], etc. Such persons will be always op-
> posed to a teaching that humiliates them, and will become full of
> passion and hatred. Consequently, the teaching and study of the
> doctrine, that has such an unfavorable result, cannot be of help
> for the attainment of felicity and salvation.[99]

Note that compassion also includes knowing when *not* to teach,
because teaching the inappropriate material, at the inappropriate time,
or to a student unprepared to receive the teaching, will cause negative
results. In Buddhism, teachings are never kept from the student in
order to maintain the teacher's superiority. Nor should the dharma be
forced upon anyone merely to "spread the teachings." A dharma teaching should only be given if it will benefit the student.

Jamgön Kongtrul summarizes this section by quoting Buton:

> Therefore, because those qualities are complete, if the wisdom
> teacher explains the dharma, it will be pleasant-sounding and
> beautiful to the people of his retinue, and will function as [lead-
> ing them on] the path. It is said in *The Ornament of the Mahayana
> Sutras*:
>
> > Because the bodhisattva is possessed with a good intellect, is
> > without sadness, is kind, highly renowned (*snyan-par rab grags*),
> > and knows the rituals (*cho-ga; sādhana*) well, the bodhisattva is
> > well spoken; giving explanations, he is like a blazing sun among
> > people.[100]

Method of explaining any topic

Here Kongtrul writes that when teaching the dharma the teacher
should give both an overview and a detailed explanation of the subject matter.

How to give a general explanation

Kongtrul begins this section by referring to Asanga's *Compendium of Knowledge* (*Chos-mngon-pa kun-btus; Abhidharma-samuccaya*). That text enumerates six points that should be included when one is teaching a subject:

> 1) The subject matter which one should thoroughly know (*yongs-
>   su shes-par-bya*)

2) Its meaning

3) The cause for knowing it

4) Thorough knowing

5) The result of knowing

6) Higher knowing (*rab-tu shes-pa*) [which is the result of the knowing]

Neither Kongtrul nor Buton expanded upon these points, so the following is based on an oral commentary by Khenpo Tsultrim Gyamtso Rinpoche and substantiated by examples found in *The Commentary to the Compendium of Knowledge* (*Chos mngon-pa kun-las-btus-pa'i bshad-pa; Abhidharma-samuccaya-bhāṣya*).[101]

When teaching the dharma, the wisdom teacher must first clearly state the subject of the discourse. For example, the subject might be a description of the skandhas, dhatus (*khams; dhātu*), and ayatanas (*skye mched; āyatana*). Next, the teacher should describe the essential meaning of the subject—in this case he might explain that the skandhas, ayatanas, and dhatus are all characterized by the three marks of impermanence, suffering, and non-self. Third, the wisdom teacher should explain how the student can experience this truth: the student should guard the doors of the senses; that is, practice discipline and keep the vows unimpaired. Fourth, the teacher should explain the topic thoroughly, perhaps elaborating on the thirty-seven dharmas that are the factors of awakening. Fifth, the teacher should explain to the student the results that would ensue—the attainment of liberation. Finally, the teacher should explain the attributes that would result, such as the kinds of knowledge or view experienced through liberation.

Kongtrul mentions that there are other ways to explain the dharma, including the fourteen approaches referred to in Buton's text. These "fourteen doors" will be given here in their entirety, even though Kongtrul does not include them in his text, since they are relevant to the subject at hand and are not widely available in English:

1) The door of abridged explanation

2) The door of concentration [of teaching] upon one subject

3) The door of taking recourse to minute details

4) The door of communicating the different degrees of perfection, each of which is respectively the foundation of higher and still higher [virtues]

5) The door of exclusion [of all that does not come under the category in question]

6) The door of changing the meaning of [ordinary] words [into technical terms]

7) The door of demonstrating matters worldly and unworldly [in regard to each other]

8) The door of indicating the individual [to whom one intends to teach]

9) The door of analysis of the stuff

10) The door of the six modes [which are: the mode of the absolute truth (*de-kho-na'i don gyi tshul*); the mode of attaining (*'thob-pa'i tshul*); the mode of explaining the latter (*bshad-pa'i tshul*); the mode of teaching without recourse to the two extremes (*mtha'-gnyis spangs-pa'i tshul*); the mode of intended meaning (*dgongs-pa'i tshul*)]

11) The door of [enlarging upon] the full apprehension of the truth, etc

12) The door of showing the power [of each word taken separately to indicate an idea] and the impotence [if one word is omitted, of others to render the contents intelligible]

13) The door of repeated teaching

14) The door of evident proofs[102]

Kongtrul then continues excerpting from Buton in his description of how the wisdom teacher should explain the dharma through the use of a system attributed to Chimpa (mChims-pa).[103] Chimpa describes the teaching of the dharma as taking place in three parts: The wisdom teacher should teach the meaning of the text in a general way. At the end of the teaching the wisdom teacher should give a conclusion, identifying the salient points of the teaching. The wisdom teacher should make sure that the students understand what has been taught by answering all their questions; it is helpful if the teacher answers questions by quoting the scriptures, using reasoning, and giving examples.

How to give a detailed explanation

Kongtrul now gives a detailed explanation of how to teach the dharma. He again bases his remarks on Buton's writings.[104] In describing how the teacher should teach, six points are given from the *Principles of Elucidation*; Kongtrul mentions that this is the standard method for explaining this topic. He then excerpts Buton's commentary, also adding commentary of his own. This section is very terse and I have not been able to locate further written commentary. What appears here is the oral commentary of Khenpo Tsultrim Gyamtso Rinpoche, who kindly explained some of the points in this section.

Kongtrul Rinpoche states that according to the *Principles of Elucidation* the detailed explanation is given in six points. The wisdom teacher will at first describe:

1) The general and specific explanation of the purpose (*dgos-don*) [of the teaching]

2) The two parts to the synopsis (*bsdus-don*) that has six good qualities

3) The literal meaning (*tshig-don*) [explained in terms of] the three things: the subject [to be explained]; by what means; [and how the explanation is] done. [First seek] the meaning [dependent upon] the words (*sgra-don*).

4) There are two points to the connection (*mtshams-spyor*): [it should be] easily understood (*go-bde*) and connected ('*brel-chags*).

5) Responses to objections will be supported by scripture

6) and by reasoning.

The wisdom teacher should first describe the purpose of the teachings and the benefits of listening to them. This is done to capture the interest of the student. Next, the teacher should sequentially cover the entire text, focusing upon the main points, but not yet giving a word-by-word explanation. It is suggested that references to other sutras and commentaries, as well as the reasoning of the teacher himself, are appropriate if they facilitate the understanding of the material. It is important that this summary of the text is kept simple so that the student can easily understand the material.

Tibetan texts have many divisions (*sbyi-sdom*), subdivisions (*nang-gses*), and branches (*yan-lag*). It is important that the teacher lay these out clearly, without confusing the classifications or having them contradict each other. Khenpo Tsultrim Gyamtso Rinpoche explains this with an example from Maitreya-Asanga's *Discriminating the Middle from the Extremes* (*dBus-mtha' rnam-'byed; Madhyānta-vibhāga*), which is divided into three main divisions (*sbyi-sdom*):

1) The unparalleled practice (*sgrub-pa bla-na-med-pa*)

2) The unparalleled focus (*dmigs-pa bla-na-med-pa*)

3) The unparalleled correct accomplishment (*yang-dag 'grub-pa bla-na-med-pa*)

Under unparalleled practice there are six subdivisions (*nang-gses*):

1) Genuine practice (*dam-pa'i sgrub-pa*)
2) Practice of mental cultivation (*yid-byed sgrub-pa*)
3) Practice in accordance with dharma (*rjes-su mthun-chos sgrub-pa*)
4) The practice of giving up the two extremes (*mtha'-gnyis spangs-pa'i sgrub-pa*)
5) Practice with a special trait (*khyed-par-can sgrub-pa*)
6) Practice without a special trait (*khyed-par-med sgrub-pa*)

Under the six subdivisions there are numerous branches (*yan-lag*). Therefore, the teacher must separate them out clearly, and then bring them together without mixing up the meaning.

The third aspect of teaching, the "literal meaning," is to explain the meaning of the technical terms. After giving an explanation of the literal meaning of the syllables, the teacher may give synonyms or describe the etymology of the terms.

The fourth aspect deals with the relation between syllables and words, and the relation between the terms and the meaning of the text. The teacher might explain a term and its grammatical relationship to the terms preceding it in order to clarify the meaning. After clarifying the connections between the words, he then focuses upon the relationship of the meaning. For example, the text may say "all phenomena are empty of self." First, the teacher may explain the genitive particle *of*. Is it indicating possession or modification? Next, the teacher would explain how this connects to the meaning of the text. So, if all phenomena are empty of self, then there are no eternally existing phenomena, and so forth.

Finally, the fifth and sixth points are that the teacher must be able to answer any questions the students may still have. This is accomplished through the use of reason and by citing scriptures. The teacher should never give responses that contradict the scriptures or that are self-contradictory.

How to teach the dharma

Kongtrul writes:

> For great intellects, teach using profound and extensive teachings. For lesser intellects, explain using words easy to remember, simple and easy to understand. Afterwards, precisely and subtly cut the connections which are contradictory. To those who are faint-hearted, uplift them; if their minds are excited or drowsy, turn them away from all those faults.

Kongtrul explains that the wisdom teacher should adapt the teaching to the abilities of the students. If they are very intelligent and have a general understanding of the subject matter, the teacher may give an extensive and profound explanation. If, however, the students are unfamiliar with the subject or are less intelligent, the wisdom teacher should try to keep the material simple and enjoyable. As the students' understanding increases, the teacher should go into greater and greater detail.

Many students lack confidence in their ability to understand and practice the dharma. Kongtrul suggests that the teacher should try to strengthen their confidence by reminding them that they possess buddha-nature, or by teaching them that the accumulation of even a small amount of merit will help them obtain better and better rebirths, eventually leading to full enlightenment. Sometimes a student's mind may become agitated or dull. Kongtrul explains that the antidote for an agitated mind that actively craves the busyness of samsara is instruction on three of the four thoughts that turn the mind towards dharma practice: impermanence, karma, and the three kinds of suffering. Instruction on the precious human existence is an antidote to drowsiness. Kongtrul states:

> For those whose minds are distracted (*g.yengs*) and excited (*rgod-pa*) by longing (*zhen*) for the affairs of this life and the five aspects of sense desire, present a discussion of impermanence, the disadvantages of the five aspects of sense desire, the fear of lower states of rebirth, and so forth. Then their minds will be changed to the dharma.

If the student is lethargic, or if his mind tends towards drowsiness during meditation, the teacher should give instructions on the spiritual biographies or *namthar* (*rnam-thar*) of the enlightened masters, such as Padmasambhava, Yeshe Tsogyal, Shabkar, and Milarepa. Namthar literally means "complete liberation." These are spiritual biographies which depict the life of an enlightened master; we follow his life from a spiritual perspective as displaying the path to enlightenment. These stories are replete with dharma teachings in the form of the example set by the person himself, and also by teachings given in the form of vajra songs.[105] Also, the teacher should instruct the student in the faults and consequences of lethargy, such as wasting the precious human existence in this life, and potential rebirth in the animal realm.

How the student should listen to the dharma teaching

Here, Jamgön Kongtrul describes that which hinders effective learning, and the attitudes the student should cultivate. This section is primarily excerpted from Buton's discussion of the characteristics of the method of study,[106] which he divides into three parts:

1) [The character] of the student
2) The means of study
3) The manner of study

Kongtrul excerpts parts one and two in a condensed form with a brief commentary of his own. He does not refer to part three.

The character of the student

Here, Kongtrul describes the different types of obstacles impeding the student from properly listening to the dharma. Buton separately lists "thirteen defects," "six stains," and "three faults," of which Kongtrul treats only the latter two categories.

The three faults Kongtrul explains the three faults in the context of the following famous sentence, said by the Buddha throughout the sutras:

> While [having eliminated being unfocused, defilements, and sadness], listen well, closely, and so that you will remember, and I will explain to you....[107]

Kongtrul uses the traditional metaphor of the three faults of listening, likening the student who does not listen to an upside-down container, a dirty container, and a leaky container. He says that when the student has removed the fault of being like an upside-down container she can "listen well." If water is poured into a glass that is upside-down, nothing will be retained; likewise, if a student follows a teaching but does not listen, nothing will be learned. Kongtrul advises:

> [The teaching will not enter the student if he] is lacking eagerness for the dharma when listening; if his mind is distracted (*g.yeng-ba*) towards [outer] objects (*yul*); and if he has gone under the influence of drowsiness (*gnyid-rmugs*). Therefore, collecting your mind while having eliminated not focusing (*gtod-pa*) your ears on the dharma is called listening.

If clean water is poured into a dirty glass, it will also become dirty. Likewise, if a student listens to the pure dharma with the wrong motivation or with wrong views, then the dharma teaching will become distorted. Kongtrul explains that when the student removes the fault which is like a dirty vessel, then she can "listen closely" (*rab-tu-nyon*). Also, one should not listen to the dharma with the intention of gathering information in order to give workshops or lectures, nor to obtain fame, prestige, etc. Kongtrul states:

> If you listen to the dharma with a mind conjoined with the stain of passions, then it does not do any good for the mind-stream of yourself or others. Therefore, eliminating attitudes such as the passions of pride, non-faith, and so forth is called listening.

The student should listen to the dharma with the motivation of bodhicitta. In *The Oral Instructions of My Excellent Lama*, Patrul Rinpoche describes how the student should listen to the dharma:

> When listening to the dharma, if you listen with the wrong motivation, such as the desire to become great or famous, or if your listening is intermingled with discursive thoughts of the five poisons, such as attachment, anger, and ignorance, not only will the dharma be of no benefit to your mind, but it will even turn into something that is not the dharma. This is analogous to pouring excellent nectar into a vessel containing poison. For this reason the Indian master Padampa Sangye said:
>
>> When listening to the dharma you should be like a deer listening to a sound.
>> When reflecting upon it you should be like a northerner shearing sheep.
>> When meditating upon it you should be like a dumb person experiencing taste.
>> When practicing the dharma you should be like a hungry yak devouring grass.
>> When attaining fruition you should be like the sun, free from the covering of clouds.
>
> When listening to the dharma you should listen like a deer so infatuated by the sound of a *piwam*, he does not notice a hunter shooting his poisonous arrow at him from the side. You should listen with every hair on your body standing on end, tears streaming from your eyes, palms together, and uninterrupted by any other thoughts. It is pointless to listen with merely your body present at the dharma teaching, while your mind chases after thoughts, your speech opening a storehouse of idle gossip—saying whatever comes to mind, and with your eyes darting everywhere. When listening to the dharma you should even stop all types of virtuous activity, such as praying, counting on your *mala*, and so forth. So, even though you have listened [properly to the dharma], you should bear in mind the meaning of what has been said without forgetting it, and continuously practice it.[108]

The third fault of listening is compared to a leaky container. If a glass is broken, then no matter how much water is poured into it nothing will be retained. Likewise, if a student makes no effort to concentrate on the teaching, or allows herself to be overwhelmed by feelings such as sadness or depression, nothing that was heard will be remembered. Kongtrul says that when the student removes the fault that is like a container which has a hole in it, then she can "listen so that she remembers."

The six stains Next, Kongtrul and Buton list the six stains (*dri-ma*), which interfere with the student's ability to listen to the teaching of the dharma. This list comes from Vasubandhu's *Principles of Elucidation*.[109] These hindrances to learning are:

1) Being arrogant and full of pride
2) Not having faith in the wisdom teacher and the dharma
3) Not making an effort to learn and understand the dharma teaching
4) Having one's attention outwardly distracted (such as by street traffic)
5) Being inwardly distracted, such as day-dreaming
6) Being sad and depressed because it is difficult to concentrate when one is overwhelmed by emotions

Although Kongtrul does not mention this, a commentary on these six stains can be found in Patrul Rinpoche's *The Oral Instructions of My Excellent Lama*. After quoting the above verse from *The Principles of Elucidation*, Patrul Rinpoche gives the following brief explanation:

> You should abandon the six defilements: overbearing pride of thinking that I am superior to the lama who is explaining the dharma; lacking faith in the dharma and the lama; not applying yourself to the dharma; your mind being distracted by external objects; the five sense gates being withdrawn; and sadness, thinking "these teachings are taking too long," and so forth.[110]

Patrul Rinpoche says that arrogance and jealousy are the two most difficult hindrances to recognize. Arrogance obstructs one from noticing one's defects, and without noticing them, there is no opportunity for removing them. Arrogance also blinds one to the virtue of others. Patrul Rinpoche emphasizes that while eliminating arrogance the student must also develop humility.

By lacking faith in the dharma one is cut off from the teachings and methods that can lead to enlightenment. The student should thoroughly and honestly test the teachings with her intellect and experience. In this way faith in the buddhadharma will naturally arise.

Patrul Rinpoche also emphasizes that the student must make an effort to concentrate on and understand the teaching. He summarizes the type of effort needed as follows:

> Listen to the dharma with great interest, disregarding all difficulties such as heat and cold.[111]

Patrul Rinpoche warns us of the danger of allowing the mind to wander from external object to external object. We are very interested in all of the fleeting distractions in the world around us, but there is nothing there that we can permanently depend on. Instead, we should make a special effort to focus our undistracted attention on the dharma, which is the only real object we can depend on. To do so will benefit us in this and future lives, while allowing our minds to run wild is of no benefit at all. Patrul Rinpoche continues:

> Furthermore, whenever you listen to or teach the dharma, or do meditation practice, you should give up examining your past habitual tendencies, chasing after future passions, and being distracted by your present situation and surroundings.[112]

He urges us to focus our attention on the teaching we are listening to by illustrating the futility of constantly thinking of the past, present, and future. He quotes Gyalsay (rGyal-sras) Rinpoche:

> Past joys and sorrows are like drawings on water,
> they leave no trace, do not follow after them.
> If you continue to recall them, reflect upon the [eventual] loss of
>   everything acquired, and the parting of all that meets.
> Is there anything more reliable than the dharma, Maniwa?
>
> Your plans for the future are like casting a fishing net into a dry
>   riverbed,
> they will never bring you what you want, so lessen your desires.
> If you continue to recall them, reflect upon the unpredictability of
>   your time of death.
> Do you have time to do anything besides the dharma, Maniwa?
>
> Your present activity is like housekeeping in a dream,
> since it is meaningless, cast it aside....[113]

Patrul Rinpoche concludes:

> Therefore, since numerous concepts about the past and future will
> achieve nothing and are the cause for distraction, it would be good
> to abandon them and listen to the dharma with mindfulness, at-
> tention, and care.[114]

Patrul Rinpoche comments on the fifth stain, in which the mind is
distracted inwardly. In this case the mind is self-absorbed, and is very
dull and sleepy, in contrast to the previous state, in which the mind is
agitated and overactive. It is important for a student listening to a
dharma teaching to keep his mind relaxed but not dull, alert, but not
agitated. To illustrate this, Patrul Rinpoche paraphrases the famous
story of Ananda's student Shrona (Śroṇa) the musician, who had
trouble attaining any realization in his meditation:

> Once upon a time, Ananda was teaching meditation to Shrona.
> Correct meditation would not come to Shrona because he was
> sometimes too tense and sometimes too loose. He went to see the
> Buddha, and the Buddha asked, "When you were a householder,
> weren't you skilled at tuning the piwam?"
> "Yes, I was extremely skilled at tuning it."
> "Did a melodious sound arise from the piwam when it was
> very tight or very loose?"
> "It arose when it was neither too tight nor too loose."
> "It is the same for your mind," said the Buddha, and with this
> advice, Shrona attained the result.[115]

The sixth stain is to listen to the dharma while sad or depressed.
Quite often we suffer through physical hardships while listening to
the dharma, such as pains in our knees and back, hunger and thirst, or
feeling too hot or too cold. These may make us feel depressed and
distract us from the teaching. Patrul Rinpoche gives us a way to change
such an unpleasant circumstance into a happy and pleasurable one.
He writes:

> At present, you should be happy that you have obtained the free-
> doms and endowments of this privileged human birth, have met
> with a qualified lama, and can listen to his profound instructions.
> This is the result of gathering the accumulations throughout count-
> less kalpas. You now have the opportunity to listen to the holy
> dharma, which is like having a meal every hundred years. For
> the sake of the dharma you should persevere through whatever
> hardship comes about, such as heat or cold, and you should lis-
> ten with joy and delight.[116]

Buton quotes an alternative list of six stains given in the same section
of *The Principles of Elucidation* as the previous list:

1) Defects in one's acts
2) Absence of faith
3) Disrespect
4) Inappropriate thoughts
5) Discord
6) Defects in apprehending[117]

Buton comments on the meaning of these stains as follows:

> As concerns the defects in one's actions, such may be corporeal—immoral behavior; or oral and corporeal—not making due efforts with body, speech, and mind, or lack of desire to study.
>
> The defects that consist in inappropriate thoughts are: to seek brawls and to think how to escape a controversy.
>
> The defects arising from discord are five in number: absence of reverence for the dharma by not taking it to be the path that leads to liberation; [absence of reverence] for the word of [the dharma], considering such to be unconnected speech, etc.; disregard for the teacher, by finding fault with him, his conduct, and the manner of teaching; contempt for [the teacher's] lineage; and, last of all, self-deprecation: thinking oneself unable to understand the meaning of the dharma and to act according to the latter.
>
> The defects in apprehending are likewise five: apprehending wrongly; getting no clear conception of the meaning; misunderstanding the words; disregarding the grammatical forms; and getting no full apprehension of the matter.

Listening with the proper frame of mind

It is important that the student be in the proper frame of mind when attending a dharma teaching or while studying, and be able to apply the teaching to his experience. Kongtrul mentions that many metaphors are suggested in *The Sutra Arranged Like a Tree* to help put the student in the proper frame of mind. The full section from the sutra, which is not given by Kongtrul, is as follows:

> Think of yourself as sick, and think of spiritual friends as physicians; think of their instructions as medicines, and think of the practices as getting rid of disease. Think of yourself as a traveler, and think of spiritual friends as guides; think of their instructions as the road, and think of the practices as going to the land of your destination. Think of yourself as crossing to the other shore, and think of the spiritual friend as a boatman; think of the instruction as a ford, and think of the practices as a boat. Think of yourself as a farmer, and think of spiritual friends as water spirits; think of

the instructions as rain, and think of the practices as the ripening of the crops. Think of yourself as a pauper, and think of spiritual friends as the givers of wealth; think of their instructions as wealth, and think of the practices as getting rid of poverty. Think of yourself as an apprentice, and think of spiritual friends as mentors; think of their instructions as arts, and think of the practices as accomplishments. Think of yourself as fearless, and think of spiritual friends as heroic warriors; think of their instructions as attack, and think of the practices as vanquishing enemies. Think of yourself as a merchant, and think of spiritual friends as ship captains; think of their instructions as treasure, and think of the practices as obtaining treasures. Think of yourself as a good child, and think of spiritual friends as parents; think of their instructions as the family business. Think of yourself as a prince, and think of spiritual friends as the chief ministers of a spiritual king; think of their instructions as the precepts of kingship, and think of the practices as putting on the turban of truth adorned with the crest of knowledge, and overseeing the capital of the spiritual sovereign.[118]

Although Kongtrul does not comment on this sutra, Patrul Rinpoche explains that the student must not only make the four assumptions (i.e., student as patient, dharma as medicine, etc.), but must also *not* make four contrary assumptions. He quotes these four from *The Treasury of Precious Qualities* (*Yon-tan rin-po-che'i mdzod*), followed by his own commentary:

It is said in *The Treasury of Precious Qualities*: "An evil-natured person who cunningly speaks with devotion approaches the lama as if he were a musk deer: After acquiring the musk-like holy dharma, he throws away his samaya with his complete joy in hunting." In that way, he perceives the lama as a musk deer, perceives the dharma as musk, perceives himself as the hunter, and perceives intensive practice as the arrow or snare used to kill the musk deer. Such persons do not practice the teachings received; and without regard for the kindness of their lamas, only negative actions are accumulated from their reliance on the dharma. This becomes an anchor that plunges them into the lower realms.[119]

How both should put the six perfections into practice

Training in the six perfections (*pha-rol-tu phyin-pa; pāramitā*) is the method for bodhisattvas to attain full enlightenment. Gampopa quotes from the *Sutra Requested by Subahu* (*Lag-bzangs kyis zhus-pa'i mdo; Subahuparipṛcchā-sūtra*):

Subahu, in order to become swiftly and perfectly enlightened, a bodhisattva mahasattva must always and continuously fully complete these six perfections. What are these six? They are the perfection of generosity, the perfection of moral discipline, the perfection of patience, the perfection of diligence, the perfection of meditation, and the perfection of wisdom.[120]

Both the wisdom teacher and the student are advised to apply the six perfections during the teaching in the following manner: For the first perfection, generosity (*sbyin-pa; dāna*), the teacher gives the gift of the dharma and the student offers gifts to the teacher. Gampopa describes four aspects to giving the dharma. First, it should be given to those who are worthy of receiving it, such as those who want and respect it. Second, the wisdom teacher should have a pure motivation, not be motivated by selfish desires such as wealth or fame. Third, the wisdom teacher should teach the dharma in a way that helps students understand its meaning; that is, the teacher should in no way distort the teachings with his own misguided ideas. Gampopa quotes from *The Stages of the Bodhisattva*:

> The gift of dharma is teaching the dharma in the right way; teaching the dharma appropriately; and enabling the disciple to adhere to the pure foundation of training.[121]

For the perfection of discipline (*tshul-khrims; śīla*), both teacher and student should remove any factors that may be in conflict with teaching or listening. Buton explains practicing discipline in this way:

> Suppress sinful inclinations and remove all the defects [that hinder one from becoming] a worthy receptacle of the dharma.[122]

The third perfection, patience (*bzod-pa; kṣānti*), includes the ability to withstand uncomfortable situations which arise during practice or teaching sessions. Buton states that a student who has patience is able to endure difficulties such as fatigue or being uncomfortable.[123]

Diligence (*brtson-'grus; vīrya*) involves enthusiasm while teaching and listening. Diligence is the gathering of one's energy together for the purpose of overcoming any obstacle hindering attainment of one's goal. The teacher wishes to help the student attain enlightenment, therefore he joyfully applies himself to the task. The student's wish is to attain enlightenment for the benefit of all sentient beings. Therefore she joyfully tries to exert herself in the study and practice of the dharma.

For meditative concentration (*bsam-gtan; dhyāna*), focus one-pointedly on the teaching.

The practice of wisdom (*shes-rab; prajñā*) is using one's intellect to analyze the meaning of the subject matter. Buton describes the perfection of wisdom in regards to the student listening to the teaching as comprising three levels:

The highest degree—the attainment of wisdom; the intermediate—
apprehension, preservation in memory, and analysis, in following
the word; and the lowest—the five immeasurable feelings.[124]

Patrul Rinpoche, in *The Oral Instructions of My Excellent Lama*, ad-
dresses the need for the student to practice the six perfections in regards to receiving teachings from the lama. He quotes from *The Tantra
of Thorough Realization of the Instructions on All Dharma Practices (mNgon-
par rtogs-pa)*:[125]

It is said in *The Tantra of Thorough Realization of the Instructions on
All Dharma Practices*:

Offer flowers, a seat, and so forth.[126]
Control your behavior and arrange the area.[127]
Do not harm any living creature.[128]
Have complete devotion in the lama.[129]
Undistractedly listen to the lama's instructions.[130]
Ask questions in order to remove doubts.[131]

The listener should have these six aspects [of the perfections].

WHAT SHOULD BE DONE AFTER THE TEACHINGS

At the conclusion of the teaching, the wisdom teacher and student
each need to do three things. The wisdom teacher should confess to
the Buddhas all the faults and mistakes he has committed while teaching. This confession is usually done in the form of a standard prayer of
confession. Kongtrul Rinpoche gives the following prayer as an example:

Whatever negative actions (*sdig-pa*) I have done by being under
the influence of the [obscurations] of the mind, after having come
into the presence of the Buddha, I confess them.[132]

Next, the teacher dedicates to all sentient beings whatever virtue
he may have gathered from teaching the dharma. This is done by the
recitation of any of the numerous dedication prayers. Kongtrul uses
Arya Asanga's prayer as an example:

From this explanation of the precious holy dharma of the excellent vehicle, whatever endless merit we have obtained, by that,
may all sentient beings become vessels of the precious and stainless holy dharma of the excellent vehicle....[133]

The dedication of merit at the conclusion of a teaching or practice session is considered indispensable from the Mahayana perspective. In
The Torch of Certainty Kongtrul states:

At the close of each meditation session, dedicate the merit.[134]

By clinging to the merit for oneself, whatever has accumulated will eventually be depleted. If one dedicates one's accumulated merit to all sentient beings with a motivation unstained by selfishness, then the merit becomes inexhaustible.

After the offering of merit, the wisdom teacher concludes with the offering of the three spheres. The "three spheres" refer to the subject, object, and action of the offering. From the perspective of the ultimate truth, these three spheres are seen as empty of solidity and inherent existence. Resting the mind in this natural state is considered to be the highest offering.

At the end of the teaching the student should show her gratefulness to the wisdom teacher by offering prostrations and an offering mandala. This should be followed by dedicating the merit accumulated through participating in the teaching to all sentient beings.

Finally, the student should study and thoroughly learn what she has just been taught, otherwise the teaching will have little benefit. Kongtrul suggests that the student should go somewhere quiet and compose herself so that her mind is not agitated or drowsy. This can be done by doing calm abiding meditation, concentrating attention on the breath for five minutes. Then the student should diligently study the material that was just taught, and if questions arise, they should then be brought back to the lama for further clarification. Questions based upon careful thought and actual meditation practice are the best, and tend to lead to answers that have immediate relevance for the student. In this way the dharma becomes part of the student's experience, and is not merely an uncritical belief system. Questions that simply pop into the student's mind are usually discouraged, because they are generally considered to be superficial.

THE BENEFITS OF LISTENING TO AND TEACHING THE DHARMA

In the final section of the chapter, Kongtrul briefly refers to the many acknowledged benefits of listening to and teaching the dharma, classified in six categories:

1) General benefits of listening and reflecting on the teaching
2) Specific benefits of listening to the teaching
3) Specific benefits of teaching the dharma
4) Specific benefits of understanding the teaching

5) Specific benefits of listening and teaching
6) Benefits of putting the teaching into practice and integrating study and practice[135]

The benefit of listening to and reflecting upon the dharma is that the student will begin to understand the basic teachings that form a foundation for practice. Kongtrul quotes from the *Scripture on Discernment* (*Lung rnam-'byed; Vinaya-vibhaṅga*):

> There are five advantages in being knowledgeable. These are: being knowledgeable in the *skandhas*; knowledgeable in the *dhatus*; knowledgable in the *ayatanas*; knowledgeable in interdependent origination; and [knowledgeable in] the instructions [on how to meditate on the above four topics], which make [understanding and meditation] increase, so you are not dependent on a teacher [instructing you during retreat; i.e., you can meditate on your own].[136]

Through attending a teaching and studying the material, the student will intellectually come to understand the functioning of his mind and his situation in samsara. For instance, the student may become intellectually familiar with the five skandhas, which account for the workings of our psycho-physical constitution in the absence of a permanent "self" (*ātman*). This intellectual understanding of the skandhas is the basis for a classic analytic meditation practice (*vipaśyanā*) in which the student investigates each skandha and tries to locate a permanent self. Not able to find this entity, the student gradually replaces intellectual knowledge with experiential understanding.

Jamgön Kongtrul says that the second benefit of listening to dharma teachings is that the student also begins to understand the eighteen dhatus, which include the six sense faculties (*dbang-po*), the six corresponding sense objects (*yul*), and the six consciousnesses (*rnam-shes*). Understanding these also prepares the student for the process of analytic meditation described above, which leads to the understanding that one's consciousness and "external" objects are interdependent, and that both lack inherent existence.

The third general benefit of listening and reflecting is that the student understands the twelve ayatanas, which include the six sense faculties with their corresponding sense objects.

The fourth advantage is understanding dependent origination (*rten 'brel-bar 'byung-ba; pratītya-samutpāda*). This enables the student to understand how the person and the world function, without a need to postulate a first cause, such as a creator god.

The final general benefit of learning and reflecting is that the student will receive instructions (*gdams-ngag*) from the teacher on how to meditate upon these topics, so that her intellectual understanding becomes part of her experience. Khenpo Tsultrim Gyamtso Rinpoche explains that with these instructions the student is able to practice analytic meditation on her own, without being dependent upon visualization meditation guided by her teacher. If the student becomes sufficiently skilled in the subject matter she can practice alone. For instance, once you have the outline and subdivisions of the skandhas, then you can receive instructions on how to meditate on this, and how to increase your understanding. Then, upon becoming very skillful, you can practice on your own.

Next, Kongtrul describes the specific benefits of listening to the dharma. It should be noted that Kongtrul does not give an extensive commentary on this, or on the previous section; he limits his remarks to one quotation from sutra per section, not because the topic is unimportant, but because for most Tibetan Buddhist practitioners these benefits would be obvious. So, Kongtrul states that the advantages of listening to the dharma have been mentioned by Buddha throughout all the sutras and tantras. He illustrates this with the five advantages found in the *Principles of Elucidation*:

> The Blessed One spoke of five advantages in listening to the dharma:
>
> 1) That which is heard will be heard.
> 2) That which is heard will be completely experienced.
> 3) Doubts will be eliminated.
> 4) The view will be corrected.
> 5) By wisdom (*prajñā*) the words and profound meaning will be understood.

Next, Kongtrul mentions the numerous advantages of teaching the dharma: It functions as the best among offerings to the Buddhas. It functions as the best kind of generosity to sentient beings. It functions as [an excellent way of] increasing merit and obtaining the [six] superknowledges (*mngon-shes; abhijñā*).

Teaching the dharma is considered the foremost offering to the Buddhas and the best gift to sentient beings, because through this gift sentient beings attain enlightenment and are permanently released from suffering.[137] Although Kongtrul does not elucidate this topic, Gampopa explains that giving the gift of the dharma falls within the perfection of generosity of the bodhisattva. He discusses generosity under three headings: material goods, fearlessness, and giving dharma teachings. In this case, when giving the gift of the dharma teaching, the bodhisattva must have the proper intention—to teach the dharma out of compassion, and without consideration of worldly gain. He must be careful to communicate the meaning of the teachings without distortion. Finally, he should only teach when requested by the student, unless he knows the student well, in which case he can teach even without being asked.

In addition, Kongtrul writes that through the merit gained by teaching, the teacher obtains the six super-knowledges: godlike insight (*lha'i mig*); godlike hearing (*rna-ba shes-pa*); knowledge of other's thoughts (*pha-rol-gyi sems shes-pa*); recollection of previous lives (*sngon-gyi-gnas rjes-su-dran-pa shes-pa*); miraculous powers (*rdzu-'phrul-gyi bya-ba*); and knowledge of having overcome obscurations (*zag-pa zad-pa shes-pa*).[138]

He now returns to the discussion of the advantages gained by the student, stating that merely by understanding the meaning of the teaching a student accumulates a great amount of merit.

Jamgön Kongtrul next explains the great advantages of listening to and explaining the Mahayana dharma:

> During the phase of the ground—to outshine the virtue [or discipline] of the Hinayana. During the phase of the path—to eliminate all hindrances without exception. During the phase of the result—to obtain complete awakening.

Next, he emphasizes that to put one's understanding of the dharma into practice is far better than understanding the meaning of the teaching. To actually experience emptiness, for example, is of greater value than to merely understand the idea of emptiness. While Kongtrul stresses the importance of supplementing study with experience, he also suggests that practice should be accompanied by study, supporting this with a reference to the *Ornament of the Mahayana Sutras*:

> So, whatever meditation the yogi (*rnal-'byor-can*) does is not useless. Likewise, the teachings of the Sugatas are not useless. But if you could perceive the truth simply by means of studying, then the meditation [of the yogi] would be useless. If you could engage in meditation without studying, then the teachings [of the Sugatas] would be useless. [Therefore, both study and practice are necessary.]

All schools of Tibetan Buddhism posit that study (*thos*), reflection (*bsam*), and meditation (*sgom*) are all essential elements for the student. However, schools vary in the emphasis they place on the various elements. For example, the Kagyu and Nyingma schools emphasize meditation practice. In these schools the student is encouraged to study just enough to understand the meaning, and to concentrate on practice for the actual experience. It is believed that too much study with too little practice will present an obstacle to realization.

On the other hand, the Gelug and Sakya schools emphasize the importance of rigorous study and reflection. Here it is believed that the student should thoroughly study the sutras, tantras, forms of debate, and so forth, before entering into any extensive tantric practice. Lack of study is seen as hindering one's understanding of the scriptures, thus presenting an obstacle to practice.

Buton gives a detailed explanation of the importance of combining both study and reflection with meditation practice:

> Extensive study must always be connected with pure morals and analysis of the meaning and profound meditation. It is said in a passage of scripture concerning the monks who have got a firm stand in the principles of the dharma: "By study and analysis only, without the practice of meditation, one is unable to get a firm stand in the dharma. Likewise this is impossible if one merely practices meditation and does not take recourse to study and investigation. But if both parts are resorted to and accepted as a foundation, one gets a firm stand in the dharma."[139]

Buton then quotes the same section of the *Ornament of the Mahayana Sutras* as Kongtrul above.

Kongtrul warns that teaching based on reading and studying alone is worthless at best, citing a discussion in the *Sutra That Arouses Superior Intention* (*Lhag-pa'i bsam-pa bskul-ba; Adhyāśaya-sañcodana*) of the twenty faults incurred by delighting in idle talk of this kind.[140] Atisha cites the same list in his *A Lamp for the Path*.[141] Atisha begins by describing the need for a wisdom teacher to possess the six superknowledges in order to teach effectively; then he explains the dangers of teaching the dharma if one lacks the qualifications and merely has a penchant for glibness and talk. Atisha states:

> It is absurd to explain the [Buddha's] teaching and to gather disciples, having only your own insight from study—when you have not yet acquired the super-knowledges or developed the insight born of meditation (*bsgom-pa'i shes-rab*).[142]

Atisha then quotes the twenty faults and negative karma incurred through idle talk about the dharma:

> Proud of his learning he has no respect; he loves conversations with dispute and debate; he becomes unmindful and loses deliberateness—these are the evils of liking to talk.

His inner thought is quite far away; neither his body nor mind
become very pure; his arrogance is turned into great humiliation—these are the evils of liking to talk.

He is a child too frail to reflect on the dharma; his thoughts turn
unfriendly and become very harsh; he is a long way off from
calmness (*zhi-gnas*) and insight (*lhag-mthong*)—these are the
evils of liking to talk.

He is ever disrespectful to his guru, and he finds delight in
obscene conversation; pointless he lives and lacking in
insight—these are the evils of liking to talk.

At the hour of death this child makes moan: "Alas! My
meditation's so weak! What shall I do?" So with the depths
unfathomed, his suffering is great—these are the evils of liking
to talk.

Like grass in the wind he is blown to and fro; his only conviction
is that he's in doubt; firmness of mind will never be his—these
are the evils of liking to talk.

He is an actor before a crowd watching his play: he declaims the
hero's virtues while his own character grows weak—these are
the evils of liking to talk.

He is a hypocrite and in despair; he is remorse-stricken ever-
afterwards; he is far off from the noble and holy dharma—
these are the evils of liking to talk.

Of little ability, he is delighted by attention, and his ignorance
makes him impulsive; his mind is as restless as a monkey's:
these are the evils of liking to talk.[143]

Kongtrul Rinpoche ends this section by stating that studying, reflection, and meditation depend on each other and naturally give rise
to each other.

IN CONCLUSION: THE BASIC QUALIFICATIONS OF TEACHER AND STUDENT

Kongtrul shows us that there are very precise measures that can be
taken in order to make the student's relationship with the teacher
and practice of the dharma effective. The student must evaluate the
qualifications of the teacher before entering the relationship, using
established criteria for training with an authentic teacher on the three
levels of the pratimoksha, bodhisattva, and vajrayana vows.

He states that at the very minimum, a qualified teacher must have
the intention that is authentically compassionate; that is, all actions of
the wisdom teacher in relation to the student must be done solely for
the benefit of the student and all sentient beings. This is essential. A
teacher who is motivated by self-interest should be avoided.

Jamgön Kongtrul also precisely describes the characteristics that qualify a student to train at each of these levels. The minimum qualification of a suitable student is genuine eagerness for practicing the dharma. This qualification is always within our power and ability to engender.

PART II
The Root Verses

Jamgön Kongtrul Lodrö Thayé

The Explanation of the Master and Student Relationship, How to Follow the Master, and How to Teach and Listen to the Dharma

While [abiding in the world it is difficult to hear] the Victorious One's teaching, which is the source of benefit and happiness. When entering [into the teaching] for the purpose of making your leisure and opportunity worthwhile, in the beginning seek and then follow the wisdom teacher.

By following inferior [teachers] you will degenerate; by following those on the same level you will stay the same. By following someone higher you will obtain holiness. Therefore, you should follow someone higher than yourself.

Seek the justification [for following a wisdom teacher] by way of scripture, reasoning, and example.

The general categories [of wisdom teachers] are the ordinary person, the bodhisattva, the emanation [body of the Buddha], and the complete [enjoyment body of the Buddha], which are related to one's own four circumstances.

The characteristics of the [wisdom teacher] who is an ordinary person are [given as] eight, four, or two good qualities.

The specific categories are pratimoksha [master], bodhisattva [master], and secret [mantra master], explained sequentially.

The five [types of pratimoksha masters are]: the preceptor or khenpo (*mkhan-po*), [ritual] master, private instructor, reliance or reading [master], [and novice monk] master.

They are praised as lamas who possess morality; know the vinaya rituals; are compassionate to a sick person; have pure followers; strive to do benefit in dharma and material things; and give timely instructions (*'doms-pa*).

Follow the wisdom teacher who has tamed [his mind]; peacefully [resides]; has pacified [delusion]; has noble qualities which are significantly [greater than yours]; is conjoined with diligence; who, through [knowledge of] the scriptures, is wealthy; fully realizes suchness; speaks with skill; whose nature (*bdag-nyid*) [is full of] caring; and who eliminates depression.

Furthermore, being endowed with the twelve qualities of being learned and so forth is best.

The vajra master is steadfast; [his mind is] tamed, intelligent, patient, and without deception. He knows the practice of mantra and of tantra; he has compassion and loving kindness for others; he is learned [in the scriptures]. He has completed the ten essential points, is skilled in the activity [of drawing] the mandala, and knows how to explain the mantra.

Alternatively, [the master of the Vajrayana vow] has the three treasures, the complete river [of empowerments], eagerness for looking out after the suitable vessels. He is wise in tantra, skilled in the activity [of the ritual], and holds the [sign of] realization.

In short, he has the [unbroken] lineage, [unimpaired] *samaya*, the special oral instructions, and he knows the meaning of the tantras. From the three types, the [lama who is a] fully ordained monk is best.

In particular, the "glorious lama" is able to generate in the mind-stream [of the disciple] union and indestructible primordial wisdom (*vajrajñana*).

To go astray from the characteristics of [the above] is to have the fault [of not being a qualified wisdom teacher]. Abandon [such a teacher].

Also, it is rare for all [the qualities] to be complete. [Therefore, one should] take a lama with more noble qualities.

Someone who is a [suitable] vessel for the pratimoksha vow is [a person] without obstacles to the vow.

The student endowed with the following should be known as being endowed with the attribute of diligence and remaining in the vow: devotion to the master (*slob-dpon*); correctly taking the moral code; meditative concentration; diligence in recitation; a taut and disciplined [mind]; and patience.

To be a vessel of the bodhisattva vow is to be endowed with faith, compassion, and an intellect [for realizing emptiness]; acceptance in practicing the practices; not seeking the benefit of peace for oneself; diligence; and delight in hearing about emptiness.

In addition to those [characteristics explained above], the suitable vessel of [secret] mantra is devoted to the lama; tantrically capable; has a vast intellect; is diligent in the *samaya* and accomplishment.

Abandon faults. In regard to [a student with] a mixture [of faults and noble qualities, the lama] should take on someone who is endowed with faith and so forth.

The master and student, who are like precious jewels, should examine their relationship.

With an attitude which] desires liberation, [follow the wisdom teacher by applying yourself in terms of] material things, honoring, paying respect, and practice.

In relying on the present wisdom teacher—which is pure conduct (*tshangs-spyod; brahmacarya*); it is pure, unadulterated, complete, and pure—I see [him as] the proof of liberation from suffering. Thus it has been said by the Victorious One.

Aside from that, there are many advantages of following the friend.

The harmful friend is one of bad temperament, of little pure vision, great in dogmatism; holds [his own view] as highest, praises himself, and denigrates others.

One should recognize (*ngo-shes*) the obstacle of mara, conquering it with the antidotes (*gnyen-po*).

Generate clear-minded, trusting, and longing faith.

In regard to the preparation for explaining the holy dharma: the lama should make arrangements, annihilate mara's faction, and purify his behavior.

The student should offer a gift, attend to his conduct, and meditatively cultivate a joyous frame of mind.

There are three things to be learned in regard to the main subject matter.

The wisdom teacher must have the two kindnesses and the three patiences.

The wisdom teacher explains the dharma utilizing the six doors of explanation, or...

The wisdom teacher will at first describe the general and specific explanation of the purpose [of the teaching].

There are two parts to the synopsis that has six good qualities.

The meaning of the words is explained in terms of the three: the subject to be explained; by what means; and how the explanation is done. First seek the meaning dependent upon the words.

There are two points to the connection: easily understood and connected.

Responses to objections will be supported by scripture, and by reasoning.

For great intellects, explain using profound and extensive teachings. For lesser intellects, explain using words easy to remember, simple, and easy to understand. Afterwards, precisely and subtly cut the connections which are contradictory.

To those who are fainthearted, uplift them; if their minds are excited or drowsy, turn them away from all those faults.

Remove the three faults and six stains of the vessel, and so forth. Then establish the perception of the patient, the medicine, and the doctor.

Both wisdom teacher and student should practice teaching and listening in possession of the six perfections.

Subsequently, the teacher asks for forgiveness of faults, then dedicates all virtue, and extensively offers.

[The three things to be done] by the student are: offer gifts, make a dedication prayer, make mindfulness and vigilance firm.

[In general], the advantages of having heard and contemplated [the dharma are fivefold. In particular, the advantages of] listening, explaining, grasping the meaning, putting into practice, and intermingling the dharma are limitless.

This ends the commentary of the first section of Volume Two, Division Five of *The Treasury of Knowledge*, explaining "The characteristics of the teacher and student relationship, the method of teaching and listening to the holy dharma."

PART III

The Auto-commentary

*The Textual System Which Encompasses
All That Needs to Be Known, Which Liberates
by Means of a Few Words, Including All That Is Well-Spoken,
the Ocean of Infinite Things That Are Known*

Preface

So, when entering into the Victorious One's precious teachings which are flourishing in the world, alone, at the beginning, the basis and support of all realization—which is the holy freedom—is that [the student] should follow (*bsten*) well the wisdom teacher, and should train in the three vows. Therefore, the higher ethics training (*lhag-pa tshul-khrims kyi bslab-pa*) is divided into stages: four sections in the fifth division of Volume Two:

1) The explanation of the characteristics of the master and student [relationship], how to follow [the master], and how to teach and listen [to the dharma]
2) Classifying the pratimoksha vows (*so-thar gyi sdom-pa*)
3) Describing the bodhisattva trainings (*byang-sems kyi bslab-pa*)
4) A general explanation of the vows of the *vidyadhara* (*rig-'dzin gyi sdom-pa*)

Section one, the section on the explanation of the characteristics of the master and student relationship, how to follow the master, and how to teach and listen to the dharma, has ten chapters:

1) How to Seek the Wisdom Teacher
2) The Justification for Following the Wisdom Teacher
3) Categories and Characteristics of the Master Who Should Be Followed
4) The Way in Which One Enters into and Goes Astray—Which Follows from the Characteristics of the Master

5) The Characteristics of the Student Who Follows
6) How to Follow
7) The Necessity of Following the Wisdom Teacher in That Way
8) Avoiding Contrary, Harmful Companions
9) Creating Faith as a Favorable Condition
10) The Way That the Wisdom Teacher Should Explain and the Student Should Listen to the Holy Dharma

1 How to Seek the Wisdom Teacher

> While [abiding in the world it is difficult to hear] the Victorious One's teaching, which is the source of benefit and happiness. When entering [into the teaching] for the purpose of making your leisure and opportunity worthwhile, in the beginning seek and then follow the wisdom teacher.

And so, while abiding in the world, it is difficult to hear even so much as the name of the Victorious One's hundred ways of the precious teaching, which is the source of continuous benefit and complete happiness. The intelligent people who enter [the teaching] in the beginning seek the wisdom teacher who has the characteristics [of a qualified wisdom teacher].[1] They do this so as not to let go to waste, and for the purpose of making worthwhile, their attainment of the human body, which is like the wish-fulfilling jewel, endowed with the qualities of leisure and opportunity. Then, on finding him, they should properly follow him.[2]

[There are] three parts to this:

1.1 The dharma is the source of all benefit

From *Alternating Praises* (sPel-mar bstod-pa):

> One way and pleasant methods, properly connected and without misdeeds (nyes-pa), in the beginning, middle, and end, it is virtuous. Nothing like your teaching is found anywhere else.

There is one way as the path to freedom, and having entered into the pleasant methods[3] of undertaking it, then connect to only the excellent result, without faults (*skyon*) of attachment etc., or misdeeds. Because the teaching, at all times—in the beginning, hearing (*thos-pa*), in the middle, reflecting (*bsam-pa*), and in the end, meditating (*sgom-pa*)—functions as the sole cause of exaltation and sublimity, it is virtuous.

Because of [all of the above], the source[4] of all benefit and happiness in all ways is, alone, the Buddha's teaching. Because of that, in the teachings of other teachers, such as the *rishi* Serkya (Ser-skya; Kapila)[5] etc., [all of this] is not found.

The son of the Victorious One, Shantideva (Zhi-ba lha; Śāntideva) illustrated this [in *The Guide to the Bodhisattva's Way of Life*] by composing this aspiration prayer:[6]

> May the teaching, which is the sole medicine for the suffering and the source of all happiness of beings, be the object of gain and respect, and come to remain for a long time.

1.2 Have faith and engage in the teaching

It is said in *The Sutra of the Meeting of the Father and the Son* (*Yab-sras mjal-ba'i mdo; Pitā-putra-samāgamana-sūtra*):[7]

> After having fully abandoned all eight obstacles and having obtained what is rare to find—the fulfillment of leisure—the wise ones (*mkhas-pa*), who have gained faith in the Sugata's teachings, practice the suitable spiritual practice.[8]

Obtaining the human body, which has leisure and opportunity, and making it meaningful, is just to have faith and engage in the teaching.

1.3 Attaining full enlightenment depends upon approaching, following, and respecting the wisdom teacher

It is said in *The Noble Eight Thousand Verse Perfection of Wisdom Sutra* (*'Phags-pa brgyad-stong-pa; Aṣṭasāhasrikā-prajñāpāramitā*):

> So, the bodhisattva, the great being, who wishes to manifestly and fully awaken to supreme, right, and full awakening, first of all should approach the wisdom teachers, follow them, and honor them.

If you ask, "What kind of wisdom teacher shall we seek?" It states in *The Collection of High Utterances* (*Ched-du brjod-pa'i tshom; Udānavarga*):[9]

> By following inferior [wisdom teachers] you will degenerate; by following those on the same level you will stay the same. By following someone higher you will obtain holiness. Therefore, you should follow someone higher than yourself.

Also, regarding that wisdom teacher, by following someone who is even inferior in noble qualities to yourself in regard to morality (*tshulkhrims*), erudition (*mang-du thos*), meditative one-pointedness (*ting-nge-'dzin*), etc., many faults are created for the people who follow, and no noble qualities whatsoever arise. Therefore, they will degenerate. And [following someone] on the same level means that by following a person with noble qualities equal with yourself you will stay unchanged, without increasing or decreasing [in noble qualities]. By following one who is greater in noble qualities than yourself, you will obtain holiness; in other words, the highest goal that is desired. Therefore, you should follow someone higher than yourself, who is greater and nobler in all respects.

From the same text [*The Collection of High Utterances*]:[10]

> Whoever is best, in terms of morality, peacefulness, and the most excellent wisdom,[11] follow that one. If you do that, you become better than the best.

2 The Justification for Following the Wisdom Teacher

> **Seek the justification [for following a spiritual friend] by way of scripture, reasoning, and example.**

Seek for the justification,[12] or in other words, the need to follow the wisdom teacher, by way of scripture, reasoning (*rigs; yukti*), and example.[13]

There are three parts:

2.1 Justification by way of scriptural authority

It is said in *The Perfection of Wisdom Sutra* (*Phags-pa sdud-pa; Prajñā pāramitā-saṃcaya*):

> The good disciples, those who are devoted to the lama, should always follow the wise lama. Why? Because the good qualities of a wise person arise from [the wise lama].

And it is said in the *Sutra Arranged Like a Tree* (*sDong-po bkod-pa'i mdo; Gaṇḍhavyūha-sūtra*):

> Son of the lineage, all your virtuous qualities arise from the spiritual friend. After you find those spiritual friends who have gathered the accumulations of merit and wisdom during all the ocean of kalpas, you will obtain the dharma. Otherwise, it is more difficult to meet the wisdom teacher than to find the supreme jewel. Therefore, you should honor them with constant devotion (*guspa*), and not be discouraged.

Thus an infinite number of scriptures make this point.

2.2 Justification by way of reason[14]

The subject (*chos-can*) is that person who wishes to become omniscient. The proposition (*dam-bca'*) is that you must follow the spiritual friend. The reason (*gtan-tshig*) is because you yourself do not know how to gather the accumulations and how to purify obscurations. The example, which is in accordance with that [proposition], is that of the Buddhas of the three times [who, by following wisdom teachers, attain complete enlightenment]. The counter-example is that of the solitary sages [who, by not following wisdom teachers, do not attain complete enlightenment]. It is thus shown through many examples.[15]

2.3 Justification by means of example[16]

From *The Life Story of Paljung* (*dPal-byung-gi rnam-thar; Śrīsaṃbhava*):

> Because the wisdom teacher leads us upon the path of the perfections, he is like a guide.[17]

And also from *The Life Story of Upasika Acala* (*dGe-bsnyen-ma Mi-g.yo-ba; Upāsikā Acalā*):

> Because the wisdom teacher accompanies us to the state of being omniscient, he is like an escort.[18]

And from the *Sutra Arranged Like a Tree*:

> Because the wisdom teacher transports us over the great river of samsara, he is like a ferryman.

It is thus shown with many quotations, and so forth.

3 Categories and Characteristics of the Master Who Should Be Followed

There are two parts to the explanation of the kind of master who should be followed:

3.1 General explanation
3.2 Specific explanation

There are two points to the first part:

3.1.1 General categories
3.1.2 General characteristics

3.1 General explanation

3.1.1 General categories

> The general categories [of wisdom teachers] are the ordinary person, the bodhisattva, the emanation [body of the Buddha], and the complete [enjoyment body of the Buddha], which are related to one's own four circumstances.

In regard to the number of general categories of the wisdom teacher, there are four types:[19]

1) The ordinary person
2) The bodhisattva
3) The emanation body of the Buddha (*sangs-rgyas sprul-pa'i sku; nirmāṇakāya*)

4) The complete enjoyment body of the Buddha (*longs-spyod rdzog-pa'i sku; sambhogakāya*)

They are related to one's own four sorts of circumstances. [Namely,] while one is a beginner, one lacks the ability to follow the Buddhas and high-level bodhisattvas, therefore one follows spiritual friends who are ordinary people. When one has mostly exhausted the obscurations (*sgrib-pa*) of karma, then one is able to follow spiritual friends who are high-level bodhisattvas. When one dwells above the greater path of accumulation,[20] one is able to follow spiritual friends who are emanation bodies of the Buddha. When one dwells upon the highest level,[21] then one is able to follow spiritual friends who are complete enjoyment bodies [of the Buddha].

Among those [four circumstances],[22] while we who are beginners sit in the dungeon of karma and passions (*nyon-mongs-pa*), we do not even have a glimpse of their faces, let alone being able to follow spiritual friends who are higher ones. Because of our meeting with spiritual friends who are ordinary people, the lamp of their speech illuminates the path from which we shall meet the spiritual friends who are superior. Therefore, the kindest of all is the ordinary person who is a spiritual friend.

3.1.2 General characteristics

> The characteristics of the [wisdom teacher] who is an ordinary person are [given as] eight, four, or two good qualities.

The other three wisdom teachers will not help the beginner, therefore it is not necessary to mention their characteristics.[23] As to the characteristics of the wisdom teacher who is an ordinary person, [the root verse] declares that it is necessary to possess the eight, four, or two good qualities.[24]

A bodhisattva is known as a wisdom teacher, perfect in every way, if he possesses eight [qualities]:[25]

1) Possessing [a bodhisattva's] morality (*tshul-khrims-ldan*)
2) Being very learned [in the *Bodhisattva-piṭaka*]
3) [Having some personal] realization (*rtogs-pa; abhisamaya*)
4) [Being fully] compassionate and loving
5) Possessing fearlessness
6) Being patient

7) Being without sorrow

8) Being [skillful in] using words

Thus it has been summarized, [with the full] explanation located in *The Stages of the Bodhisattva (Byang-chub sems-dpa'i sa; Bodhisattva-bhūmi)*.

The Ornament of the Mahayana Sutras (mDo-sde rgyan; Mahāyāna-sūtrālaṃkāra) explains that there are four [good qualities in regards to] the wisdom teacher *(ston-pa)*. The four are:

1) He makes extensive teachings[26] because he is very learned.

2) He cuts off the doubts of others because of his great wisdom.

3) Because he engages in the activity of a holy man, he is praiseworthy.

4) He is able to show the actual *(de-kho-na-nyid)* characteristics of both afflicted [phenomena] and completely purified [phenomena].[27]

As it has been said in *The Bodhisattva's Way of Life (Byang-chub sems-dpa'i spyod-pa la 'jug-pa; Bodhisattva-caryāvatāra)*, the two [good qualities] are:[28]

> The wisdom teacher is always learned in the meaning of the Mahayana; and will not relinquish, even for the sake of his life, the most excellent conduct *(brtul-zhugs)*[29] of the bodhisattva.

Accordingly, [the wisdom teacher who is an ordinary person] is learned [in the meaning of the Mahayana] and possesses the [bodhisattva] vow.[30]

3.2 The specific explanation also has two points:

3.2.1 Specific categories

3.2.2 Individual characteristics

3.2.1 Specific categories

> The specific categories are pratimoksha [master], bodhisattva [master], and secret [mantra master], explained sequentially.

If the specific [categories of the wisdom teacher who is an ordinary person] are classified by means of the source from whom the three vows are taken, then the categories are the pratimoksha master *(so-sor-thar-pa slob-dpon)*, the bodhisattva master *(byang-chub sems-dpa' slob-dpon)*, and the secret mantra master *(sngags-kyi slob-dpon)*. Those characteristics should be explained sequentially.

3.2.2 Individual characteristics

After making that scheme, there are three points to the second [part, the individual characteristics]: The explanation of the pratimoksha, bodhisattva, and tantric masters.

3.2.2.1 The pratimoksha master[31]

> The five [types of pratimoksha master are]: the preceptor or khenpo, [ritual] master, private instructor, reliance or reading [master], [and novice monk] master.

From that list, we have, first of all, the khenpo (*mkhan-po*; *upādhyāya*),[32] who bestows the initial monastic ordination (*rab-byung*), and the higher monastic ordination (*bsnyen-rdzogs*), only in connection with the vinaya; the ritual master (*las-byed-pa slob-dpon*); the private instructor (*gsang-ste ston-pa; rahas-nuśāsaka*);[33] and the reliance or reading master (*gnas-klog-pa'i slob-dpon*), making four.[34] On top of those, if you add the novice monk master (*dge-tshul gyi slob-dpon*), then you explain it as five.

Those general characteristics are explained in *The Three Hundred Verses* (*Sum-brgya-pa*):

> They are praised as lamas who possess morality; know the vinaya rituals; are compassionate to a sick person; have pure followers; strive to do benefit in dharma and material things; and give timely instructions.

Because ten years have passed since higher ordination (*bsnyen-par-rdzogs; bhiksu*) and no mistakes have arisen,[35] he possesses morality, which is "the branch of steadfastness" (*brtan-pa*). The "branch of learning" is knowing from the undeluded intellect the rituals (*cho-ga*) of the vinaya pitaka (*sde-snod 'dul-ba*). The "branch of doing benefit" is being compassionate to the disciple, who is like a sick person; and because his followers possess morality, they are pure. Also, he strives to do benefit by means of the two benefits—dharma and material things; and he gives timely instructions to those to be taught. In that way, he is described as a pratimoksha lama.

The specific characteristics are that the khenpo possesses four branches which are: being steadfast, learned, a venerable monk [or nun], and doing benefit. They can also be combined together in regards to steadfastness and learnedness, or in regards to the 105 [qualities of the khenpo]. You should understand this as it is explained in *The Great*

Commentary to the Root Sutra (*mDo-rtsa'i 'grel-chen*) and as explained by the Venerable Pema Karpo (Pad-ma-dkar-po).[36] In regard to doing benefit, it is explained in twelve branches:

1) Compassion
2) Patience
3) [Having a] pure inner circle [of followers] (*nang-'khor*)
4, 5) Striving to do the two benefits
6, 7) [Having the] corresponding characteristics and view (*lta-ba*)
8) Knowing how to speak
9) Understanding the meaning
10) Not being crazy[37] [the three conventions][38]
11) [Having an] ordinary body
12) [Residing] naturally on the earth

The ritual master:

1) Has the completely pure full monk's (*dge-slong*) vow
2) Has the corresponding characteristics
3) Has the corresponding view
4) Possesses the three conventions
5) Inhabits an ordinary body
6) Resides naturally on the earth

On top of these six qualities, he is learned in imparting the pratimoksha] vow.

The private instructor, on top of these six qualities, is learned in interrogating [for possible] hindrances.

The reliance master, by imparting the transmission of what is to be accepted and rejected, is the one who is able to purify the mind-stream of the disciple, as well as having the qualities of the khenpo.

The reading master is the one who clarifies the understanding [of the student] according to the word of the dharma master.

3.2.2.2 The master of the bodhisattva vow

It has been said in *The Ornament of the Mahayana Sutras* that a student needs a wisdom teacher who possesses ten qualities:[39]

> Follow the wisdom teacher who has tamed [his mind]; peacefully [resides]; has pacified [delusion]; has noble qualities which are significantly [greater than yours]; is conjoined

with diligence; who, through [knowledge of] the scriptures, is wealthy; fully realizes suchness; speaks with skill; whose nature (*bdag-nyid*) [is full of] caring; and who eliminates depression.

One ought to rely upon a wisdom teacher who:[40]

1) With the good bridle—which is the moral training[41]—has tamed the wild horse of the mind.

2) With the training in samadhi (*ting-nge 'dzin; samādhi*), by mindfulness (*dran-pa*) and vigilance (*shes-bzhin*)[42] he peacefully resides (*zhi-bar gnas-pa*) within the mind.

3) He relies upon peaceful residing, in which the mind is workable. With the wisdom arisen from that, which is the analytic examination upon the true meaning, he has pacified delusion (*rmongs-pa*).

4) His noble qualities, not being inferior or equal to the disciple, are significantly greater.

5) He is energetic for the benefit of others, conjoined with constant diligence (*brtson-'grus*).

6) Through knowledge of the scriptures, which involves being learned in the Tripitaka, he is wealthy.

7) By virtue of hearing, contemplating, and meditating,[43] he has fully realized (*rab-tu rtogs-pa*) the suchness (*de-kho-na-nyid; tathatā*)[44] of all dharmas.

8) He speaks on the gradual path which conforms with the intellectual capacities of those to be tamed, so he is endowed with skill in explaining.

9) By the pure motivation, which teaches the dharma with compassion while not looking for gain, fame, and so forth, his nature itself is full of caring for others.

10) He eliminates depression by not being weary from repeatedly explaining [the dharma], and by being patient when someone is angry, etc.

Furthermore, taming [the wild horse of the mind] [1], peacefully residing [within the mind] [2], pacifying [delusion] [3], and fully realizing reality [7], are the branches of realization. "Through knowledge of the scriptures...he is wealthy" [6] is the branch of scripture. Including the "significantly greater" noble qualities [4], these six aspects are the noble qualities that are obtained by oneself.[45] The four remaining ones [5, 8, 9, 10] are the noble qualities that are directed towards others. Someone endowed with those qualities is designated a great person (*skye-bu chen-po; mahāpuruṣa*).

Furthermore, being endowed with the twelve qualities of being learned and so forth is best.

Furthermore, being endowed with the twelve noble qualities, which are being learned[46] and so forth, has been said to be best. As the noble Nagarjuna (kLu-sgrub; Nāgārjuna) said:

> Being very learned; being endowed with great wisdom; not striving for material gain;[47] not striving for fame; having bodhicitta; having great compassion; enduring difficulty; enduring lesser depression; having received a lot of special oral instructions (*man-ngag*); being liberated from the path;[48] being skilled in [teaching each] family[49] [of beings appropriately]; knowing their faculties (*drod-tshad*). You should follow a wisdom teacher who possesses these twelve good qualities.

3.2.2.3 The mantra master

[As it is said in *The Fifty Verses on Guru Devotion*:][50]

> **The vajra master is steadfast; [his mind is] tamed, intelligent, patient, and without deception. He knows the practice of mantra and of tantra; he has compassion and loving kindness for others; he is learned [in the scriptures].**
>
> **He has completed the ten essential points, is skilled in the activity [of drawing] the mandala, and knows how to explain the mantra.**

The categories of the vajra master of mantra (*sngag-kyi rdo-rje slob-dpon*) are explained below.[51] Although these characteristics are spoken of as vast, the summary of the common characteristics, according to the explanation in the *Fifty Verses on Guru Devotion*, is as follows:[52]

1) Because his body, speech, and mind do not swirl around, he is steadfast.
2) Because he possesses mind training, his mind is tamed.
3) He has the intellect that fully analyzes phenomena.
4) By being patient towards the behavior of his disciples, he is not angry.

5) By being without the deception of concealing faults [from himself; or]

6) the trickery of teaching the wrong meaning with the intention of misleading another, he is honest.

These six [are the common characteristics]. The special characteristics are:

1) He knows the practice of the mantra, such as the four activities and so forth.

2) He knows the practice of the tantra, such as the six extremes,[53] and so forth.

3) He cares for others.

4) He is also reasonably learned in the common systems (*thun-mong-ba'i gzhung lugs*).[54]

[The master of the Vajrayana] has completed the ten essential points (*de-nyid*). Because he comprehends the duties of the empowerment (*dbang-bskur-ba; abhiṣeka*), and has pure practice and so forth, he is skilled in the activity of drawing the mandala. He knows how to explain the mantra in accordance with the manner of the highest, middling, and inferior faculties. For the ten essential points just described, after classifying in three sets, then by adding, you get nine. By adding the two groups, common and special, you get fifteen.

If we classify the ten essential points into three subdivisions, then the first of the three is, as it appears in *The Consecration Tantra* (*Rab-tu gnas-pa mdor-bsdus-pa'i rgyud; Supratiṣṭha-tantra-saṃgraha*),[55] "the ten essential points that are requirements[56] for the vajra master." These are:[57]

> (1) Mandala (*dkyil-'khor; maṇḍala*); (2) samadhi (*ting-'dzin; samādhi*); (3) mudra (*phyag-rgya; mudrā*); (4) ritual dances;[58] (5) sitting posture ('*dug-stangs*); (6) reciting [mantras] (*bzlas-brjod*); (7) fire offering (*sbyin-sreg*); (8) torma offering; (9) performing the activities (*las la sbyar*);[59] (10) the reabsorption stage[60]

The "ten essential points of the ritual" appear in *Dombi-pa's Ten Verses on the Essentials of the Sphere of Wisdom Mind* (*Gur-gyi dgongs-pa Dom-bi-pa'i de-nyid bcu-pa*):

> The ten essential points are: (1) protection (*srung-ba*); (2) giving empowerment; (3) torma; (4) recitation (*bzlas*); (5) meditation (*bsgom*); (6) diverting [obstacles]; (7) mandala; (8) siddhi (*sgrub-pa*); (9) purifying misdeeds; (10) requesting [the deities] to depart (*gshegs-su gsol-ba*). Those are the ten essentials. Thus it has been said by the Victorious Ones.

The "ten essential points of suchness (de-kho-na-nyid)," as they appear in *The Blazing Gem: The Wisdom Mind of the Five Hundred Thousand Tantras (rGyud 'bum-lnga'i dgongs-pa rin-chen 'bar-ba)* are:

> Know the ten essentials as: (1) vajra; (2) bell; (3) primordial wisdom; (4) deity; (5) mandala; (6) fire offering; (7) mantra; (8) colored sand [used for making mandalas]; (9) torma; (10) giving empowerment; thus it is said.

So, the thirty essential points are complete.

Alternatively, the list of ten external essential points that are spoken of in *The Vajra Essence Ornament (rDo-rje snying-po rgyan; Vajrahṛdayālaṃkāra)*[61] is similar to the list that appears [above] in the *Consecration Tantra*; and the sayings which are in accord with those [ten external essential points above] from the *Tattvasarasaṃgraha*,[62] are the system of the *yoga* [class of tantras].

As it appears in *The Vajra Essence Ornament*,[63] the ten secret essential points are:

1, 2) The ritual of the two reversals

3) The secret initiation (*gsang-ba*)

4) The wisdom (*shes-rab ye-shes*) initiation

5) The ritual of unifying and dividing[64]

6) Torma

7) Vajra recitation (*rdo-rje'i bzlas-pa*)

8) The ritual of the wrathful accomplishment

9) Consecration of images

10) Accomplishment in the mandala

The unsurpassable point of view as asserted by father Mikyod (Mibskyod) [the eighth Karmapa][65] and his spiritual sons appears in the *Tantra of Completely Mastering the Good Qualities of the Lama (bLa-ma'i yon-tan yongs-bzung gi rgyud)*, the *Nyamjor Commentary (Sangs-rgyas mnyam-sbyor)*, the *Man-nye (Man-snye)*, etc.

> **Alternatively, [the master of the Vajrayana vow] has the three treasures, the complete river [of empowerments], eagerness for looking out after the suitable vessels. He is wise in tantra, skilled in the activity [of the ritual], and holds the [sign of] realization.**

Alternatively, the explanation from the school of the early translations (*snga-'gyur*) of mantra[66] [speaks of the vajra master of mantra as] having the three holy treasures (*mdzod-gsum*), namely, the view (*lta-ba*), which is realizing (*rtogs-pa*) the indivisibility of the two truths (*bden-pa*); the samadhi (*ting-'dzin*) which consummates the generation (*bskyed-pa*) and completion (*rdzogs-pa*) stages; and not transgressing (*las mi-'da'-ba*) the general and specific samayas (*dam-tsig*). Alternatively, he is wise (*mkhas-pa*) in the three treasuries, which are the treasury of generation, Mahayoga; the treasury of completion, Anuyoga; and the treasury of the view, Atiyoga.[67]

[The vajra master of mantra] has completed the river of the profound empowerment which has benefits and abilities; does not give up the secret mantra; has eagerness for looking after the suitable vessel; is wise in the tantra class and in uncovering the meaning of the scriptures; is skilled in activity (*phrin-las*)—that is to say, in arranging the accomplishment ritual (*sgrub-pa'i cho-ga*); holds the sign of realization (*drod-rtags 'chang-ba*), which is the experience (*nyams-su myong-ba*) according to the special oral instructions (*man-ngag*) of the hearing lineage (*nyan-brgyud*).

It is said in *The Gradual Path of Guhya-buddha* (*Sangs-rgyas gsang-ba'i lam-rim*) that by enumerating the three treasures separately, the vajra master possesses eight natures (*rang-bzhin*).

> **In short, he has the [unbroken] lineage, [unimpaired] samaya, the pith instructions, and he knows the meaning of the tantras. From the three types, the [lama who is a] fully ordained monk is best.**

In short, if you collect all that has been explained about the characteristics of the lama up until now:[68] He has not broken the lineage (*brgyud-pa*) which ripens [through empowerment] and liberates [through oral instructions], from Dorje Chang through the present. He has not entered into the fault of violating the *samaya*. He adheres to the conduct (*brtul-zhugs*) of the vows (*sdom-pa*) and the samaya (*dam-tshig*).[69] He possesses the special oral instructions (*man-ngag*) that have been passed down through the lineage.[70] He knows (*rig-pa*) the meaning of the Buddha-word (*bka'*),[71] the *shastras* (*bstan-bcos*), and the general and specific tantras (*rgyud*). All the characteristics are condensed into having a compassionate mind which benefits others.

The support for being endowed with those characteristics is being either a layman (*dge-bsnyan*), a novice monk (*dge-tshul*), or a fully ordained monk (*dge-slong*). From among those three, the first one is the layman, excluding those laymen who have attained the [first] bodhisattva level (*sa; bhūmi*). From the *Vajra Essence Commentary*:

The king should not take as a lama one who is a householder (*khyim-pa*), except for one who has attained the [first] *bhumi*.[72] Thereupon, by entirely understanding what was heard, whenever one makes offerings to the householder who is a master, excluding someone who possesses the marks of having attained the [first] bhumi, you become without devotion in the Buddha, the dharma, and the sangha.

The second type is part of the monastic grouping and therefore it is nobler than the previous one; however the fully ordained monk is the best.[73] As it has been said in the *Kalachakra Root Tantra* (*Dus-'khor rtsa-rgyud; Kālachakra-mūlatantra*):

The ten essential points are entirely known; from among the three statuses, the fully ordained monk is the best. It is said that the middle one is the novice monk, and the householder (*khyim-gnas*) is the lowest.

In particular, the "glorious lama" is able to generate in the mind-stream [of the disciple] union and indestructible primordial wisdom.

In particular, one is called a "glorious lama" (*dpal-ldan bla-ma*) who functions as the auxiliary cause of the supreme siddhi (*mchog gyi dngos-grub*), because he is able to generate in the disciple's mind-stream (*rgyud*) that which is union (*zung-'jug*), mahamudra (*phyag-rgya chen-po; mahāmudrā*), and indestructible primordial wisdom (*rdo-rje ye-shes; vajrajñāna*). His characteristics, according to the *Compendium Tantra*:[74]

The "glorious lama" is the one in whose mind and face abides the face of the Buddha [the fourth empowerment].[75]

According to the elucidation in *The Commentary on the Bodhisattva* (*Byang-chub sems-dpa'i 'grel-pa*), the glorious lama is able to guide the disciple's mind into the path of union, the fourth empowerment (*dbang-bzhi*), which is being in the face or presence of the Buddha, with the certainty of this transmission coming from the Buddha.[76] And through the certainty of mantra he is able to transfer (*spo-ba*) the realization of the blessings (*byin-rlabs*) into the mind-stream of the disciple, because he resides in the heart (*thugs*) of the different kinds of samadhi. The lama who has attained the first bhumi is the "glorious lama" who distinctly becomes even greater than the other types of lamas.[77]

4 The Way in Which One Enters Into and Goes Astray—Which Follows from the Characteristics of the Master

> To go astray from the characteristics [of the above] is to have the fault [of not being a qualified wisdom teacher]. Abandon [such a teacher]. Also, it is rare for all the qualities to be complete. [Therefore one should] take a lama with more good qualities.

To go astray (*ldog*) from the characteristics of what was said above, or to have strayed from the Buddha's doctrine (*bstan-pa*), is to have the fault of not having the characteristics [of a qualified teacher]. Therefore, however great a lama's social status, fame, reputation, and so forth may be, those students who possess discernment examine [the wisdom teacher carefully]. Even if one is already connected to the lama, ignore him. If one is not connected from the start, while rejecting him, abandon him.

From the Great Sakya Pandita [Sa-skya pan-chen]: "One who does not act according to the Buddha's doctrine, even though he is a lama, ignore him." Furthermore, in the *Compendium Tantra* (Kalachakra Tantra):

> Disciples who are overcome by arrogance (*nga-rgyal dang-ldan*) and anger (*khro-ba*), are separated from samaya, long for material things, and are also uneducated—these disciples are eager to be deceived, their minds deteriorate from the state of supreme

happiness, and they do not get empowered. The lamas who cling to enjoyments, are careless, use harsh words, and are endowed with desiring the objects of the sense faculties (*dbang-po*)—those people should be rejected by intelligent disciples, as if rejecting hell as a cause for complete awakening.

Therefore, as there are other illustrations of the manifold ways in which this happens, abandon that kind of lama.

It is very rare for all the excellent characteristics to be complete; therefore, even if you have not found a wisdom teacher like that, because time is short, you should take as a lama one who has few faults and more noble qualities.

As it has been said in *The Ultimate Service* (*Don-dam bsnyen-pa; Paramārthasevā*):[78]

On account of the *kalpa* of quarreling (*rtsod-ldan*)[79] the lama's faults (*skyon*) and good qualities are mixed together. He is not separate from misdeeds (*sdigs-pa*) in every respect. Therefore, investigate well for a lama who has more noble qualities [than faults]. Then the disciple should follow him.

5 The Characteristics of the Student Who Follows

There are also two parts to the explanation of the characteristics of the student who follows:

5.1 *Those who should follow* (bsten-bya)
5.2 *The things to be abandoned, with their subsidiaries*

To the first part there are three points:

5.1.1 *The suitable vessel* (snod-rung) *of the pratimoksha* (so-thar)
5.1.2 *The suitable vessel of the bodhisattva* (byang-sems)
5.1.3 *The suitable vessel of the mantra* (sngags)

5.1 Those who should follow

5.1.1 Those who should follow: the suitable vessel of the pratimoksha vow[80]

> Someone who is a [suitable] vessel for the pratimoksha vow
> is [a person] without obstacles to the vow.

Someone who is a suitable vessel for the pratimoksha vow must be someone who is free from the four dharmas which would cut the vow,[81] or, in other words, are obstacles (*bar-chad*), negative conditions (*'gal-rkyen*), and inharmonious factors to the vow. In general, that person is the basis for the growth of the vow.

In particular, it has been said in *The Three Hundred Verses*:

> The student endowed with the following should be known as being endowed with the attribute of diligence and remaining in the vow: devotion to the master; correctly taking the moral code; meditative concentration; diligence in recitation; a taut and disciplined [mind]; and patience.

For a student to be known as being endowed with the attribute of being capable of diligence and remaining unfailingly in the pratimoksha vow, he should be possessed of constant devotion (*gus-pa*) to the khenpo, and especially to the reliance and reading master. By having abandoned the four causes of the arising of moral downfall (*lhung-ba*), he has the ability to correctly take the moral code. He should have meditative concentration (*bsam-gtan*) which eliminates [defilements]; diligence in recitation (*'don*), or [in other words], reading [aloud] and reciting [by heart]. His mind is taut, and his mind-stream and behavior are naturally disciplined (*dul-ba*). He has patience (*bzod-pa*) towards the guidance by the master and injury done by another.

5.1.2 Those who should follow: the suitable vessel of the bodhisattva vow

> To be a vessel of the bodhisattva vow is to be endowed with faith, compassion, and an intellect [for realizing emptiness]; acceptance in practicing the practices; not seeking the benefit of peace for oneself; diligence; and delight in hearing about emptiness

The student who has become a vessel of the bodhisattva vow is possessed with faith in the Mahayana Pitaka and in the spiritual friend (*dge-ba'i bshes-gnyen*); compassion (*snying-brtse-ba*) for sentient beings, and an intellect (*blo-gros*) for realizing the profound (*zab*) and the extensive (*rgya-che-ba*); patience (*bzod-pa*) in the practice (*spyod-pa*); in other words, she is not discouraged in regard to extensive practices such as the four means of conversion, the six perfections, and so forth. She does not seek merely the level (*go-'phang*) of peace and happiness for herself alone, but delights in the crossing over[82] of all sentient beings. She is endowed with uninterrupted diligence (*brtson-'grus*). If she hears the profound [Mahayana dharma], which is the subject of emptiness, then joy arises in her mind. It has been said that these are the indications of someone whose family (*rigs*)[83] has been activated.

In *Sutra of the Ten Noble Dharmas* (*Chos-bcu-pa'i mdo; Daśadharmaka-sūtra*) it is said:

> One knows the family of the intelligent bodhisattva from the pure characteristics he possesses ; just as from smoke one knows fire, and from a riverbank one knows there is water.

Furthermore, in [Aryadeva's] *The Four Hundred* it is said : "It has been taught that an amenable vessel is objective, intelligent, and eager."[84]

Because she is impartial, which means not being attached to her own way (*lugs*) and not being angry against another's way, she is objective (*gzu-bor gnas-pa*). She has the intelligence that knows how to distinguish the well-spoken path, which is correct, and the wrongly-spoken path (*nyes-bshad-lam*), which is counterfeit. She is endowed with great eagerness (*don-gnyer*) for the Mahayana.

If the disciple is endowed with those three, then, on one hand she will see the noble qualities of the wisdom teacher as noble qualities [and therefore engage in a proper relationship with the spiritual friend]. If the disciple is not endowed with those three qualities, then, on the other hand the great number of noble qualities of the wisdom teacher will be seen as faults [and a proper relationship will not develop].

5.1.3 Those who should follow: the suitable vessel of the mantra vow

> In addition to those [characteristics explained above], the suitable vessel of [secret] mantra is devoted to the lama; tantrically capable; has a vast intellect; is diligent in the samaya and accomplishment.

Those who are suitable vessels, who are given the ripening (*smin*) [empowerments] and liberating (*grol*) [instructions] of secret mantra, are summed up by these kinds of qualities, in addition to those just explained [for the pratimoksha and bodhisattva vows]: The disciple should be very devoted (*gus-pa*) to the lama; tantrically capable in the profound view and practice, and so forth; have a vast intellect which is without doubt in the aim of the secret mantra and which realizes reality (*de-nyid*); be capable of diligence in keeping the samaya and in the practice (*sgrub-pa*) of what needs to be rejected and accepted. This is extensively spoken of in the *Compendium Tantra, Exposition Tantra* (*bShad-rgyud*), in the *Vajra Garland* (*rDor-phreng*),[85] and so forth.

It has been said in the *Magical Display*,[86] a tantra of the early translation period (*snga-'gyur gyi rgyud*):[87]

> A suitable vessel should be endowed with the characteristics of
> making offerings to the wisdom teacher; diligence; clear [mind
> delving into the view to be] realized; unimpaired samaya; know-
> ing the mantras and mudras; and [favorable material] requisites.[88]

By offering to the wisdom teacher—the lama—the suitable vessel
gradually obtains the empowerments. By diligence (*brtson-'grus*) that
is devoted (*gus-sbyor*)[89] and steadfast, he does not give up hearing [the
dharma] and contemplating [its meaning]. The suitable vessel should
have an undistortedly clear mind (*blo-gros*), which intensively delves
into the view that should be realized. The root and branch samayas
are unimpaired.[90] He should comprehend the topics of mantra, mudra,
and so forth. He has the required favorable conditions. These characteristics are shown as having the capacity for making the disciple enter into the path.

5.2 The explanation of the things to be abandoned along with their subsidiaries

> **Abandon faults. In regard to [a student with] a mixture [of
> faults and noble qualities, the lama] should take on some-
> one who is endowed with faith and so forth.**

Turning away from some of the good qualities of the student [men-
tioned above] is being with fault; therefore you should abandon that.
As it has been said in the *Chakrasaṃvara Tantra*:

> The lama should always avoid students who lack compassion,
> are angry and malicious, arrogant (*khengs*) and undisciplined, have
> vacillating minds, are violent, deluded (*rmongs-pa*), indolent, are
> without affection for the lives of others, and who openly yearn
> for another's property.[91]

And in *The Five Stages* (*Rim-pa lnga; Pañcakrama*):[92]

> Do not describe the stage of oral instruction (*gdams-pa*) to one who
> has contempt for the lama, one who is dishonest, faithless, con-
> ceited by praise, arrogant by being book-learned,[93] faithless, or
> who belittles the empowerments.

In regard to a student who has a mixture of faults and good qualities,
although all the characteristics of the suitable vessel are incomplete, the
lama should take on someone who possesses eagerness from amongst
[the list given above that begins with] "faith" and so forth.[94] As it has
been said in *The General Tantra* (*sPyi-rgyud*):

A disciple who is physically intact, has exceptional noble qualities, is free from illness, is from a respectable family,[95] has faith, and possesses the vows (*btul-zhugs*), is rare. In summary, these are great sentient beings who have faith in the three jewels (*dkon-mchog*), delight in the system (*lugs*) of the Mahayana, and who possess merit. Therefore, the disciple who is eager and strives to practice the Sugata's secret mantra, although possessing an inferior form and not possessing noble qualities, because of being intelligent, should be brought onto the path.

6   How to Follow

There are two parts to the explanation:

6.1 At first examine the relationship ('brel)
6.2 Then follow

6.1 At first, examine the relationship

> **The master and student, who are like precious jewels, should examine their relationship.**

When the master and student—who are like precious jewels, possessed with noble qualities which have been explained above—have come together, they at first should thoroughly examine their relationship; any way you look at it, it is very important. It is said in *The Fifty Verses on Guru Devotion*:

> Because the lama and student will fail together in the samaya, in the beginning the warrior (*dpa'-bo*) should examine the relationship of the master and the student.[96]

And, as it has been said in *The Essence of Mahamudra* (*Phyag-chen thig-le*):

> A lama who is like that should examine the student assiduously, just as a person who is skilled examines gold by burning and so forth, [and finds that it is] precious. Just like [examining] the blissful girl (*bde-ldan bu-mo*), just so, the lama should examine the disciple.

Therefore, both must be very assiduous and examine each other. If it is not like that, there will be problems.

In particular, if the secret mantric lama gives the empowerment to just anybody, without having examined the student, then, because the unfit vessel is incapable of performing the samaya, the lama degenerates in both this and the next life; the samaya will become impaired; one's *siddhi* (*dngos-grub*) will be long delayed; plenty of faults (*nyes-pa*) arise, such as injury due to [demonic] obstacles (*bgegs*).

Meanwhile, if the disciple receives the empowerment from just anybody, without having examined the characteristics of the lama, then disadvantages will plentifully arise, such as: The disciple will be deceived (*bslu-pa*) by the misleading spiritual friend (*log-pa'i bshes-gnyen*). By not being able to keep the samaya, the root of siddhi will be cut. Because he will be entangled in a bad path, the eight leisures and the ten opportunities will be wasted, and so forth.

6.2 Then follow

> [With an attitude which] desires liberation, [follow the spiritual friend by applying yourself in terms of] material things, honoring, paying respect, and practice.

There are two parts to that:

6.2.1 Attitude (bsam-pa)
6.2.2 Application (sbyor-ba): *the manner of honoring the spiritual friend*

6.2.1 Attitude

As it has been said in the *Compendium* (*sDud-pa; Ratnaguna-samcayagāthā*):

> On account of that, the wise one, who is endowed with a strong attitude which is seeking holy enlightenment, certainly conquers pride. As the multitudes of patients follow the doctor in order to be healed, the student should follow the wisdom teacher without wavering.

After planting (*gting-tshugs*) the attitude that eagerly desires the holy level of enlightenment, which is unsurpassable liberation, sincerely honor [the wisdom teacher].

6.2.2 Application: the manner of honoring the wisdom teacher

Also, concerning the manner of honoring the wisdom teacher, as it is said in the *Ornament of the Mahayana Sutras*: "The student should follow the wisdom teacher in terms of material things, honoring, paying respect (*rim-gro*), and practice."

6.2.2.1 Giving material things and honoring the wisdom teacher

The first that is discussed among the three topics is giving material things. If one has food and clothes, etc., and they are handy, enthusiastically offer whatever the master wishes. Besides that, it is said that the student ought to offer even to the extent of his child, wife, and his own body.

The stages of honoring are prostrating on sight (*mthong-phyag*), rising [when the wisdom teacher enters the room], uttering praises (*bsngags-pa brjod-pa*), and so on. One follows the wisdom teacher with behavior that is always respectful; and if one should not even walk on the shadow of his body, what need to mention anything else. In regard to his clothing, seat, wearing his shoes, [using his] consort, and so on, unless you have the order, do not wear or use them. Eliminate all aspects of deportment that are disrespectful, such as sleeping in his presence, lying down, blowing your nose, expressing secret disparagement [behind his back], and so on.

6.2.2.2 Offering your services (*rim-gro*)

With prostrations as preliminary, one should calmly, graciously, and collectedly do all the immediate duties, such as bathing, anointing, massaging, wiping off, and so forth.

6.2.2.3 Follow in terms of practice (*sgrub-pa'i sgo-nas bsten*)

Cheerfully practicing all the commands given by the lama, and assiduously practicing whatever possible in the way of listening, contemplating, and meditating upon all the dharma teachings, is better worship than the ways previously mentioned, because the authentic wisdom teacher is pleased by the offering of practice, and not by material things and so forth.

Also, as it is said in the *Sutra Arranged Like a Tree*:

> You should not be sad in seeking (*'tshol*) the wisdom teacher. Even after finding him you should practice according to him and show respect, which is not forgetting. You should generate the idea that you are like the earth, because you are not saddened by all the burdens. You should generate the idea (*'du-shes*) that you are like a slave in listening to whatever he commands...[97]

and so forth.

7 The Necessity of Following the Wisdom Teacher in That Way

There are two parts in this section:

7.1 Establish the necessity by proof (rigs-pa)
7.2 The advantages as explained in the scriptures (lung)

7.1 Establish the necessity by proof

> **In relying on the present wisdom teacher—which is pure conduct; it is pure, unadulterated, complete, and pure—I see [him as] the proof of liberation from suffering. Thus it has been said by the Victorious One.**

By following the wisdom teacher—in other words when I follow the present spiritual friend—it is pure conduct,[98] pure (*ril-po*), unadulterated, perfect, and pure throughout; I see him as the proof, or example of easy liberation from the suffering of craving (*sred-pa*). Thus it has been said and given as advice by him, the Victorious One, the Wisdom Teacher, the Compassionate One. From sutra:

> Ananda, it is like this: the wisdom teacher, or the wholesome companion (*dge-ba'i grogs-po*), is the fulfillment of pure conduct.

And it is said in [Nagarjuna's] *A Letter to a Friend* (*bShes-pa'i spring-yig*; *Suhṛllekha*):

> Because the Sage (*thub-pa*; *muni*) has said, "The pure conduct of following the wisdom teacher is perfect," follow the wisdom teacher; and after following the wisdom teacher, very many disciples have obtained peace.[99]

7.2 The advantages as explained in the scriptures

> Aside from that, there are many advantages of following the friend.

Aside from that [way of knowing], the sutras and tantras speak boundlessly of the many advantages of following the wisdom teacher. As it has been shown in the *Sutra Arranged Like a Tree*:

> The bodhisattvas who are favored by the wisdom teacher will not fall down into lower realms (*ngan-'gro*); they do not let themselves get into things that shouldn't be done; they turn away from the state of carelessness; they are extricated from the city of samsara; they are not in contradiction with the bodhisattva training; they are sublime above all [people] of the world; it is difficult for them to be affected by karma and passions. Therefore, son of the family, as we just discussed, you should go like that into the presence of wisdom teachers with uninterrupted attentiveness.[100]

As it has been said from the mouth of the Omniscient One Drime Ozer (Kun-mkhyen Dri-med 'od-zer),[101] who summarizes the points of the scriptures:

> The noble qualities of following the lama are limitless. One enters into the correct path; distinguishes (*rnam-phyed*) objects that are to be accepted or rejected (*blang-dor*); completes the [two] gatherings; purifies obscurations (*sgrib*); and pacifies obstacles (*bar-chad*). After one obtains the status (*gnas*) of a noble person (*skye-bo dam-pa*), then one goes quickly to the city of liberation.

In addition, it is said that by following the wisdom teacher the student approaches the level of Buddhahood; pleases the Victorious Ones; is not impoverished in regard to wisdom teachers; does not fall into lower realms; it becomes difficult for him to be affected by bad karma and afflictions; he is not in contradiction with the bodhisattva way of life (*spyod-pa*) and is mindful of it. Thereby he grows higher and higher with the accumulation of good qualities, and all provisional and ultimate aims are attained.

Furthermore, it is said that by honoring the wisdom teacher great advantages are obtained which outshine the virtuous roots of having made offerings to the measureless numbers of Buddhas. For example, karma which has the potential to cause lower realms of rebirth is experienced as a little bit of harm to body and mind in this life, or is even experienced as being in a dream. Because of that karma having been uprooted,[102] it will then be exhausted.

If you turn away from the [right] way of following, then you will experience [the turning away] in this life as injury by illness and lots of demonic spirits (*gdon*), and in subsequent lives as a measureless amount of suffering in the lower realms, and noble qualities that have not been created will not be created. Then it will also ensue that those noble qualities that have already arisen will deteriorate. Therefore it appears in the *Vajrapani Empowerment Tantra* (*Lag-na rdo-rje dbang-bskur-ba'i rgyud; Vajrapāṇi-ābhiṣeka-mahātantra*):[103]

> O Lord Guhyapati (*gSang-ba'i bdag-po*),[104] if you ask, "How should the disciple view the wisdom teacher?" Just as you would view the Buddha Bhagavat, [view the wisdom teacher] like that.

And in the sutras and vinaya of the Mahayana it has also been spoken like that; therefore, eliminate discursive thoughts about [the master's] faults, and follow with great devotion which exceeds what you have for the Buddhas.

The advantages of offering to the lama are inconceivable. As it appears in the *Guhyasamaja Tantra* (*gSang-dus-ba; Guhyasamāja-tantra*): "There is greater merit through offering to a pore of hair of the lama, than offering to the Buddhas of the ten directions and the three times."[105] It appears in the *The Life Story of Paljung*: "If you please the wisdom teacher, you will obtain the enlightenment of a Buddha." And so say other scriptures as well.

In summary, you will obtain immeasurable noble qualities of dharmas which are visible and invisible, such as completing the accumulations of merit (*bsod-nams kyi tshogs*) and wisdom (*ye-shes kyi tshogs*), pacifying all obstacles of bad conditions (*rkyen*), great prosperity and leisure, swiftly obtaining buddhahood, and so forth.

In general, whatever actions you do for the lama, who is the highest object [of respect], for a khenpo, master, a sick person, a dharma speaker,[106] a bodhisattva who is in his last life (*srid-pa tha-ma-pa*) [non-returner], a noble shravaka, noble pratyekabuddha, and parents, whether they are meritorious or demeritorious, will be very powerful.

It also appears in the *Abhidharmakosha* (*Chos-mngon-pa'i mdzod; Abhidharmakośa*):[107]

> Although they are not Noble Ones (*ārya*), [the advantages of] benefiting parents, sick people, a dharma speaker, and a bodhisattva who is a last-lifer (*skye-mtha'*),[108] are said to be measureless.

8   Avoiding Contrary, Harmful Companions

There are two parts in this section:

8.1   Obstructions of a harmful friend (sdig-pa'i grogs)
8.2   Obstructions of mara (bdud-kyi bar-chad)

8.1   Obstructions of a harmful friend

> **The harmful teacher is one of bad temperament, of little pure vision, great in dogmatism; he holds [his own view] as highest, praises himself, and denigrates others.**

In general, the nonspiritual teacher (*mi-dge-ba'i bshes-gnyen*) is a lama, teacher (*mkhan-slob*), dharma brother [or sister] (*grogs-mched*), and so forth—all those who are attached to the phenomena (*snang*) of this life, and who get involved in unvirtuous activity. Therefore, one must abandon the nonspiritual friend. In particular, although they have the manner of goodness in appearance, they cause you to be obstructed in your liberation.

The nonspiritual teacher has a bad temperament, little pure vision (*dag-snang*), is very dogmatic (*phyogs-ris*), holds as highest his view (*lta-ba*) as the only dharma, praises himself, slanders others, implicitly denigrates and rejects others' systems (*lugs*) of dharma, and slanders the lama—the true wisdom teacher—who bears the burden of benefiting others. If you associate with those who are of this type, then, because one follows and gets accustomed to the nonspiritual teacher and his approach, his faults stain you by extension, and your mind-stream (*rgyud*) gradually becomes negative. Illustrating this point, it has been said in the *Vinaya Scripture*:[109]

> A fish in front of a person is rotting and is tightly wrapped with kusha grass. If that [package] is not moved for a long time, the kusha itself also becomes like that. Like that [kusha grass], by following the sinful teacher, you will always become like him.[110]

Therefore, as it has been said in *The Sutra of the True Dharma of Clear Recollection* (*mDo dran-pa nyer-bzhag; Saddharmānusmṛiti-upasthāna*):

> As the chief among the obstructors (*bar-du gcod-pa*) of all virtuous qualities is the sinful teacher, one should abandon being associated with him, speaking with him, or even being touched by his shadow.

In every respect one should be diligent in rejecting the sinful teacher.

8.2 The obstructions of mara

One should recognize the obstacle of mara, conquering it with the antidotes.

The obstacle of mara will arise when meeting the real dharma and lama, and when participating in hearing, contemplating, and meditating. It is said in the *Compendium* (*sDud-pa; Ratnaguṇa-saṃcayagāthā*):

> There is a lot of damage to the precious dharma and the three jewels. Those sentient beings whose intellectual abilities are low, who have newly entered into the vehicle—some of them do not even find this precious rare one. In order to create obstacles for them, mara will be energetic.

Also on that subject, it has been said in sutra that in general, there are four maras, the *kleshas* and so forth;[111] and it has been said in the oral instructions (*man-ngag*) that in particular, there are six outer maras, three inner maras, eighteen secret maras, etc.[112] [It can also be discussed from the perspective of] the causes for the entering of those maras: karma, the objects of engagement,[113] the marks of being blessed by [mara], and the ordinary and extraordinary means of pacification. Out of all that wealth of detail, in this context [the maras are]: (1) thinking about the faults of the wisdom teacher, and not desiring to exert oneself in hearing and contemplating; (2) relying on divisiveness, foolish talk, and so forth, which are the causes of anger; (3) distractions of food, drink, a [comfortable] bed, business, and so on; (4) sinking under the influence of sleepiness and laziness; (5) coming under the influence of discursive thoughts (*rnam-tog*)[114] such as attachment and so forth.

While [the sutras and oral instructions] have caused us to recognize these as maras which obstruct us in our liberation, they also will make us skilled in conquering mara by possessing the armor of the antidotes to these maras, such as faith and devotion in the lama and dharma brother; diligence in hearing, contemplating, and meditating; trust (*yid-ches*), which is without doubt in the dharma; and not slipping under the power of discursive thought and agitation.[115]

9 Creating Faith as a Favorable Condition

Generate clear-minded, trusting, and longing faith.

In general, faith is the preliminary of all positive qualities,[116] and in particular, generating the three aspects of faith (*dad-pa*)[117] is very important at the beginning of both following the wisdom teacher and being diligent on the path.[118] It has been said in the *Precious Talala Sutra* (*dKon-mchog ta-la-la'i mdo; Ratnolkā-nāma-dhāraṇī sūtra*):

> Faith is generated as the preliminary. It dispels doubt (*dogs-pa sel*) and transports across (*las-sgrol*) rivers. Faith is the maker of a prosperous city (*bde-legs grong-khyer*).[119]

And the sutra continues.

> As to the essence (*ngo-bo*) of clear-minded faith (*dang-ba'i dad-pa*):[120] the intellect which discerns what is to be rejected and accepted, and [knows] the objects to be involved with and avoided, is clear. If we further classify faith, then it has been said in the *Abhidharma*.[121]

What is faith? Manifest trust in karma and result, the [four noble] truths, and the three jewels; longing; and a clear mind (*sems dang-ba*).

According to that, there are clear-minded faith, trusting faith (*yidches-pa'i dad-pa*), and longing faith (*'dod-pa'i dad-pa*). Clear-minded faith is relying upon the objects of the three jewels, which means being respectful (*mos*) and having a clear mind towards the three jewels and towards the lama. Trusting faith is having trust in karma, cause, and result. Longing faith is [recognizing] unsurpassable enlightenment [itself as something very special, then] with devotion for the sake of obtaining it, training in the path.[122]

From that same text [*The Compendium of Abhidharma; Chos-mngon-pa kun-btus; Abhidharma-samuccaya*]:

> Someone who does not violate (*mi-'da'*) the dharma by desire (*'dun*), anger, fear, and stupidity (*rmongs-pa*)—he is called "one who has faith," and he is an excellent vessel (*snod*) for higher attainment.[123]

Not giving up the dharma for the sake of attachment (*chags*),[124] anger, delusion, and so forth, is the measure of the extent that faith has been born. The advantages of having faith are endless; for example, the mind of the higher person arises,[125] the eight unfortunate places of rebirth are abandoned, and so on.[126] And if you are endowed with faith, then the Tathagatas, after you have gone into their presence, teach the dharma.

In the *Precious Talala Sutra*:

> When faith in the Victorious One and the Victorious One's dharma has come about, and you have faith in the way of life of the bodhisattvas, and when faith in the unsurpassable enlightenment has come about, then the mind of the great person arises.[127]

And as it has been said in the *Bodhisattva-pitaka* (*Byang-sems-kyi sde-snod; Bodhisattva-piṭaka*) :

> The bodhisattvas who abide in faith are known by the Buddhas to be fit vessels for the Buddha's doctrine. So coming before [the Buddhas, the bodhisattvas] are taught the bodhisattva path.

To summarize, because faith is the basis of all positive qualities, you should try to rely on (*bsten*) the causes and conditions which create and increase faith, eliminate the causes and conditions which decrease faith, and you should strive to stabilize faith.

10 The Way That the Wisdom Teacher Should Explain and the Student Should Listen to the Holy Dharma

There are four parts to this section:

10.1 What should be done as preparation
10.2 What should be done as the main subject matter
10.3 What should be done afterwards
10.4 Mentioning the benefits of explaining, listening, and so forth

10.1 What should be done as preparation

There are two points to the first part:

10.1.1 What should be done on the part of the master
10.1.2 What should be done on the part of the student

10.1.1 What should be done on the part of the master

> In regard to the preparation for explaining the holy dharma, the lama should make arrangements, annihilate mara's faction, and purify his behavior.

There are three points to this.

10.1.1.1 Making arrangements (*bkod-bsham*)[128]

Accordingly, as it has been extensively said in *The Lotus Sutra* (*Dam-chos pad-ma dkar-po; Saddharma-puṇḍarīka*):

Excellently arrange a fine throne in a place which is clean and pleasing. After putting on good, pleasing, clean clothing, place many kinds of things [on the throne], such as a fine multi-colored cloth and so on, then sit on the raised throne.[129] Within a gathering of a circle of students who are listening one-pointedly (*rtse-gcig*), while not thinking about procuring material things and fame, teach without laziness, and with kindly thoughts....

And the sutra continues.[130]

10.1.1.2 Annihilating mara (*bdud tshar-gcod*)

What one should do according to what has been said in *The Sutra Requested by Sagaramati the Naga King* (*bLo-'gro rgya-mtshos zhus-pa'i mdo; Sāgaramati-paripṛcchā-sūtra*):[131]

Generate the five notions, namely: oneself as the doctor; the dharma as the medicine, the listener as the patient, the holy person as the Tathagata, and that the activity of dharma will reside for a long time; recite loudly the mantra[132] so that the deities of mara's faction can't come within one hundred miles.[133]

10.1.1.3 The master should purify his behavior (*kun-spyod*)[134]

In regard to the body, abandon lying in bed, lounging, stretching your legs, and so forth, so that you comport yourself in the way the King of Shakya [Buddha] does in the turning the wheel of dharma (*chos-kyi 'khor-lo bskor-ba*).

In regard to speech, abandon talking too much, repetition (*zlo-pa*), speaking in a feeble voice, high and low pitched sounds, and so forth, so that you explain [the dharma] clearly and purely with the excellent facets of melodious speech.[135]

In regard to mind, abandon attachment and aversion, so that you think, "I will cause a rain of dharma," conforming with the topics such as emptiness, deity samadhi (*lha'i ting-'dzin*),[136] and so forth, and with the attitude of desiring to place all sentient beings in a state which is beneficial and happy.

10.1.2 What should be done by the student in regard to preparation[137]

The student should offer a gift, attend to his conduct, and meditatively cultivate a joyous frame of mind.

From among the three things that the disciple should do, the first is:

10.1.2.1 Offering a pure gift

With preliminary prostrations, that is, bowing the five places to the ground, offer a pleasing gift and a mandala which is extensively visualized.

10.1.2.2 Follow with respectful conduct (*spyod-lam*)

According to the saying in the *Jataka Tales* (*sKyes-rab; Jātakamālā*):[138]

> You should sit on a very low seat, create the glory of discipline, and look with a joyful eye. The words [of the teaching] are like drinking nectar. Creating with devotion a stainless and very clear mind, you should one-pointedly bow. Like the patient listening to the doctor's word, showing respect,[139] you should listen to the dharma.
>
> Also, you should give up lying down, leaning, and turning your back to the master, and so on. While squatting or kneeling, possessed with respectful conduct, fall silent, listening with a one-pointed mind.

10.1.2.3 Meditatively cultivate (*bsgom-pa*) joy in the favorable conditions you have accumulated

As it has been said in the *Sutra on the Inconceivable Secret* (*gSang-ba bsam-gyis mi-khyab-pa*):[140]

> Buddha[dharma] very rarely appears in the world. The human body is very difficult to acquire. Oh! Have faith and listen to the dharma. Conditions like this are very rare in the world.[141]

After the conditions have been gathered, listen with joy and cheerfulness that you have the capacity to listen to the dharma.

10.2 What should be done as the main subject matter

There are three parts to the main subject matter:

10.2.1 The master explains well
10.2.2 The way in which the student listens with devotion
10.2.3 Both should be endowed with the six perfections

10.2.1 The master explains well

There are three points to this:

10.2.1.1 The characteristics of explaining
10.2.1.2 The method of explanation based upon the object
10.2.1.3 How to teach the dharma

10.2.1.1 The characteristics of explaining

There are also three points to the first part, the characteristics of explaining:

10.2.1.1.1 Wisdom related to being knowledgeable (mkhas-pa'i shes-rab)
10.2.1.1.2 Attitude of loving kindness (btse-ba'i bsam-pa)
10.2.1.1.3 Possessed with patient practice (sbyor-ba bzod-pa)

10.2.1.1.1 Wisdom related to being knowledgeable

> **There are three things to be knowledgeable regarding the main subject matter.**[142]

Regarding the main subject matter, which is explaining the holy dharma, the first among the eight characteristics[143] of the wisdom teacher (*'chad-pa-po*) is the three things he should be knowledgeable in. The wisdom teacher should be knowledgeable in:

10.2.1.1.1.1 The subject is to be explained (bshad-bya)[144]
10.2.1.1.1.2 Teaching ('chad-byed)
10.2.1.1.1.3 Conduct (kun-spyod)

10.2.1.1.1.1 Being knowledgeable in the subject to be explained

It is indeed excellent if one is knowledgeable in what is to be made known (*shes-bya*), or in all the *pitakas* (*sde-snod; piṭakas*). However, in regard to this, it is necessary for someone knowledgeable to understand the words (*tshig*) and their meanings (*don*), scriptures (*lung*), logic (*rigs*), and special oral instructions (*man-ngag*) of the subject to be explained. Thereby the wisdom teacher is able to cut through doubts of the disciples (*gdul-bya*).

10.2.1.1.1.2 Being knowledgeable in teaching

The three aspects related to speech are: (1) Grammatically correct language; (2) citations from sources that are relevant to the teaching; (3) the length of the explanation being just right. These three aspects are valid for any explanation, and are communicated with a pleasant voice that others take pleasure in. Moreover, it is said in *The Ornament of the Mahayana Sutras:*[145]

> Appropriate words, teaching, and analysis cut through doubt. The amount of teaching given depends upon whether the student understands simply by being told the title or through a detailed explanation. The teachings of the Buddhas are pure in the three spheres [of subject, object, and action].[146] This should be

understood as freedom from the eight faults (*nyes-pa brgyad*) of speech: (1) laziness; (2) lacking understanding [of the topic]; (3) discourse not suited for the occasion; (4) being uncertain (*ma-nges*); 5) not cutting through the doubts [of the disciples]; (6) or confirming the absence [of doubt];[147] (7) sadness; (8) stinginess. These are defined as the eight faults of discourse. The Buddha's teaching is unsurpassable because it is without these eight faults.

Buddha's teaching is free from the eight faults of discourse, therefore it is a teaching in which the three spheres are pure. Alternatively, it is explained in the *Principles of Elucidation* (*rNam-bshad rigs-pa; Vyākhyā-yukti*)[148] that there are twenty aspects of dharma discourse which are the antidotes of the eleven faults of speech.[149]

10.2.1.1.1.3 Being learned in conduct[150]

The wisdom teacher is deserving of honor by everyone for his virtue of the three doors [body, speech, and mind]. Therefore, he is skilled in his own conduct, and skilled in the disciple's conduct, which means knowing the *ayatanas* (*skye-mched; āyatana*), *dhatus* (*khams; dhātu*), and unmanifest latent tendencies (*bag-la nyal; vāsanā*).[151] Therefore the dharma explanation which is suited to that disciple is meaningful.[152]

10.2.1.1.2 Attitude of loving kindness

The teacher must have the two kindnesses...

The higher one is the compassion which is the desire to place all sentient beings in the great enlightenment (*byang-chub; bodhi*). If the teacher is lacking that, then it is certainly necessary to have the compassion which explains the dharma with the desire to benefit [all sentient beings], disregarding material things, and excellently knowing the meaning of what is to be explained.[153] Therefore, while your explanation functions as [placing the disciple on] the path, if you lack the desire to benefit all sentient beings and instead have an eye for material things and so forth, your explanation becomes the shortcoming of selling the dharma.

10.2.1.1.3 Possessed with patient practice

...and the three patiences.

The wisdom teacher is able to be: (1) patient (*bzod-ba*), which is being without sadness (*skyo-ba*) in regards to fatigue when teaching and doing difficult work; (2) patient in regard to questioning by the student; (3) patient and willing to give an answer to arguments put forth by others.[154]

With these three abilities the wisdom teacher will be able to embrace the disciple. Therefore, because those qualities are complete, if the wisdom teacher explains the dharma, it will be pleasant-sounding and beautiful to the people of his retinue, and will function as [leading them on] the path.

It is said in *The Ornament of the Mahayana Sutras*:

> Because the bodhisattva is possessed with a good intellect, is without sadness, is kind, highly renowned, and knows the rituals (*choga; sādhana*) well, the bodhisattva is well-spoken; giving explanations he is like a blazing sun among people.[155]

10.2.1.2 The method of explanation based upon the object

There are two parts to the method of explanation:

10.2.1.2.1 The explanation in general
10.2.1.2.2 The explanation divided into particulars

10.2.1.2.1 The explanation in general
10.2.1.2.1.1 Explaining the dharma utilizing six doors

> The teacher explains the dharma utilizing the six doors of explanation, or...

In the *Compendium of Knowledge* it is said that one explains the dharma by [utilizing] six [doors]:[156] (1) The subject matter which one should thoroughly know (*yongs-su shes-par-bya*); (2) its meaning; (3) The cause for knowing it; (4) thorough knowing; (5) result of knowing; (6) higher knowing [which is the result of the knowing].

Or, it is said [in the *Compendium of Knowledge*] that one explains the dharma by the twelve doors, "The door which is the collection of complete explanations (*rnam-par bshad-pa bsdus-pa*)," and so forth.[157]

10.2.1.2.1.2 Explaining the dharma utilizing three doors[158]

In some texts, it is explained that one explains the dharma by means of three doors: (1) the usefulness (*dgos-don*); (2) a synopsis (*bsdus-don*); (3) the words (*tshig*) and their meanings (*don*).

10.2.1.2.1.3 Explaining the dharma utilizing two doors

Others say that one explains the dharma by means of two points:

(1) the general meaning; (2) the branch meaning.

10.2.1.2.1.4 Chimpa (mChims-pa) claims that explaining the dharma is to:

10.2.1.2.1.4.1 Teach the meaning
10.2.1.2.1.4.2 Explain the texts
10.2.1.2.1.4.3 Make it certain[159]

10.2.1.2.1.4.1 Teach the meaning

One should teach by imparting the bare meaning of the words of the text; that is to say, make [the bare meaning of the words of the text] certain, by showing where the connection comes from,[160] how the usefulness is established, and what is the subject matter being taught. Thereby, the student will become good at the meaning of dharma.

10.2.1.2.1.4.2 Explain the texts

[Help the student] understand the particular topic by enumerating [the salient points of the text] at the end. In other words, having explained the dharma, which works distinctively in terms of being a method which eliminates the doubtful points, whatever way you teach in regard to the literal meaning or implied meaning, in that way, you make the student knowledgeable in the terms.

10.2.1.2.1.4.3 Make it certain

Although the students have understood the meaning of the text, nevertheless it is possible that an opponent who has not been refuted may raise an objection, thinking, "That which has already been explained [in the text] and [what comes later in the text are] contradictory," or, "[The same meaning has been] repeated,"[161] or, "There is no connection [between what was said earlier and later]."[162] You should give answers which dispel this way of thinking, eliminating these doubts concerning the intended meaning (*don-dgongs-pa-can*)[163] by giving answers drawn from other scriptures and reasoning. Thereby, according to Chimpa, the student will obtain certainty in the meaning of the text.

10.2.1.2.2 The explanation divided into particulars

The teacher will at first describe the general and specific explanation of the purpose [of the teaching].

There are two parts to the synopsis that has six good qualities.

> The meaning of the words is explained in terms of the three: the subject to be explained; by what means; and how the explanation is done. First seek the meaning dependent upon the words.
>
> There are two points to the connection: easily understood and connected.
>
> Responses to objections will be supported by scripture, and by reasoning.[164]

This, according to what has been said in the *Principles of Elucidation*, is the contemporary method of explanation, which is well known. Also, in regard to that:

10.2.1.2.2.1 The general and specific explanation of the purpose (*dgos-don*) of the teaching

Because the purpose of the teaching is stated, the listener will be encouraged to remember what he will listen to. Therefore, first describe the general purpose of the teaching, which is the advantages of listening and explaining, and the specific purpose of the teaching, which is the connection to the dharma to be explained.

10.2.1.2.2.2 There are two parts to the synopsis (*bsdus-don*):

10.2.1.2.2.2.1 The meaning, which is a synopsis of the words

The wisdom teacher first explains the synopsis of the meaning of the words, "The meaning of the text is such and such." Thus, explanations from the actual [quotations] from the text are presented in successive order. If it is useful, besides giving the textual meaning, by scripture[165] and reasoning cite from other texts, and give a synopsis of the words which is itself easy to understand and simple to grasp.

10.2.1.2.2.2.2 The individual synopsis (*so-so'i bsdus don*)

While making the entirety of the text an object of intellect, individually establish large main divisions. Expose the classifications of the subdivisions (*nang-gses*) so that they are not contradictory.[166] Explain the branches (*yan-lag*) so that the summaries are not mixed up.[167]

The synopsis is possessed of six excellent qualities.[168] The general overview[169] and specific textual meaning are both combined together, so they are: (1) easy to understand; and dependent on that they are (2) clearly worded; (3) pleasantly expressed; (4) precisely stated; (5) the explanation is equally weighted [among the topics]; and (6) easily remembered.

In short, if what one expresses is easy for others to understand, and it is pleasant to hear for the ears of both [the speaker and the listener], then one is a learned teacher.

10.2.1.2.2.3 The literal meaning

The literal meaning in Sanskrit is explained in terms of the three: the agent [one who does the explaining], the object [subject matter], and the action; and, it is also explained in terms of letters, affixes, adverbial endings, and so forth.[170]

In Tibetan, the three aspects one combines are the subject that is to be explained; by what means it is explained;[171] and how the explanation is done.[172] Namely, at first you must seek the meaning (*don*) dependent upon the terminology (*sgra*) or the words (*tshig*), by means of making yourself skilled in the expansions of the nouns, adjectives, and syllables, as explained in the common Abhidharma (*thun-mong-ba mngon-pa*), and the nouns, adjectives, and syllables which appear in the extraordinary Abhidharma (*thun-mong ma-yin-pa mngon-brjod*)[173] and the *Grammatical Treatise* (*brDa-sprod-kyi bstan-bcos*), and so forth. Not mixing together the parts of the words, distinguish them individually; that is how one teaches (*bstan*).

Therefore, whatever the topic of the text is, explain its meaning without confusion, not adding to it and not leaving anything out.

10.2.1.2.2.4 The connections

There are also two points regarding the connection:

10.2.1.2.2.4.1 The connection of the words[174]

You may not be able to draw out the meaning of the latter by the [case ending] of the former word, or even if you are able to do that, it may not be entirely clear, or, even if it is clear, there are various difficulties in understanding the way in which the words are joined.[175] In this case, the teacher explains in a way which is easily understood, such as, "The former and latter words are connected in this way."

10.2.1.2.2.4.2 The connection of the meaning (*don-gyi mtshams-sbyor*)

After briefly teaching like that,[176] extensively explain the thing itself, according to quotation (*zhe-pa lta-bu*), or according to what is contradictory and what is connected, or that which should be rejected and the antidote, or the cause and the result, and so forth. Mutually connect [their meanings] and explain the text as related (*'brel-chags*) with these things.[177]

10.2.1.2.2.5 Objections (*brgal*) and responses (*lan*)

There are some textual meanings which are difficult for the student to understand. The student sincerely raises doubts and questions such as, "How is such and such meaning not contradictory, or is it?" You should eliminate contradictions, seeking the meaning with answers for those questions that are explanations, and are not contradictory. With scriptures and reasoning seek the textual meaning, and settle the doubts.

10.2.1.3 How to teach the dharma[178]

> **For great intellects, explain using profound and extensive teachings. For lesser intellects, explain using words easy to remember, simple, and easy to understand. Afterwards, precisely and subtly cut the connections which are contradictory.**
>
> **To those who are faint-hearted, uplift them; if their minds are excited or drowsy, turn them away from all those faults.**

To the students who are of sharp faculties and great wisdom (*shes-rab*), explain with words that are steady and well-suited, so that the meaning is profound (*zab*) and extensive (*rgya-che*). To those of dull faculties and lesser intellect, explain using words which are easy to remember and simple to understand, so that the meaning is easily comprehended and pleasing to the ear.

When the students are able to analyze the subject matter, and can relate the word and the meaning a little bit, then teach the subject subtly and precisely. Afterwards, cut the contradictions[179] of the meaning of the words, and explain them.

To those who are fainthearted, thinking, "My mind is dull and old, and I am short-lived and so on. I am not able to study and meditate; or although able, I have no time," you should teach the story of the noble Lampenten (Lam-phran-bstan; Cūḍa-panthaka).[180] Furthermore, it has been said:

> You should also teach that your awareness will pass away the day after tomorrow.[181] Although you have not become learned in this life, trust [that you will become learned] in future lives, in accord with holding oneself to be wealthy.[182]

Remember this, and uplift them.

For those whose minds are distracted (*g.yengs*) and excited (*rgod-pa*) by longing for the affairs of this life and the five aspects of sense desire, present a discussion of impermanence, the disadvantages of the five aspects of sense desire, the fear of lower states of rebirth, and so forth. Then their minds will be changed to the dharma.

For those who have gone under the influence of drowsiness (*rmugs*) and so forth, you should explain in whatever way is suitable the wondrous stories, the faults of drowsiness, and you should turn them away from all those faults.[183]

10.2.2 The way in which the student listens with devotion (*gus-pa*)

> Remove the three faults and six stains of the vessel, and so forth. Then establish the perception of the patient, the medicine, and the doctor.[184]

10.2.2.1 Remove the three faults

Furthermore, it has been said in sutra:

> While [having eliminated being unfocused, defilements, and sadness,] listen well, closely, and so that you remember, and I will explain to you....[185]

As for the meaning of that, the student should listen to the teaching after removing the three faults of the vessel:[186] the meaning of the phrase "listening well" (*legs-par-nyon*), is to eliminate the fault which is like an upside-down container. Just as juice will not go into an upside-down container, [the teaching will not enter the student if he] is lacking eagerness for the dharma while listening, if his mind is distracted towards outer objects, or if he is under the influence of drowsiness. Therefore, collecting your mind while having eliminated not focusing your ears to the dharma, is called listening.

The meaning of the phrase "listening closely" (*rab-tu-nyon*) is to eliminate the fault which is like a dirty container. Just as pouring juice into a dirty container does not do anyone any good, if you listen to the dharma with a mind conjoined with the stain of passions (*nyon-mongs*), then it does not do any good for the mind-stream of yourself or others. Therefore, eliminating the attitudes (*bsam-pa*) such as the defilements of pride, non-faith, and so forth, is called listening.

The meaning of the phrase "listening so that you remember" (*yid-la-zung la nyon*) is to eliminate the fault which is like having a hole in a container. Just as juice does not stay in a container which has a hole in it, [the teaching is not retained by the student] when he is discouraged while listening to the dharma, since he cannot exert himself in regard to understanding the words and meaning, so the teaching does not do any good. Therefore, striving to eliminate sadness that is incapacitating is called listening.

10.2.2.2 Remove the six stains

The six stains (*dri-ma drug*) have been explained in the *Principles of Elucidation:* "Listening is stained by (1) pride; (2) non-faith; (3) not striving; (4) mind distracted towards outside [objects]; (5) mind distracted inwardly; (6) being sad."[187]

Those six stains are condensed into the three faults of the vessel, and what is included in "and so forth" [in Kongtrul's verse above], are the precepts of abandoning and taking.

Furthermore it is said in the same text:[188] "Listen to the dharma with the sixteen kinds of antidotes of the thirteen faults. The [first] six are: (1) sloppy behavior;[189] (2) disrespect; (3) not making offerings [to the lama]; (4) [negative] intention [in listening to the teaching];[190] (5) that which is in disharmony; (6) not taking it in. The last two each have five subdivisions.

10.2.2.3 Listen with the proper frame of mind

There are numerous examples in the *Sutra Arranged Like a Tree* showing that when listening to the dharma the student should establish the perception of the patient as himself, the medicine as the dharma, and the doctor as the lama; also, the passenger as himself, the boat as the dharma, and the ferryman as the lama; furthermore, himself as lacking familiarity [with the way], the mount as the dharma, and the guide as the lama, and so forth.[191] Then he should listen to the teaching.

10.2.3 Both should be endowed with the six perfections

> Both teacher and student should practice teaching and listening in possession of the six perfections[192]

At the time of explaining and listening to the dharma, both the teacher and listener of the dharma should be endowed with the six perfections (*pha-rol-tu phyin-pa*). Namely, (1) generosity (*sbyin-pa*) by the teacher is giving the word of the dharma, and by the student is offering a gift and so forth for the sake of receiving the dharma. (2) Discipline (*tshul-khrims*) is eliminating discordant factors of listening and explaining. (3) Patience (*bzod-pa*) is not being sad in the difficult practices of body and speech. (4) Diligence (*brtson-'grus*) is enthusiasm towards listening and explaining. (5) Meditative concentration (*bsam-gtan*) is one-pointedness (*rtse-gcig*) towards the dharma. (6) Wisdom (*shes-rab*) is analyzing the words and their meanings. The teacher and student should practice teaching and listening in possession of these six perfections.

10.3 What should be done afterwards

There are two parts to what should be done afterwards:

10.3.1 What should be done by the wisdom teacher
10.3.2 What should be done by the student

10.3.1 What should be done by the wisdom teacher

> **Subsequently, the teacher asks for forgiveness of faults, then dedicates all virtue, and extensively offers.**

"Subsequently" means after finishing listening and explaining the dharma.

10.3.1.1 Ask for forgiveness for faults

The first of the three suitable things for the wisdom teacher to do is to ask for forgiveness for faults:

> Whatever negative actions I have done by being under the influence of the obscurations of the mind, after having come into the presence of the Buddha, I confess (*bshag-pa*) them.[193]

and so forth. [You should ask for forgiveness concerning] whatever is appropriate.

10.3.1.2 Dedicate virtue to enlightenment

You should make a pure dedication prayer, such as, "By this merit may we become omniscient (*thams-cad gzigs-pa*)," and so on,[194] or recite the verse from Arya Asanga ('Phags-pa Thogs-med; Ārya Asaṅga):

> From this explanation of the precious holy dharma of the excellent vehicle, whatever endless merit we have obtained, by that may all sentient beings become vessels of the precious and stainless holy dharma of the excellent vehicle...

10.3.1.3 The extensive offering, which is objectless (*dmigs-med*)

As it is said in *Entering into the Conduct of the Bodhisattva* ('Byang-chub sems-dpa'i spyod-pa-la 'jug-pa; Bodhisattva-caryāvatāra),[195] extensively offer with the wisdom that does not conceptualize the three spheres:

"Emptiness of the act of giving, what is to be given, the taker, and giver, is called 'the perfection which surpasses the world.'"

10.3.2 What should be done by the student[196]

[The three things to be done] by the student are: offer gifts, make a dedication prayer (*bsngo-smon*), and make mindfulness (*dran-pa*) and vigilance (*shes-bzhin*) firm.

There are three things that need to be done by the student:

10.3.2.1 Offer a gift which is an offering of thanks

Recollecting the kindness of the wisdom teacher, you should offer whatever amount of prostrations and thanks-offering mandalas that are suitable.

10.3.2.2 Dedicate virtue to enlightenment

Change the word "explanation" in the above-mentioned quotation [from Asanga] to the word "listening," [and then recite the prayer].

10.3.2.3 Rely on the continuity of mindfulness and vigilance (*dran-shes*)[197]

Having gone into isolation with the memory of the meaning of the words of the dharma talk, eliminate agitation, drowsiness, and so forth. Then the dharma talk that you just heard should be contemplated over and over. You should read it over and over. You should write it over and over. You should question the lama concerning all your doubts. After having finished the dharma teachings, you will please the lama with an offering of thanks in hand. You should do as is said above in the *Door Entering into the Dharma* (*Chos-la 'jug-pa'i sgo*).

10.4 Mentioning the advantages of explaining, listening, and so forth

[In general], the advantages of having heard and contemplated [the dharma are fivefold. In particular, the advantages of] listening, explaining, grasping the meaning, putting into practice, and intermingling the dharma are limitless.

10.4.1 General advantages

In general, the advantages of having heard and contemplated the dharma are as they appear in the *Scripture on Discernment* (*Lung rnam-'byed; Vinaya-vibhaṅga*):[198]

There are five advantages in being learned. These are: (1) being learned in the *skandhas* (*phung-po*); (2) learned in the *dhatus* (*khams; dhātu*); (3) learned in the *ayatanas* (*skye-mched; āyatana*); (4) learned in interdependent origination (*rten-cing 'brel-bar 'byung-ba; pratītya-samutpāda*); (5)[knowing] the instructions [on how to meditate on the above four topics] which make [understanding and meditation] increase, so you are not dependent on a wisdom teacher [instructing you during retreat; i.e. you can meditate on your own].[199]

[The advantages] also extensively appear in the *Jataka Tales* and so forth.

10.4.2 Specific advantages

10.4.2.1 Advantages of listening to the dharma

Specifically, the advantages of listening to the dharma, as they are explained in the *Principles of Elucidation*:

The Blessed One spoke of five advantages in listening to the dharma: (1) That which is heard will be heard; (2) that which is heard will be completely experienced (*yong-su byang ba*); (3) doubts will be eliminated; (4) the view will be corrected; (5) by wisdom (*prajñā*) the words and profound meaning will be understood.

In general, it has been said [by the Buddha] in all sutras and tantras that the advantages of hearing the dharma are inconceivable.

10.4.2.2 Advantages of explaining the dharma

Also, the advantages of explaining the dharma are very many:

1) It functions as the best among offerings to the Buddhas.

2) It functions as the best kind of generosity to sentient beings.

3) It functions as [an excellent way of] increasing merit and obtaining the six super-knowledges (*mngon-shes; abhijñā*).[200]

Expanding upon that, the list of twenty advantages of giving the dharma are explained in the *Sutra That Arouses Superior Intention*[201] and so forth.

10.4.2.3 The advantages of grasping the meaning of the dharma

It extensively appears in the *Secret Teachings of the Tathagatas* (*De-bzhin gshegs-pa'i gsang-ba bstan-pa; Tathāgata-acintya-guhya-nirdeśa*):

Concerning the merit of grasping the holy dharma: all the Buddhas can earnestly speak about this merit for ten million *kalpas* but not reach the end.

10.4.2.4 The advantages of participating in listening and explaining

In particular, the advantages of listening and explaining the Mahayana dharma extensively appear in the scriptures: during the phase of the ground, to outshine the virtue[202] of the Hinayana; during the phase of the path, to eliminate all hindrances[203] without exception; during the phase of the result, to obtain complete awakening.

10.4.2.5 Putting the dharma which is comprehended into practice

Putting the dharma of realization into practice is more exalted than those noble qualities [stated above].[204] It has been said that even to contemplate the selflessness of phenomena (*chos bdag-med*) inconceivably surpasses the merit of taking seven steps in the direction of a monastery (*dgon-pa*).[205]

Being immersed in mere explanations which are disconnected from practice is entirely meaningless. Therefore, the *Sutra* [*That Arouses Superior Intention*] discusses twenty faults, such as delighting in speaking,[206] and so forth. On the other hand, you might participate in practicing discipline, meditative concentration, and so forth,[207] but without studying; in that case you are similar to a blind man entering the path. Therefore a practitioner who has both studied and practiced the teachings is one with the most sublime noble quality.

As it has been said in the *Ornament of the Mahayana Sutras*:

> So, whatever meditation the yogi (*rnal-'byor-can*) does is not useless. Likewise, the teachings of the Sugatas are not useless. But if you could perceive the truth simply by means of studying, then the meditation [of the yogi] would be useless. If you could engage in meditation also without studying, then the teachings of the Sugata would be useless. [Therefore both study and practice are necessary].[208]

10.4.2.6 Advantages of intermingling listening to teachings and then practicing

Therefore, the noble qualities of intermingling listening to the teachings and then practicing the dharma that has been explained are said to be beyond comprehension. It has been said by Arya Nagarjuna (Ārya Nāgārjuna):

> Making wisdom increase is studying, and together with contemplation, if you have both, then from them meditation excellently arises. Therefore, you attain unsurpassable enlightenment.

This ends the commentary of the first section of Volume Two, Division Five of *The Treasury of Knowledge*, explaining the characteristics of the wisdom teacher and student relationship, the method of explaining and listening to the holy dharma.

Notes

ABBREVIATIONS AND KEY TO CITATIONS

Kg   Kangyur (bKa' 'Gyur), numbers correspond to Tohoku Catalogue

Tg   Tangyur (bsTan 'Gyur), Narthang Edition

mDo   Sutra, Narthang Edition

Ot   Tibetan Tripitaka, Peking Edition in the Library of the Otani University

Toh   Catalogue of the Tibetan Buddhist Canons published by Tohoku Imperial University

<#>   Refers to the page in the Tibetan text: Kong-sprul yon-tan rgya-mtsho, *Shes-bya kun-khyab* (Lhasa: Mi-rigs dpe-skrun-khang [Ethnic Minority Press], 1982), 1-33. This edition is based on the dPal-spungs block prints.

NOTES TO PART I

1. *sLob-dpon dang slob-ma'i mtshan-nyid dang bsten-tshul 'chad-nyan bcas bshad-pa'i skabs.*

2. This chapter is located in Volume II of *The Textual System Which Encompasses All That Needs to Be Known, Which Liberates By Means of a Few Words, Including All That Is Well-Spoken, the Ocean of Infinite Things That Is Known* (*Shes-bya kun-la khyab-pa'i gzhung-lugs nyung-ngu'i tshig-gis rnam-par 'grol-ba legs-bshad yongs-'du shes-bya mtha'-yas-pa'i rgya-mtsho zhes-bya-ba*). This text will be referred to here as the *Shes-bya kun-khyab.*

3. This work was translated from the Tibetan by E. Obermiller in two volumes:

—E. Obermiller, *The Jewelry of Scripture of Bu-ston* (Delhi: Sri Satguru Publications, 1986).

—E. Obermiller, *The History of Buddhism in India and Tibet by Bu-ston* (Delhi: Sri Satguru Publications, 1986).

All passages from Buton quoted here are Obermiller's translations. For further information on Buton see Stcherbatsky's introduction to *The Jewelry of Scripture,* 3-4. See also: D. Snellgrove, *Indo-Tibetan Buddhism* (Boston: Shambhala, 1986), vol. 2, 506-507; and Tulku Thondup Rinpoche, *Buddhist Civilization in Tibet* (London: Routledge and Kegan Paul, 1987), 87.

4. Gampopa, *Dam-chos yid-bzhin nor-bu thar-pa rin-po-che'i rgyan.* Throughout this book numerous quotations have been taken from this text. I translate the title as *An Ornament to Precious Liberation,* and this will be used to cite the text in the main body of this book. In the notes, citations which refer to *"Nor-bu thar-pa rin-po-che'i rgyan"* always refer to my translation from the original Tibetan; the page numbers refer to: *Dam-chos yid-bzhin nor-bu thar-pa rin-po-che'i rgyan dang zhal-gdams rin-po-che phreng-ba, The Jewel Ornament of Liberation: The Precious Garland of the Supreme Path by Gampopa* (Rumtek, Sikkim: The Students' Welfare Union of Karma Shri Nalanda Institute, 1991). Citations which refer to *"Jewel Ornament"* always refer to Guenther's translation: Herbert V. Guenther, trans., *The Jewel Ornament of Liberation by sGam-po-pa* (Boulder: Prajña Press, 1981).

For a further discussion of Gampopa's life, see: Guenther, *Jewel Ornament* , ix-xiv; Nālandā Translation Committee, trans., *The Rain of Wisdom* (Boston: Shambhala, 1982), 330-331; Jampa Mackenzie Stewart, *The Life of Gampopa* (Ithaca: Snow Lion, 1995).

5. For an in-depth account of Kalu Rinpoche's life story see Kenneth I. McLeod, trans., *The Chariot for Travelling the Path to Freedom: The Life Story of Kalu Rinpoche* (San Francisco: Kagyu Dharma, 1985).

6. All quotations drawn from this text are my translations from the original Tibetan: *Sems-nyid ngal-gso,* "Reproduced from a set of prints from the *A-'dzom 'brugs-pa chos-sgar* blocks by the Ven. Dodrup Chen Rinpoche," vol. 1 (Gangtok, India, 1973). For further information on Kun Khyen Longchenpa's life and work, see: Dudjom Rinpoche, *The Nyingma School of Tibetan Buddhism: Part One* (Boston: Wisdom Publications, 1991), 575-596; Tulku Thondup Rinpoche, *Masters of Meditation and Miracles* (Boston: Shambhala, 1996), 201-210; Longchenpa, *Kindly Bent to Ease Us: Part One,* trans. Herbert Guenther (Berkeley: Dharma Publishing, 1975), xiii-xxv.

7. Patrul Rinpoche, *sNying-thig sngon-'gro'i khrid-yig kun-bzang bla-ma'i zhal-lung; The Oral Instructions of My Excellent Lama.* This text is the oral instruction on the preliminary practices of the Dzogchen Longchen Nyingthig tradition. All quotations drawn from this text are my translations from the original Tibetan. For further information on Patrul Rinpoche, see: John Reynolds, *The Golden Letters* (Ithaca: Snow Lion, 1996), 297-305; Tulku Thondup Rinpoche, *Masters of Meditation*, 201-

210; Patrul Rinpoche, *The Words of My Perfect Teacher* (San Francisco: Harper Collins, 1994); Dilgo Khyentse, *The Heart Treasure of the Enlightened Ones*, trans. Padmakara Translation Group (Boston: Shambhala, 1992), 231-237.

8. Thomas Cleary, trans., *The Flower Ornament Scripture*, vol. 3 (Boston: Shambhala, 1987), 34.

9. Gampopa, *Nor-bu thar-pa rin-po-che'i rgyan*, 27.1.

10. Ashvaghosha, *Fifty Stanzas of Guru Devotion*, in *The Mahāmudrā: Eliminating the Darkness of Ignorance*, by The Ninth Karmapa Wang-Ch'ug Dor-je, trans. Alexander Berzin (Dharamsala: Library of Tibetan Works and Archives, 1989), 173, verse 22. Ashvaghosha was also commonly known as Aryashura (Āryaśūra).

11. Ibid., 175, verse 25.

12. Third Dalai Lama, *Essence of Refined Gold*, trans. Glenn H. Mullin (Ithaca: Snow Lion, 1985), 73. This is a *lam-rim* text written by the Third Dalai Lama (1543-1588). It includes a commentary by H.H. the Fourteenth Dalai Lama.

13. Patrul Rinpoche, *Kun-bzang bla-ma'i zhal-lung*, 215.

14. Gampopa, *Nor-bu thar-pa rin-po-che'i rgyan*, 136.16.

15. Ashvaghosha, *Fifty Stanzas*, 164, verse 2.

16. Cleary, *Flower Ornament*, 327.

17. The term "beginningless beginning" denotes the lack of a first cause, a lack of an original act of creation. Instead, Buddhism teaches that there is an interdependent co-origination of all existence, which is described as a twelvefold chain of interdependence (*rten-'brel bcu-gnyis*).

18. Maitreya/Asanga, *The Changeless Nature* (*Mahāyānottaratantra-śāstra*), trans. Ken Holmes and Katia Holmes (Scotland: KDDI, 1985), 31. This is a text transmitted to Asanga by Maitreya.

19. For a discussion of tathagathagarbha, see Gampopa, *Jewel Ornament*, 1-13. For an in-depth handling of tathagathagarbha, see Maitreya/Asanga, *Changeless Nature*. Also available is a commentary on this text by Thrangu Rinpoche, *Buddha Nature*, trans. Erik Pema Kunsang (Kathmandu: Rangjung Yeshe Publications, 1988). The *Mahāyānottaratantra-śāstra* is an important text for the Kagyu lineage, functioning as the philosophical basis for Mahamudra practices.

20. *Theg pa chen po'i rgyud bla ma'i bstan bcos* (China: Cultural Printing Press, 1987), p. 187 (my translation). For a discussion of the impurities which veil one's buddha-nature, see *Changeless Nature*, trans. Holmes and Holmes, pp. 51-67.

21. Patrul Rinpoche, *Kun-bzang bla-ma'i zhal-lung*, 10-11.

22. For an excellent elucidation of the three vows, see H.H. Dudjom Rinpoche, *Perfect Conduct: Ascertaining the Three Vows* (Boston: Wisdom, 1996).

23. The three trainings (*bslabs-gsum*) are one mode for the classification of the 151 trainings, i.e., all the trainings.

24. Gampopa, *Nor-bu thar-pa rin-po-che'i rgyan*, 181.1.

25. Based on Peking Edition. See Tulku Thondup Rinpoche, *Buddhist Civilization*, 76.

26. Chogyam Trungpa, ed., *The Rain of Wisdom*, trans. Nālandā Translation Committee (Boulder: Shambhala, 1980). This is a translation of the *bKa'-brgyud mgur-mtsho*. It consists of the spiritual songs (*dohā*) of the great Kagyu masters, compiled by the Eighth Karmapa Mi-bskyod rDo-rje. The above quotation comes from the glossary definition of "oral instruction," p. 359.

27. For a discussion of the spiritual teacher in Tibet, see H. Guenther, *Tibetan Buddhism in Western Perspective* (Emeryville: Dharma Publishing, 1977), chapter entitled "The Spiritual Teacher in Tibet," pp. 178-195.

28. Jamgön Kongtrul III, *The Guru-Disciple Relationship*, trans. from Tibetan into German by Christoph Klonck (Los Angeles: Rigpe Dorje Foundation, 1991), 5. This is a transcription of a talk given at Karma Chöling in Frankfurt, Germany. The entire transcript consists of ten pages. The translator from German into English is not cited.

29. Ibid., 5.

30. The following biographical material is summarized from E. Gene Smith's introduction to Jamgön Kongtrul Lodrö Thayé, *Kongtrul's Encyclopaedia of Indo-Tibetan Culture, Parts 1-3*, ed. Dr. Lokesh Chandra (New Delhi: International Academy of Indian Culture, 1970). (This is a reproduction of the original Tibetan.) For an extensive discussion of the *Ris-med* movement and Kongtrul's role, see pp. 1-28. For a fascinating and informative discussion of Kongtrul's life, see *Jamgön Kongtrul's Retreat Manual*, trans. and intro. by Ngawang Zangpo (Ithaca: Snow Lion, 1994), 31-56.

31. For a discussion of the Bon religion, see Giuseppe Tucci, *The Religions of Tibet*, trans. Geoffrey Samuel (Berkeley: University of California Press, 1988), 213-248; and R.A. Stein, *Tibetan Civilization* (Stanford: Stanford University Press, 1972), 229-240. Tucci, in *The Religions of Tibet*, p. 213, writes:

> The Bon religion is the indigenous religion of Tibet.... Bon monasteries and Bon shrines are distributed throughout the whole country. They are especially numerous in East Tibet, and in the western border areas of the country such as bLo (Mustang) which belongs politically to Nepal but culturally and linguistically to Tibet....

32. Jamgön Kongtrul, *Encyclopaedia*, Introduction by E. Gene Smith, 28-29, note 57.

33. Ibid., 30-31.

34. Gampopa, *Nor-bu thar-pa rin-po-che'i rgyan*, 14.13.

35. Ibid., 9b.1.

36. Ibid., 9b.5.

37. H.E. Kalu Rinpoche, in *The Gem Ornament of Manifold Oral Instructions* (San Francisco: KDK Publications, 1986), 25, paraphrases point five:

...the kindness and support that one is shown by others in one's practice.

On the following page he glosses this point:

> Finally, there is the kindness and support that others show for one's practice. This is something that is quite important, because without support, be it financial or moral, one might have all the intention in the world but be unable to practice. However, in fact, that support is forthcoming from individuals who are impressed with the teachings, impressed by one's interest in and practice of the teachings, and they therefore provide support out of kindness and affection for one as a practitioner.

In *The Oral Instructions of My Excellent Lama* (*Kun-bzang bla-ma'i zhal-lung*) Patrul Rinpoche lists the fifth point as given in the Nyingma tradition:

> There is the loving [lama] who has compassion for others. (p. 36)

Patrul Rinpoche glosses this point:

> Once, when Lord Atisha came to Tibet, Khu, Ngog and Drom asked him, "For a person to attain the state of liberation and omniscience, which is more important, studying the Kangyur and Tengyur, or receiving the instructions of the lama?"
>
> "The instructions of the lama are more important," replied Atisha. "Why is that so? Because although you may know how to explain from memory the Tripitaka, and you are learned in the characteristics of all phenomena, if you do not have the practical knowledge of the lama's instructions, you and the dharma will part." (p. 39)

38. For a description of syllogism and its use in Tibetan Buddhist debates, see Daniel Perdue, *Debate in Tibetan Buddhism* (Ithaca: Snow Lion Publications, 1992); Daniel Perdue, trans., *Debate in Tibetan Buddhist Education* (Dharamsala: Library of Tibetan Works and Archives, 1976); F. Th. Stcherbatsky, *Buddhist Logic*, 2 vols. (New York: Dover Publications, 1962).

39. Gampopa, *Nor-bu thar-pa rin-po-che'i rgyan*, 34-35; Guenther, *Jewel Ornament*, 34-35.

40. For a detailed explanation of morality and vows of the bodhisattva, see Jamgön Kongtrul's *Shes-bya kun-khyab*, book 2 (*bar-cha*), section 5, chapter 3, pp. 98-134, entitled, *Byang-sems kyi bslab-pa brjod-pa'i skabs*. See also: Mark Tatz, trans., *Asanga's Chapter on Ethics: With the Commentary of Tsong-kha-pa* (Lewiston: Edwin Mellen Press, 1986); and Jamgon Kongtrul, *The Torch of Certainty*, trans. Judith Hanson (Boston: Shambhala, 1977), 60-68.

41. For a discussion of the pratimoksha vow, see Jamgön Kongtrul, *Shes-bya kun-khyab*, book 2, part 5, chapter 2, pp. 34-98: *So-thar-gyi sdom-pa rab-tu phye-ba'i skabs*.

42. For a description of the types of monastic vows, and a description of the vows, see Atiśa, *A Lamp for the Path and Commentary*, trans. Richard Sherburne (London: George Allen & Unwin, 1983), 66-85.

43. *The Mahāyāna-sūtrālaṃkāra* is one of five texts transmitted to Asanga by Maitreya. This is an important text of the Yogacara school, which discusses relative

and absolute mind. The relative mind is seen as dualistic, while the absolute mind is equated with "clear light." For a summary of this text, see Tsultrim Gyamtso Rimpoche, *Progressive Stages of Meditation on Emptiness*, trans. Shenpen Hookham (Oxford: Longchen Foundation, 1988), 82.

44. Here Kongtrul plays on the word *"dul-ba"* which also means *vinaya*—the pratimoksha code disciplining the body, which was discussed in the previous section. With regard to the bodhisattva vow, the emphasis moves from taming the body to taming the mind.

45. Nagarjuna, *Golden Zephyr: Instructions from a Spiritual Friend*, trans. Leslie Kawamura (Berkeley: Dharma Publishing, 1975), 49. Toh 4496.

46. There are Hinayana and Mahayana *piṭakas*. Each is attributed to a different compiler. For the Hinayana pitaka, Ananda compiled the Sutras; Upali compiled the Vinaya; and Mahakashyapa compiled the Abhidharma. For the Mahayana Tripitika, the bodhisattva Manjushri compiled the Abhidharma; the bodhisattva Maitreya compiled the Vinaya; and the bodhisattva Vajrapani compiled the Sutras.

47. Verses 7-9: "The vajra master is: (1) steadfast; (2) [his mind is] tamed; (3) intelligent; (4) patient; (5) without deception; (6) without trickery; (7) he knows the practice of mantra; (8) he knows the practice of tantra; (9) he has compassion and loving kindness [for others]; (10) he is learned [in the scriptures]. He has completed the ten essential points (*de-nyid*), is skilled in the activity of [drawing] the mandala, and knows how to explain the mantra."

Many writers quote from Ashvaghosha's text, including Khedrup-je, in *rGyud-sde spyi'i rnam-par gzhag-pa rgyas-par brjod*, translated by Lessing and Wayman as *Fundamentals of the Buddhist Tantras* (The Hague: Mouton, 1968).

48. I have based my commentary to these ten points on the commentary of Geshe Ngawang Dhargyey, as found in his commentary to *bLa-ma lnga-bcu-pa*, p. 169 of *The Mahāmudrā: Eliminating the Darkness of Ignorance*, by The Ninth Karmapa Wang-Ch'ug Dor-je, trans. Alexander Berzin (Dharamsala: Library of Tibetan Works and Archives, 1981).

49. Patrul Rinpoche, *Kun-bzang bla-ma'i zhal-lung*, 217-218.

50. For an in-depth discussion of *samaya* see H.H. Dudjom Rinpoche, *Perfect Conduct*. Also see Kalu Rinpoche, *Gem Ornament*, 113-127; and Keith Dowman, *Sky Dancer: The Secret Life and Songs of the Lady Yeshe Tsogyel* (London: Routledge and Kegan Paul, 1984), 28-31.

51. Kalu Rinpoche, *Gem Ornament*, 118.

52. Longchenpa, *Sems-nyid ngal-gso*, 39.

53. Patrul Rinpoche, *Kun-bzang bla-ma'i zhal-lung*, 216-217.

54. The ten stages (*sa; bhūmi*) are: (1) The Utterly Joyful (*rab-tu dga'-ba*); (2) The Stainless (*dri-ma med-pa*); (3) The Illuminating (*'od byed-pa*); (4) The Radiant (*'od 'phro-ba*); (5) Very Difficult to Train For (*shin-tu sbyang dka'-ba*); (6) The Manifesting (*mngon-du gyur-pa*); (7) The Far Going (*ring-du song-ba*); (8) The Unwavering

(*mi-g.yo-ba*); (9) Excellent Intelligence (*legs-pa'i blo-gros*); (10) Cloud of Dharma (*chos-kyi sprin*).

55. Although Kongtrul does not explain this statement, the Dalai Lama describes this briefly in *The Essence of Refined Gold*, 71.

56. Patrul Rinpoche, *Kun-bzang bla-ma'i zhal-lung*, 220-221.

57. A wooden grinder is incapable of grinding a hard substance.

58. This refers to the story of the frog in a well who told an ocean frog that his well was the largest abode imaginable. When the ocean frog brought the well frog to the ocean, the well frog fainted, cracked his head, and died. See Patrul Rinpoche's commentary in *Words of My Perfect Teacher*, 140.

59. Patrul Rinpoche, *Kun-bzang bla-ma'i zhal-lung*, 221-222.

60. Tatz, *Chapter on Ethics*, 24. This text includes a detailed discussion of the bodhisattva's ethics.

61. Kongtrul does not enumerate the four defeats. These are described in the introduction to Tatz, *Chapter on Ethics*, 11.

62. Aryadeva, *bsTan-bcos bzhi-brgya-pa zhes-bya-ba'i tshig le'ur byas-pa; Catuḥśataka-śāstra-kārikā;* Ot 5246, vol. 95.

63. Kalu Rinpoche, *The Dharma*, 120.

64. Patrul Rinpoche, *Kun-bzang bla-ma'i zhal-lung*, 240.

65. See Dilgo Khyentse, *The Wishfufilling Jewel: The Practice of Guru Yoga, According to the Longchen Nyingthig Tradition*, trans. Könchog Tenzin (Boston: Shambhala, 1988), 54.

66. Jamgon Kongtrul, *Torch of Certainty*, 123.

67. See above, page 48 of the translator's introduction, for a list of the fourteen root downfalls.

68. Longchenpa, *Sems-nyid ngal-gso*, 42.

69. Ibid.

70. Gampopa, *Nor-bu thar-pa rin-po-che'i rgyan*, 27.2.

71. Patrul Rinpoche, *Kun-bzang bla-ma'i zhal-lung*, 229-230.

72. Nagarjuna, *Golden Zephyr*, 56.

73. Nagarjuna, *Nagarjuna's Letter to a Friend*, trans. Geshe Lobsang Tharchin and Artemis Engle (Dharamsala: Library of Tibetan Works and Archives, 1979), 94-95. Toh 4496.

74. "Ultimate aim" here refers to the attainment of complete enlightenment. "Provisional aims" are those leading up to that attainment.

75. Longchenpa, *Sems-nyid ngal-gso*, 45-46.

76. *The Gem Ornament of Manifold Oral Instructions*, 73.

77. Longchenpa, *Sems-nyid ngal-gso*, 45.

78. Gampopa, *Nor-bu thar-pa rin-po-che'i rgyan*, 23-26.

79. Because most English readers are not as familiar with the text as Kongtrul's audience, I have included my entire translation of Gampopa's explanation of faith as an annotation to the translation; see note 118 in Kongtrul's auto-commentary.

80. For an English translation, see Guenther, *Jewel Ornament*, 14.

81. Ibid., 30.

82. Gampopa, *Nor-bu thar-pa rin-po-che'i rgyan*, 21.19-22.2. This passage can also be found in Shantideva, *A Guide to the Bodhisattva's Way of Life*, trans. Stephen Batchelor (Dharamsala: Library of Tibetan Works and Archives, 1992), chapter VII.14, p. 84.

83. Gampopa, *Nor-bu thar-pa rin-po-che'i rgyan*, 22.9-22.20.

84. Ibid., 98.13-98.16. For a detailed discussion of karma, cause and result, see Guenther, *Jewel Ornament*, 74-88.

85. Gampopa, *Nor-bu thar-pa rin-po-che'i rgyan*, 23.14.

86. Ibid., 24.18.

87. Ibid., 25.5.

88. Buton, *Jewelry of Scripture*, 58-90. Obermiller titles this section "The Consideration and Fulfillment of Rules Prescribed for Study and Teaching."

89. The mantra and complete quotation can be found in both Gampopa's *Nor-bu thar-pa rin-po-che'i rgyan*, 102b.2-6 (in Guenther's translation, 159), and in Buton's *Jewelry of Scripture*, 75. Also see below, page 156, note 131 of Kongtrul's auto-commentary.

90. Jamgon Kongtrul, *Torch of Certainty*, 111. For an in-depth discussion of mandala offerings in the context of the extraordinary preliminary practices, see pp. 93-111.

91. This is the same quote as in Buton. Toh 47: *De-bzhin-gshegs-pa'i gsang-ba bsam-gyis mi-khyab-pa bstan-pa; Tathāgata-acintya-guhya-nirdeśa*. Kongtrul identifies it as the *gSang-ba bsam-gyis mi-khyab-pa*. Kg dKon I, 119a7-119b1.

92. Gampopa, *Nor-bu thar-pa rin-po-che'i rgyan*, 17.3.

93. Buton, *Jewelry of Scripture*, 84-85.

94. Ibid., 65-67.

95. Ibid., 67.

96. Ibid., 68.

97. Ibid., 68-69.

98. Ibid., 69.

99. Ibid., 69.

100. Ibid., p. 69, for same quote.

101. *Abhidharma-samuccaya-bhāṣya*, Toh 4053, 129b.6. See also Buton, *Jewelry of Scripture*, 163, note 665.

102. Buton, *Jewelry of Scripture*, 70-71. Buton gets this list from the *Abhidharma-samuccaya-bhāṣya*, Tg mDo 57 129.b8-130a.1.

103. mChims 'jam pa'i dbyang was the abbot of Narthang monastery from 1254-1290 and wrote extensive and abbreviated commentaries on the *Abhidharmakosha*.

104. Buton, *The Jewelry of Scripture*, 72.

105. For a brief discussion of the nature and intent of the Tibetan biography, see *The Life of Marpa*, trans. Nālandā Translation Committee (Boston: Shambhala, 1982), xxi-xxiv.

106. Buton, *The Jewelry of Scripture*, 76.

107. *Legs-par rab-tu nyon-la yid la zungs shig dang ngas khyod la bshad-do.*

108. Patrul Rinpoche, *Kun-bzang bla-ma'i zhal-lung*, 12.3-13.5.

109. Tg mDo 58, 76a 2-8.

110. Patrul Rinpoche, *Kun-bzang bla-ma'i zhal-lung*, 14.3.

111. Ibid., 15.

112. Ibid., 15.

113. Ibid., 15-16.

114. Ibid., 17.

115. Ibid., 17.8.

116. Ibid., 18.4.

117. Vasubandhu, *rNam-bshad rigs-pa*, 76a.2-8; quoted here from Buton, *Jewelry of Scripture*, 78.

118. Cleary, *Flower Ornament*, 326-327.

119. Patrul Rinpoche, *Kun-bzang bla-ma'i zhal-lung*, 22. *The Treasury of Precious Qualities* is a *lam rim* text by Jigme Lingpa Rinpoche.

120. Gampopa, *Nor-bu thar-pa rin-po-che'i rgyan*, 182.1. *Lag-bzangs kyis zhus-pa'i mdo* is Toh 70. For a detailed discussion of the six paramitas, see Guenther, *Jewel Ornament*, 148-231.

121. Ibid., 196.16.

122. Buton, *Jewelry of Scripture*, 85.

123. Ibid., 85.

124. Ibid., 85.

125. Patrul Rinpoche, *Kun-bzang bla-ma'i zhal-lung*, 23.6.

126. Patrul Rinpoche comments (ibid., 23):

> Arrange the throne of dharma, laying out cushions on it, and make offerings such as a mandala, flowers, and so forth. This is [the perfection of] generosity.

127. Patrul Rinpoche (ibid.) explains the practice of morality for the student:

> Sweep the area thoroughly, sprinkle water to settle the dust, and so forth; and control any disrespectful behavior and so forth. This is [the perfection of] moral discipline.

128. Patrul Rinpoche (ibid.) explains the practice of patience as:

> Do not harm even the tiniest living creatures, and withstand all hardships of heat, cold, and so forth. This is [the perfection of] patience.

129. In explaining diligence, Patrul Rinpoche (ibid.) continues his commentary of the root verses of the *Tantra of Thorough Realization* (*mNgon-par rtogs-pa*):

> Abandon wrong views towards the lama and the dharma, then joyfully listen to the dharma with complete faith. This is [the perfection of] diligence.

130. Patrul Rinpoche comments (ibid.):

> Listen to the instructions of the lama with a mind undistracted by other things. This is [the perfection of] meditation.

131. Patrul Rinpoche (ibid.) concludes his commentary on the *Tantra of Thorough Realization* by explaining how the student should apply wisdom:

> Ask questions, to remove doubts and so forth, and to sever all misconceptions. This is [the perfection of] wisdom. The listener should have these six perfections.

132. *Sems kyi dbang du gyur pas na/ bdag gis sdig-pa ci bgyis-pa/ sangs-rgyas spyan sngar mchis nas su/ bdag gis de-dag bshags-par-bgyi//*

133. *Theg-mchog dam-chos rin-chen bshad 'di las/ bsod-nams mtha'-yas bdag gis gang thob-pa/ des ni 'gro kun theg-mchog dam-pa'i chos/ rin-chen dri-ma med-pa'i snod gyur cig/ ces sogs rnam-par dag-pa'i bsngo-smon bya'o//*

134. Jamgon Kongtrul, *Torch of Certainty*, 82.

135. Buton concludes his explanation of the teacher-student relationship with a lengthy discussion of the importance of study, reflection, and meditation. Kongtrul draws on Buton's handling of this material in the section, "Benefits of putting the teaching into practice and integrating study and practice."

136. Toh 3: *'Dul-ba rnam-pa-'byed-pa; Vinaya-vibhaṅga*.

137. For a discussion see Guenther, *Jewel Ornament*, 157-158.

138. For a discussion of the six super-knowledges, see Atiśa, *Lamp for the Path*, 114-123.

139. Buton, *Jewelry of Scripture*, 86.

140. Ot. 760:25; Toh 69: *Lhag-pa'i bsam-pa bskul-ba; Adhyāśaya-sañcodana.*

141. Atiśa, *Lamp for the Path*, 115-117.

142. Ibid., 115.

143. Ibid., 115-116.

NOTES TO PART III

1. "Characteristics" refers to the characteristics needed for one to be a qualified lama. See chapter three below for Kongtrul Rinpoche's discussion of the characteristics of a qualified wisdom teacher.

2. For a discussion of the precious human existence, see Guenther, *Jewel Ornament*, 14-21; and Patrul Rinpoche, *Kun-zang La-may Zhal-lung*, Part 1, trans. Sonam T. Kazi (Upper Montclair, NJ: Diamond-Lotus Publishing, 1989), 27-54.

3. This refers to the absence of asceticism in the Vajrayana.

4. For a discussion of the benefits of the buddhadharma, see Buton's *Jewelry of Scripture*, 59-62.

5. Kapila is considered the founder of the Samkhya school in India. He probably lived in the seventh century C.E.

6. Shantideva, *A Guide to the Bodhisattva's Way of Life*, trans. Stephen Batchelor, chapter X.57, p. 174.

7. Toh 60. See Gampopa, *Jewel Ornament*, 14, for a similar quotation from *The Sutra of the True Dharma of Clear Recollection* (*mDo dran-pa nyer-bzhag; Saddharma-smṛtyupasthāna*). Also see below in this chapter for a further discussion of the precious human existence.

8. For a full explication of what characterizes a precious human body, see Patrul Rinpoche, *The Words of My Perfect Teacher*, 7-37.

9. Also known as the *Dhammapada*. For an English translation of the *Ched-du brjod-pa'i tshom*, see Gareth Sparham, trans., *The Tibetan Dhammapada: Sayings of the Buddha* (London: Wisdom Publications, 1986). Chapter 25, pp. 125-128, discusses following the wisdom teacher. This passage is verse 6, p. 125. See also dGe-'dun Chos-'phel, trans. from Pali to Tibetan, *Dhammapada*, trans. into English by Dharma Publishing Staff (Berkeley: Dharma Publishing, 1985).

10. Sparham, *Tibetan Dhammapada*, 126, verse 7.

11. This refers to the three higher trainings: morality (*tshul-khrims; śila*); concentration (*samādhi*), appearing in the above passage as peacefulness (*nye-bar-zhi-ba*); and wisdom (*shes-rab; prajñā*).

12. Guenther, in *Jewel Ornament*, translates '*thad-pa* as "reasons."

13. From "Seek the justification..." to "...arise from [the wise lama]" is a direct quote from Gampopa, *Nor-bu thar-pa rin-po-che- rgyan*, 27.11. For an English translation see Guenther, *Jewel Ornament*, chapter three on "Meeting Spiritual Friends," p. 30.

14. For an explanation of syllogisms (*prayoga*), see Perdue, *Debate*, 33-53. For other sources on Buddhist logic, see Stcherbatsky, *Buddhist Logic*; the bibliography in Perdue, *Debate*, 891-900; and Kennard Lipman, "What is Buddhist Logic?" in *Tibetan Buddhism: Reason and Revelation*, Steven D. Goodman and Ronald M. Davidson, eds. (Albany: State University of New York Press, 1992).

From "The subject..." to "...the counter-example is that of the solitary sages" is a direct quote from Gampopa, *Nor-bu thar-pa rin-po-che'i rgyan*, 28.2.

15. See Guenther, *Jewel Ornament*, 30, bottom paragraph.

16. From "From the life story..." to "...he is like a ferryman" is a direct quote from Gampopa, *Nor-bu thar-pa rin-po-che'i rgyan*, 29.11; Guenther, *Jewel Ornament*, 32.

17. Gampopa, *Nor-bu thar-pa rin-po-che'i rgyan*, 29.11; Guenther, *Jewel Ornament*, 31. For an English translation of the *Gaṇḍavyūha-sūtra*, see Cleary, *Flower Ornament*. This quotation is located on p. 326.

18. For Sudhana's meeting with the girl Acala, see Cleary, *Flower Ornament*, 127-132. This quote is also found in Gampopa, *Nor-bu thar-pa rin-po-che'i rgyan*, 30.13; Guenther, *Jewel Ornament*, 32, with the context found on pp. 31-32. Also, an interesting discussion regarding the benefits of following the spiritual friend can be found on p. 37, note 9.

19. This refers to Gampopa's fourfold classification. See Guenther, *Jewel Ornament*, 32.

20. Skt. *saṃbhāramārga*. For a discussion of the five paths, see Guenther, *Jewel Ornament*, 232-238; and Longchenpa, *Kindly Bent*, 92-98, 241-244.

21. The "highest level" refers to the tenth bhumi.

22. From "Among those..." until "...ordinary person who is a spiritual friend" is a direct quote from Gampopa, *Nor-bu thar-pa rin-po-che'i rgyan*, 32.5; Guenther, *Jewel Ornament*, 33.

23. Kongtrul now skips over Gampopa's explanation of the other three types of spiritual friend, found in *Nor-bu thar-pa rin-po-che'i rgyan*, 32.15. The section skipped is as follows:

> Regarding the explanation of the qualifications of the four kinds of wisdom teachers: because the Buddha has abandoned the two kinds of obscurations he is perfect [regarding what needs to be] abandoned; and because he has the two kinds of omniscience, he is perfect in wisdom.
>
> Also, regarding the wisdom teacher who is a bodhisattva residing on the great bhumis: those residing on the first through the tenth bhumis also have the appropriate abandonments and wisdoms. In particular, those bodhisattvas residing on and above the eighth bhumi have attained the ten powers which take others into their care. These are the power over life, mind, necessities, karma, birth, will, aspiration prayers, magical displays, primordial wisdom, and the dharma.
>
> That is to say, the power over life is the ability to remain [in the world for] as long as one wishes. The power of mind is the power to rest evenly in samadhi for however long one wishes. The power over necessities is

the ability to shower a rain of immeasurable precious necessities upon sentient beings. The power over karma is the ability to change into something else the karma which would be experienced in a realm, a location, as a being, a place of birth, or other situations. The power over birth is the ability to be born in the desire realm while remaining in meditation and without leaving meditation. The power over will is the ability to transform, through will, earth into water and so forth. The power over aspiration prayer is making aspiration prayers to perfectly benefit oneself and others in whatever way is wished, and for those prayers to be accomplished. The power over miraculous displays is the ability to demonstrate immeasurable miracles which are magical displays, in order to instill admiration in sentient beings. The power of primordial wisdom is to completely know the dharma, its meaning, the correct words, and have confidence [in this understanding].The power over the dharma is to be able to fully satisfy the minds of all sentient beings by a single discourse, in accord with their respective languages, giving them exactly what and how much is necessary, presenting the dharma as found in the sutras and so forth, using the correct names, words, and phrases.

24. From "As to the characteristics..." up to "...or two good qualities" is a direct quote from Gampopa, *Nor-bu thar-pa rin-po-che rgyan*, 34.11.

25. From "if he possesses eight [qualities]..." up to "...in the *Bodhisattva-bhūmi*" is a paraphrase of the quote from Gampopa, *Nor-bu thar-pa rin-po-che'i rgyan*, 34.11-34.14; Guenther, *Jewel Ornament*, 34. In this section everything in brackets is taken from Gampopa's full quote. The eight qualities are quoted from *The Stages of the Bodhisattva* (*Byang-chub sems-dpa'i sa*; *Bodhisattva-bhūmi*) of Asanga (Thogs-med; Asaṅga). Gampopa, *Nor-bu thar-pa rin-po-che'i rgyan*, 34.14, quotes as follows:

> It is said in the *Stages of the Bodhisattva*: "If he possesses these eight qualities, then a bodhisattva should be understood to be a wisdom teacher with all the qualities complete. What are these eight qualities? They are to have the moral discipline of a bodhisattva; to be extremely learned in the bodhisattva-pitaka; to have realization; to have love and compassion; to be fearless; to have patience; to have a never-tiring mind; and the ability to use the language well."

26. Khenpo Tsultrim Gyamtso explained that *ston-pa* here refers to "the teaching," not "the wisdom teacher"; this yields the translation: "He makes extensive teachings because he is very learned."

27. Guenther translates this phrase as, "he points out the ultimately real by its primary characteristics of having defiling and purifying elements." See Guenther, *Jewel Ornament*, 37, note 16. Khenpo Tsultrim Gyamtso explained that "afflicted phenomenon" refers to samsara, and "completely purified phenomenon" refers to nirvana.

28. Shantideva's *Bodhisattva-caryāvatāra*, v.102. Gampopa also makes use of this quotation, see Guenther, *Jewel Ornament*, 34. Also see Stephen Batchelor's translation of Shantideva's work. Batchelor translates it as, "Never, even at the cost of my life, should I forsake a spiritual friend who is wise in the meaning of the great vehicle and who is a great bodhisattva practitioner."

Kongtrul directly quotes from Gampopa from, "the two [noble qualities] are..." up to "...conduct of the bodhisattva." Gampopa, *Nor-bu thar-pa rin-po-che rgyan*, 35.10.

29. Literally, *brtul* means "activity," and *zhugs* means "enter"—entering the activity, or in other words, one's discipline, behavior, or practice. *brTul-zhugs* has different meanings in reference to the three *yānas*. For instance, in the Hinayana training, *brtul* refers to subduing the afflictions, while *zhugs* refers to attaining the peace of nirvana. On the other hand, in Vajrayana training, *brtul* refers to training in the development and completion stages in order to subdue dualistic mind, while *zhugs* refers to entering into the profound samadhi of the tathagatagarbha, which is the clear light itself.

30. I expanded upon this phrase based on the original Tibetan from Gampopa, *Nor-bu thar-pa rin-po-che'i rgyan*, 35.16. Gampopa concludes chapter three, on "Meeting Spiritual Friends," with a discussion of the three ways of following the spiritual friend and the three ways of requesting dharma from the spiritual friend (p. 35.16-39). Because this discussion is relevant to Jamgön Kongtrul's text, and because Jamgön Kongtrul expected his reader to be familiar with this material, I include it here:

> The three methods of following the spiritual friend once you have found him are: (1) By honoring him and serving him; (2) by showing him devotion and respect; (3) by practicing and being assiduous. First, "following him by honoring him" means to make prostrations and rise quickly in his presence, to bow down and circumambulate him, to speak at the proper time and with affection, and to look at him again and again with a mind that will not be satisfied; for example, as the spiritual friend was respectfully received by the merchant Norzang. Also, it is stated in *The Sutra Arranged Like a Tree*, "Be insatiable to look at wisdom teachers. Why is that so? Because it is difficult to behold them, difficult for them to appear, and difficult to meet them."
>
> "Following by serving him" means to provide him, regardless of the trouble, with proper food, clothes, bedding, cushions, medicines, and other necessities for life, such as wealth and so forth; for example, just as the wisdom teacher was served by the noble Tagtunu (rTag-tu-ngu; Sadaprarudita). In *The Life Story of Paljung* (*dPal-byung-gi rnam-thar*; Śrīsaṃbhava) it says, "The enlightenment of a Buddha is obtained by serving wisdom teachers."
>
> "Following by devotion and respect" is to think of the wisdom teacher as the Buddha, not to disobey his commands, and to generate in yourself devotion, respect, and faith; for example, just as the pandit Naropa followed the wisdom teacher. Also in *The Mother of the Victorious Ones* (*rGyal-ba'i yum*) it is stated, "You should generate sincere respect for spiritual friends; you should hold them as being very precious and have faith in them." Furthermore, regarding the skillful means of the spiritual friend, you should give up misconceptions and continually generate respect; for example, as it is shown in *The Life Story of Gyalpo Mi* (*rGyal-po mi'i rnam-thar*).
>
> "Following by practicing and being assiduous" means to practice in terms of hearing the dharma teaching of the wisdom teacher, reflecting upon it, and then meditating; being assiduous is extremely pleasing to the

wisdom teacher. As it says in *The Ornament of the Mahayana Sutras* (*mDo-sde rgyan; Mahāyāna-sūtrālaṃkāra*), "He who understands the instruction as it has been given to him, makes the spiritual friend's mind extremely pleased." When the wisdom teacher is pleased, we attain the enlightenment of the Buddhas. It is said in *The Life Story of Paljung*, "When spiritual friends are pleased, we attain the enlightenment of all the Buddhas."

Asking the spiritual friend for the dharma is done in three ways: (1) the preliminary step; (2) the main part; (3) the conclusion. The preliminary step is to make the request with the mind of enlightenment (*byang-chub sems*). The main part is to generate the perception of yourself as the patient, the dharma as the medicine, and the spiritual friend as the doctor, and then to assiduously practice the dharma as the cure for the disease. As the conclusion, you should give up the defects of being like a pot turned upside down, with a leaky bottom, or filled with poison.

The advantages of following a wisdom teacher are given in *The Life Story of Paljung*:

O child of the family, bodhisattvas who are embraced by wisdom teachers will not fall into the lower realms. Bodhisattvas who are entirely guarded by wisdom teachers will not fall into the hands of harmful companions. Bodhisattvas who are sustained by wisdom teachers will not turn away from the Mahayana dharma. Bodhisattvas who are fully embraced by wisdom teachers go beyond the level of ordinary human beings.

And from *The Mother of the Victorious Ones*: "A bodhisattva mahasattva who is embraced by wisdom teachers quickly attains unsurpassable complete perfect enlightenment."

31. The following list comes from Atisha's *Lamp for the Path*, 83, note 23. Sherburne seems to have used the *Mahāvyutpatti* for the definitions of these different types of wisdom teachers. The Sanskrit list of pratimoksha masters can be found in the *Mahāvyutpatti*, 561:

The four officers required for the [ordination] ceremony are: (a) Preceptor (*mkhan-po; upādhyāya*): to sponsor and receive the novice in the name of the community. (b) Teacher (*slob-dpon; ācārya*): to instruct the novice and receive his promises at the end of the ceremony. (c) President (*las-byed-pa; karma-karaka*): to act as master of ceremonies or chairman, seeing to the proper conduct of the ritual, and to present the formal motion to the community for granting ordination. (d) Admonitor (*gsang-ste ston-pa; rahas-nuśāsaka*): to inquire privately during the ceremony about the novice's freedom from the physical impediments.

The president (*las-byed-pa; karma-karaka*) is not part of the list given by Kongtrul. Instead, we have the *gnas-klog slob-dpon*, reading-reliance master. For a discussion of the pratimoksha level of training see Atiśa, *Lamp for the Path*, 65-85.

32. The *khenpo* is the head of the monastery and monastic school. In Kagyu and Nyingma terminology the title "khenpo" is roughly equivalent to "geshe," used by the Gelugpa school.

33. The definition of the private instructor is found in the *Mahāvyutpatti*, 454: "Instructor in private, a monk or nun chosen to administer a private preparatory examination to a new initiate."

34. This master was not included in Sherburne's list on p. 83, note 23.

35. "No mistakes have arisen" means that the vows have not been broken. (Khenpo Tsultrim Gyamtso)

36. Khenpo Tsultrim Gyamtso emphasized that this information was never given to someone who was not going to become a monk or a nun, because it would be useless and of no benefit. Only monastics were allowed to study this material. Therefore he felt it is not necessary to give any further commentary on it.

37. This means not to be silly or crazy; in other words, mental normalcy. (Khenpo Tsultrim Gyamtso)

38. According to the Peking Edition p. 7.3-4, *tha-snyad gsum* is added in parentheses between *shes-pa rang-bzhin* and *gnas tha-mal lus*. "Residing in the essential nature of things" (*shes-pa rang-bzhin du gnas-pa*) is one of the three conventions. In *The Great Tibetan-Chinese Dictionary* (*Bod-rgya tshig-mdzod chen-mo*) the three conventions are given as *mi-yin-pa ngang; shes-pa rang-bzhin-du gnas-pa; 'dod-khams-pa'i sa-pa yin-pa*.

39. *Mahāyāna-sūtrālaṃkāra*, XVII.10. This quote is also found in Buton's *Jewelry of Scripture*. See the *Jewelry of Scripture* for a synopsis of the *Mahāyāna Sūtrālaṃkāra*. Buton writes:

> The *Sūtrālaṃkāra* contains an exposition of all the Mahayanistic doctrines in an abridged form: "Like wrought gold, like an unfolded lotus flower, like well-prepared food enjoyed by those that were starving, like a message agreeable to hear, or like an opened chest full of jewels, the Doctrine that is expounded here is the cause of the highest delight." In such a form its contents are presented [to the reader].

40. Buton, in *Jewelry of Scripture*, 63-64, glosses these ten points:

> Here ten qualities are mentioned. [The teacher is]: (1) Well disciplined, being endowed with pure morality. (2) Self-controlled, since he practices profound meditation. (3) has perfectly calmed all passions, through being endowed with highest wisdom. (4) Of exclusive merits, since his virtues are superior to those of others. (5) Zealous, as he is not indifferent towards the needs of others. (6) Rich in [his knowledge of] scripture, through extensive study [of the latter]. (7) Perceives the absolute truth that is to be recognized. (8) A skillful orator. (9) Merciful, since he does not look to profit. (10) Never too tired to expound the doctrine.

Buton then continues:

> And again (*Sūtrālaṃkāra* 13.8): "The Bodhisattva, the highest of human beings, is known to be greatly learned, perceiving the absolute truth, eloquent, full of compassion, and free from lassitude." Accordingly, [the teacher appears here] as endowed with five distinctive qualities. He is: (1) Greatly learned, an advantage as regards the textual transmission (*lung*). (2) Cognizes the absolute truth, an advantage that concerns realization (*rtogs-pa*). (3) An eloquent orator. (4) Merciful, since his mind is not directed toward material gain. (5) Free from lassitude in thought and action.

Moreover, four qualities are known, as follows (*Sūtrālaṃkāra* XII.5): "Extensive, clearing doubt, worthy of being heard, demonstrating the absolute truth in two aspects; such do we know to be the complement of the teaching [administered by] the bodhisattvas." Here [the bodhisattva is characterized as]:

(1) Endowed with great knowledge, by having extensively studied. (2) Clearing the doubts of the converts by his great wisdom. (3) Worthy of being accepted as a teacher, by being virtuous with regard to the three media [body, speech, and mind]. (4) Demonstrating the absolute truth, with a view to the [morally] defiling and purifying elements.

All these qualities are usually the [exclusive] attributes of a saint, and it is therefore not easy to become possessed of [all of] them. Three distinctive features are, however, indispensable. These are: (1) the high wisdom that characterizes a learned person; (2) a mind full of love and compassion; (3) virtuous acts.

Also, Geshe Ngawang Dhargyey, in his commentary to *The Fifty Verses of Guru Devotion*, 68, explains:

In general a Mahāyāna guru should have the following ten qualities: (1) Discipline as a result of his mastery of the training in the higher discipline of moral self-control. (2) Mental quiescence from his training in higher concentration. (3) Pacification of all delusions and obstacles from his training in higher wisdom. (4) More knowledge than his disciple in the subject to be taught. (5) Enthusiastic perseverance and joy in teaching. (6) A treasure of scriptural knowledge. (7) Insight into and an understanding of emptiness. (8) Skill in presenting the teachings. (9) Great compassion. (10) No reluctance to teach and work for his disciples, regardless of their level of intelligence.

Geshe Ngawang Dhargyey does not give any source of reference for this list of ten qualities, though they are very similar to the lists offered by both Kongtrul and Buton.

41. The first three points of this list refer to the three trainings which a qualified teacher should have: moral discipline (*tshul-khrims*), concentration (*bsam-gtan*), and wisdom (*shes-rab*).

42. For a discussion of mindfulness (*dran-pa*) and vigilance (*shes-bzhin*), see Shantideva, *Guide to the Bodhisattva's Way of Life*, 28-56.

43. These are the three prajnas.

44. In the Tattvartha chapter of the *Bodhisattva-bhūmi* Asanga wrote:

Again, what is that? It is the domain and the sphere of cognitive activity that belongs to the Buddha-Bhagavans and bodhisattvas who, having penetrated the non-self of dharmas (*dharmanairātmya*), and having realized, because of that pure understanding, the inexpressible nature (*nirabhilāpya-svabhāvatā*) of all dharmas, know the sameness (*sama*) of the essential nature of verbal designation (*prajñapti-vāda*) and the nondiscursive knowable (*nirvikalpa-jñeya*). That is the supreme suchness (*tathatā*), there being none higher, which is at the extreme limit of the knowable and for which all analyses of the dharmas are accomplished, and which they do not surpass.

Janice Dean Willis, trans., *On Knowing Reality: The Tattvārtha Chapter of Asaṅga's Bodhisattvabhūmi* (New York: Columbia University Press, 1979), 79.

45. The Fourteenth Dalai Lama, in his commentary to *The Essence of Refined Gold* by the Third Dalai Lama, 62-63, also states that these ten points are necessary qualifications of the lam-rim teacher.

46. According to Chandra Das, 952: *mang-du thos-pa* refers to a Buddhist monk who has heard many sermons and has read many sacred books; such a learned man has five qualifications: (1) *phung-po la khas-pa*; (2) *khams la mkhas-pa*; (3) *skye-mched la mkhas-pa*; (4) *rten cing 'brel-bar 'byung-ba la mkhas-pa*; (5) *de'i gdam-ngag dang rjes-su bstan-pa gzhan la rag las-pa ma-yin*.

47. Point three should be divided into two points: not striving for material gain and not striving for fame. (Khenpo Tsultrim Gyamtso)

48. This means being liberated to full enlightenment, which is uncontrived, beyond path and method.

49. "Family" (*rigs; gotra*) refers to the five types of sentient beings. For a discussion of *rigs*, see Guenther, *Jewel Ornament*, 3, and notes 21-25. The five families are: cut-off family (*rigs-chad kyi rigs*), dubious family (*ma-nges-pa'i rigs; aniyata-gotra*), shravaka family (*nyan-thos kyi rigs; śrāvaka-gotra*), pratyekabuddha family (*rang-sangs-rgyas kyi rigs; pratyekabuddha-gotra*); and Mahayana family (*theg-pa chen-po'i rigs; mahāyāna-gotra*). The cut-off family does not have a Sanskrit equivalent.

50. Kongtrul's verse is a paraphrase from Ashvaghosha, *Guru Devotion*, vv. 8-9, 166-168. Kongtrul then glosses these verses. The following are Ashvaghosha's verses 6-9 (Berzin trans.):

> In order for the words of honor of neither the Guru nor the disciple to degenerate, there must be a mutual examination beforehand [to determine if each can] brave a Guru-disciple relationship.
>
> A disciple with sense should not accept as his Guru someone who lacks compassion or who is angersome, vicious or arrogant, possessive, undisciplined or boasts of his knowledge.
>
> [A Guru should be] stable [in his actions], cultivated [in his speech], wise, patient and honest. He should neither conceal his shortcomings nor pretend to possess qualities he lacks. He should be an expert in the meanings [of the tantra] and in its ritual procedures [of medicine and turning back obstacles]. Also he should have loving compassion and a complete knowledge of the scriptures.
>
> He should have full expertise in both ten fields, skill in the drawing of maṇḍalas, full knowledge of how to explain the tantra, supreme pure faith, and his senses fully under control.

The Fifty Verses has also been translated by Sylvain Levi, "Autour d'Aśvaghoṣa," *Journal Asiatique*, CCXV (Oct-Dec 1929).

51. Geshe Ngawang Dhargyey, in his commentary to Ashvaghosha, *Guru Devotion*, 168, explains that:

A Tantric Master must have even more good qualities [than the Mahayana guru], as listed in the text [verses 8-9]. Most important is that he be an extremely stable person, with his body, speech, and mind totally under control. He should be someone in whose presence everyone feels calm, peaceful, and relaxed. Even the mere sight of him brings great pleasure to the mind. And his compassion must be unsurpassable.

52. Kongtrul now glosses vv. 7-9.

53. The six extremes are: (1) provisional meaning (*drang-don*); (2) definitive meaning (*nges-don*); (3) hidden meaning (*dgongs-pa-can*), (3.1) time (*dus*), (3.2) meaning (*don*), (3.3) thought (*bsam-pa*); (4) explicit meaning (*dgongs-pa ma-yin-pa*); (5) according to the letter (*sgra-ji bzhin-pa*); (6) not as it is said (*sgra-ji bzhin-pa ma-yin-pa*). (Khenpo Tsultrim Gyamtso)

(1) Provisional meaning is a means for the realization of definitive meaning. Examples of things which come under the category of provisional meaning are: meditation on the deities in their mandalas; all the various kinds of rituals; making offerings, etc. All of these are a means for attaining the definitive meaning. (2) Definitive meaning refers to the nature of mind, which is empty of dualistic clinging and is naturally luminous. This is the highest truth.

(3) Hidden meaning. There are three categories to hidden meaning: (3.1) Time. Although one becomes enlightened in one instant, this occurs after one has traversed the ten stages (*bhūmis*). Enlightenment occurs after one has purified the nadis, bindu, prana, etc. Therefore, though enlightenment occurs in one instant, it takes much work and effort to arrive at this final point. (3.2) Meaning. For example, when it says in a tantra, "You should steal the consort of the Buddha and enjoy her," this is not to be taken literally. The consort (*yum*) represents the paramitas, and the meaning is that one should meditate on emptiness. (3.3) Thought. For example, in the *Hevajra-tantra*, when it says that you should kill someone, it means that you should extinguish all conceptualization. This occurs as the wind of karma is stopped when it enters the central channel. Then dualistic perception is stopped. Therefore, one must transform one's concepts using the wind (*rlung; prāṇa*).

(4) Meaning is not hidden. For example, when you are told, "Do not kill any sentient being," this is to be taken literally, the meaning is fully explicit. (5) Literal meaning. Directions for performing rituals should be followed to the letter. One should follow instructions literally when making offerings, doing a fire puja, etc. In these cases one does exactly as the text says. (6) Not a literal meaning. This is used in secret practices. For example, "excrement" refers to Vairocana, and "urine" refers to Akshobhya. So if the text states that "you should eat Vairocana and drink Akshobhya," this means you should eat excrement and drink urine. This type of teaching is given to those who are attached to purity and impurity. Therefore these secret practices help break through deepseated fixations.

54. "Common systems" refers to all the non-tantric systems.

55. Toh 486. Chandra Das, *Tibetan-English Dictionary*, 1168: a tantra that contains the rituals of consecrating images, symbols, etc.

56. The ten essential points that the teacher needs to know are applied differently, based upon the particular sadhana and the cycle in which the teacher is involved.

57. The verse quoted by Kongtrul is very terse and was not glossed by him. Geshe Ngawang Dhargyey's gloss from Ashvaghosha, *Guru Devotion*, 169, helps to clarify the meaning, although he does not mention his source. It appears that either he is using a source similar to that which Kongtrul is quoting from (probably the *rDo-rje nying-rgyan*), or that this is a well-known list that educated lamas would know about. It is also possible he is using Kongtrul as his source. The two lists seem to be identical, except for a slight variation in point eight. At the end of these three lists Kongtrul mentions that a list of ten external essential points can be found in the *Vajra Essence Ornament* (*Do-rje snying-po rgyan; Vajrahṛdayālaṃkāra*) (Toh 451) and this list is similar to the one he quotes from the *Rab-gnas kyi gyud.*

Geshe Ngawang Dhargyey states that there are ten external and ten inner qualities which a guru needs to possess to be a complete master:

> The ten external qualities are required for teaching the *kriyā* and *caryā* classes of tantra, which stress the importance of purifying mainly external activities in connection with internal mental processes. These are expertise in: (1) Drawing, constructing, and visualizing the maṇḍala abodes of the meditational deities. (2) Maintaining the state of single-minded concentration (*samādhi*). (3) Executing the hand gestures (*mudra*). (4) Performing the ritual dances. (5) Sitting in the full meditational posture. (6) Reciting what is appropriate to these two classes of tantra. (7) Making fire offerings. (8) Making the various other offerings. (9) Performing the rituals of (a) pacification of disputes, famine, and disease; (b) increase of life span, knowledge, and wealth; (c) power to influence others; (d) wrathful elimination of demonic forces and interferences. (10) Invoking meditational deities and dissolving them back into their appropriate places.

Geshe Ngawang Dhargyey (168-169) then continues with the second set of ten qualities, which overlap with the lists Kongtrul quotes: the ten essential points of the ritual that appear in *Dombi-pa's Ten Verses on the Essentials of the Sphere of Wisdom Mind* (*Gur-gyi dgongs-pa Dom-bi-pa'i de-nyid bcu-pa*); and the ten essential points of suchness as they appear in *The Blazing Gem: The Wisdom Mind of the Five Hundred Thousand Tantras* (*rGyud 'bum-lnga'i dgongs-pa rin-chen 'bar-ba*):

> The ten inner ones are essential for teaching the *yoga* and *anuttarayoga* classes of tantra, which stress the importance of purifying mainly internal mental activities. These are expertise in: (1) Visualizing wheels of protection and eliminating obstacles. (2) Preparing and consecrating protection knots and amulets to be worn around the neck. (3) Conferring the vase and secret empowerments, planting the seeds for attaining a Buddha's form bodies.
>
> (4) Conferring the wisdom and word empowerments, planting seeds for attaining a Buddha's wisdom bodies. (5) Separating the enemies of dharma from their own protectors. (6) Making offerings such as sculptured *tormas*.

(7) Reciting mantras, both verbally and mentally; that is, visualizing them revolving around the heart.

(8) Performing wrathful ritual procedures for forcefully catching the attention of meditational deities and protectors. (9) Consecrating images and statues. (10) Making mandala offerings, performing the meditational practices (*sādhana*) and taking self-initiations.

Geshe Dhargyey (169) then makes the point that it is not enough for a lama to go through the motions of these rituals in order to be considered a tantric master; he must really be able to do them:

> It is not sufficient for a Tantric master merely to know how to perform the superficial actions of these above rituals [from both the set of ten inner and outer essential points]. He must actually be able to do them. For instance, when consecrating an image of a meditational deity, he must be able to invoke the actual deity and place it in the image, not merely recite the words of the accompanying text. If you take as your Guru a Master with all these qualifications and powers [those mentioned above for both the Mahayana guru and Tantric master], and he accepts you as his disciple, you must devote yourself fully to him. Although it is possible that out of delusion you might disagree with your Guru, never show him disrespect or despise him from the depth of your heart.

58. According to Geshe Ngawang Dhargyey, this refers to the ritual dances. (See previous note.)

59. This refers to the four activities applied to the ritual, such as a peaceful or wrathful *puja*, etc. (Khenpo Tsultrim Gyamtso)

60. This refers to dissolving the deities. (Khenpo Tsultrim Gyamtso)

61. This is the *Vajrahṛdayālaṃkāra* (Toh 451), which belongs to the father tantra of the anuttarayoga class of tantras. See F.D. Lessing and A. Wayman, *Introduction to the Buddhist Tantric Systems* (Delhi: Motilal Banarsidass, 1983), 251; this book is a translation of Khedrup-je's *rGyud-sde spyi'i rnam-par gzhag-pa rgyas-par brjod*. Also see p. 273 of the same text for a description of the sets of ten external and ten internal essential points (*daśatattva*) of the tantric teacher. According to Chandra Das, 705, *The Vajra Essence Ornament* is a tantric text which is a description of acquiring perfection. Perhaps this is the text used by Geshe Dhargyey, because it mentions the ten external essential points, and Kongtrul states that the lists are similar to those found in the *Consecration Tantra* (*Rab-gnas kyi rgyud*, Toh 486).

Khedrup-je's (mKhas Grub-rje) (1385-1438), in his *rGyud-sde spyi'i rnam-par gzhag-pa rgyas-par brjod*, states that the characteristics needed by the master who confers initiation upon the disciple are:

> ...just as said in the *Fifty Stanzas in Praise of the Guru* (*Gurupañcāśikā*), 'Steadfast, self-controlled, intelligent...' That is to say, he has the complete characteristics of the internal and external ten categories (*daśatattva*), of erudition in the expository texts (*śāstra*) of the sūtras and mantras as well as in the tantras, and so forth. Above all, they are just as said, 'He is victorious over the basic transgressions' (Lessing and Wayman, *Buddhist Tantric Systems*, 273-275).

Lessing and Wayman, 273, write:

> These [the ten external and internal essential points] are set forth and
> explained by Tsong-kha-pa in his commentary on the *Gurupañcāśikā* called
> *sLob-ma'i re-ba kun-slong* (Toh 5269), 7b3 ff. He quotes two groups of ten
> from the *Vajrahṛdayālaṃkāra* (Toh 451), as follows, with incorporation of
> some of his commentary. These are the outer ten categories: 1. The
> maṇḍala [of form and formless]. 2. Intense concentration (*samādhi*) [i.e.
> *devatā-yoga*, and of the (three) kinds beginning with "initial training"
> (*prathama-prayoga*)]. 3. Seal (*mudrā*) [e.g. the seals which apply seals to
> deities]. 4. [Male] stance [the (five) kinds, beginning with "left leg bent
> and right foot forward" (*ālīḍhastha*)]. 5. Seated position [the (two) kinds,
> beginning with "feet crossed in the diamond manner" (*vajra-paryaṅka*)]. 6.
> Muttering. 7. Burnt offering. 8. Worship. 9. Preliminary ritual [protecting,
> invitation, etc.] 10. Concluding acts [having finished the offering, prais-
> ing, etc., to pray that the gods depart]. Tsong-kha-pa states that these ten
> external essential points characterize the *vajra-ācārya* of the three lower
> tantras of kriya, carya, and yoga tantras.

62. Tg rGyud 3711: *De-kho-na-nyid kyi snying-po bsdus-pa; Tattva-sara-saṃgraha*. This
is the main tantra in the yoga class of tantras. According to 'Gos lo-tsa-ba gZhon-
nu-dpal in *The Blue Annals* (*Bod-kyi yul-du chos-dang chos-smra-ba ji-ltar byung-ba'i
rim-pa Deb-ther sngon-po*), 355, this text is a father tantra included in the
anuttarayoga class of tantras.

63. Lessing and Wayman, *Buddhist Tantric Systems*, 272, also give this list of ten
secret or inner principles from Tsongkhapa, with Tsongkhapa's commentary
included:

> 1, 2. The rites of the two "reversals" (*phyir zlog-pa*) [reversal through con-
> templation of the ten wrathful deities (*krodha*), for example; and reversal
> by means of tying, etc. after the drawing of the Knowledge being]; 3, 4.
> The [Initiation of] Secret (*guhya*) and Insight-Knowledge (*prajñā-jñāna*)
> [which imply the Flask (*kalaśa*) and the Fourth (*caturtha*) Initiations]. 5.
> The rite of "tearing apart" (*'byed*) the *saṃpuṭa* (*kha-sbyor*) [i.e. having forced
> away the enemy guardians (*dgra-bo srung-ma*), to practice *abhicāra* ("de-
> structive magic")]. 6. Devoted food offering (*bali*) [e.g. the fifteen-fold *bali*
> for the protectors of the quarters (*dik-pāla*)]. 7. Vajra recitation (*vajrajāpa*)
> [of mind and speech]. 8. The rite of accomplishing the fierce act (*drag-shul*)
> [i.e. tying down the gods with the magic nail (*kīla*)]. 9. Consecration
> (*pratiṣṭhāna*). 10. Accomplishing the maṇḍala [of the deities generated in
> front; extending them offerings and praises; entering the maṇḍala, and
> then receiving Initiation and being favored with permission (*anujñā*)].

64. According to Lessing and Wayman, *Buddhist Tantric Systems*, "the ritual of
tearing apart ('*byed*) the *saṃpuṭa* (*kha-sbyor*)."

65. For a description of Mi-bskyod rdo-rje (1507-1554) see: Nālandā Translation
Committee, *Rain of Wisdom*, 310-313; Nik Douglas and Meryl White, ed., *Kar-
mapa: The Black Hat Lama of Tibet* (London: Luzac, 1976), 73-78; Karma Thinley,
The History of the Sixteen Karmapas of Tibet (Boulder: Prajña Press, 1980), 89-95.

66. This refers to the Nyingma school.

67. Mahayoga emphasizes *bskyed-rim,* Anuyoga emphasizes *rdzogs-rim,* and Atiyoga emphasizes *lta-ba,* in which neither *bskyed-rim* nor *rdzogs-rim* are considered essential.

68. This refers to all the lists of the characteristics of the lama which Jamgön Kongtrul has explained up until now. For references on the summary of characteristics see: Longchenpa, *Kindly Bent to Ease Us;* Dalai Lama III, *Essence of Refined Gold;* Patrul Rinpoche, *Kun-zang La-may Zhal-lung;* Buton, *Jewelry of Scripture;* Jamgon Kongtrul, *Torch of Certainty.*

69. *Dam-tshig* only refers to the Vajrayana commitments. *Dam-pa* means "holy" and is short for *skye-bu dam-pa,* a holy person. In this case a "holy person" refers to a Buddha, and only in the Vajrayana is the teacher seen as a Buddha. *Tshig* means "word"; the words that the holy being gives must be kept. Therefore, *dam-tshig* is a promise the student makes to a holy being upon receiving a tantric empowerment. If this promise is not kept, then a transgression has occurred, and the disciple will deteriorate. (Khenpo Tsultrim Gyamtso)

70. Literally, "from lineage to lineage."

71. *bKa'* is a synonym for *sūtra (mdo).*

72. For a discussion of the ten bhumis, see Guenther, *Jewel Ornament,* 239-256.

73. See Atiśa, *Lamp for the Path,* 7, v. 21, and p. 74.

74. *bsDus-pa'i rgyud,* Kg rGyud-'bum, Toh 362; the full title is *mChog gi dang-po'i sangs-rgyas las phyung-ba rgyud kyi rgyal-po dpal dus-kyi-'khor-lo; Paramādi-buddhoddhṛta-Śri-kālacakra-nāma-tantrarāja.*

75. The four faces of Kalachakra represent the four empowerments *(dbangs)* and the four views. These views are received directly from the lama. (Khenpo Tsultrim Gyamtso)

76. In other words, the glorious lama *(dpal-ldan bla-ma)* is one who has realized the fourth empowerment [the path of union] in his heart, and can transfer this realization to the mind of his disciple. For this to occur the lama must have full realization, like Kalu Rinpoche. *Zhal-la gnas-pa* means that if he realizes this, it resides in his face [*zhal,* which here refers to heart], and if the disciple has devotion, it can be transferred to him. (Khenpo Tsultrim Gyamtso)

77. This describes the qualifications of a lama who can teach the highest levels of tantra. The Fourteenth Dalai Lama confirms this in *Essence of Refined Gold,* 71.

78. *Śri-Paramārthasevā,* Tg rGyud 1348.

79. One of the four great kalpas, in which it is very difficult to find a lama whose good qualities and faults do not appear mixed together. (Khenpo Tsultrim Gyamtso)
    For an account of the different kalpas, see Jamgön Kongtrul, *Shes-bya kun-khyab,* book 1. This section has been translated into English under the title *Myriad Worlds,* by Jamgön Kongtrul Lodrö Taye (Snow Lion, 1995).

80. For a detailed explanation of the three vows, see Jamgön Kongtrul, *She-bya kun-khyab*, book 2, ch. 2-4, 34-134.

81. The four defeats of the pratimoksha vow, each of which causes expulsion of a monk or nun, are sexual intercourse, theft, murder of a human being, and false claim to spiritual achievement. See Tatz, *Asaṅga's Chapter on Ethics*, 11. On p. 161 Tatz quotes Chandragomin (seventh century C.E.) from *The Twenty Verses*:

> (5) That which, developed from severe defilement, functions as destruction of the vow, the four transgressions of it, are considered similar to defeats.
>
> (6) With attachment to gain and respect, praising oneself and deprecating another; stingily not giving doctrine and wealth to the suffering, [poor] and forsaken.

And on p. 163 Tsong-kha-pa describes the four defeats:

> So there are four defeats: (1) Attachment to gain and respect. (2) Stinginess in goods. (3) Thoughts of harm toward sentient beings. (4) The stupidity of abusing the doctrine.

82. "Crossing over" means liberation.

83. In this context *rigs* refers to the awakening of one's inherent buddha-nature. For a discussion of the five *rigs* and their relationship to tathagatagarbha, see Guenther, *Jewel Ornament*, 3-8. A discussion of *rigs* can also be found in: Jamgön Kongtrul, *Shes-bya kun-khyab*, book 2, ch. 10, and ch. 2 on the bodhisattva vows, p. 98; Thrangu Rinpoche, *Buddha Nature*, trans. Erik Pema Kunsang (Kathmandu: Rangjung Yeshe Publications, 1988); Maitreya/Asanga, *Changeless Nature*, ch. 4.

84. Aryadeva, *bsTan-bcos bzhi-brgya-pa zhes-bya-ba'i tshig le'ur byas-pa; Catuḥśataka-śāstra-kārikā*; Ot 5246, vol. 95.

85. *rDo-rje 'phreng-ba; Vajramālā*, Kg rGyud-'bum, Toh 445.

86. Tg rGyud 2513: *rGyud-kyi rgyal-po chen-po sgyu-'phrul dra-ba'i rgya-cher-bshad-pa; Māyājāla-mahātantra-rājaṭīka-akhya*.

87. The "early translation period" refers to the Nyingma school.

88. This means having favorable material conditions.

89. Textual discrepancy: The text published by the International Academy of Indian Culture (IAIC) has *lus-sbyor* (p. 16), while the Peking Edition has *gus-sbyor* (p. 14). *Gus-sbyor* appears to be correct, because this term is also used in the root text, and the meaning makes sense.

90. For a discussion of the root and branch samayas see Dudjom Rinpoche, *Perfect Conduct*, 100-141.

91. *dPal bde-mchog 'byung-ba shes-bya-ba'i rgyud-kyi rgyal-po chen po; Śrī-mahāsaṃbarodaya-tantrarāja*, Tg rGyud 373.

92. Tg rGyud 1802.

93. This means being arrogant through extensive studying of the sutras and tantras without the corresponding experiences gained through meditation.

94. This refers to the list of general qualifications of a student for the Mahayana training, listed above.

95. This refers to the Mahayana family (*rigs*).

96 Ashvaghosha, *Guru Devotion*, 166, v. 6.

97. Kongtrul is probably summarizing and paraphrasing from memory the section of the *Gaṇḍavyūha-sūtra*, located in Cleary, *Flower Ornament*, 324-326. The full quote from Cleary, 324, is:

> Therefore you should not tire of seeking spiritual friends and benefactors, should not weary of meeting spiritual friends and benefactors, should not become complacent about questioning spiritual friends and benefactors, should not give up the determination to contact spiritual friends and benefactors, should not cease striving to respectfully follow spiritual friends and benefactors, should not misconstrue or resist the advice or instruction of spiritual friends and benefactors, should not be irresolute in acquiring the qualities of spiritual friends and benefactors, should not doubt the ways of emancipation shown by spiritual friends and benefactors, should not malign the acts of spiritual friends and benefactors adapting to the world to expedite their work, should not give up increasing pure faith in spiritual friends and benefactors.

The sutra then explains the numerous reasons why one should do this, beginning with, "It is from spiritual benefactors that enlightening beings [bodhisattvas] learn the practice of enlightening beings" (Cleary, 324), until "the charitable works of all enlightening beings originate from spiritual friends" (325).

Kongtrul ends the reference with "You should generate the idea that you are like the earth...." The full quote is:

> Therefore, thinking in this way, you should continue to approach spiritual benefactors, with a mind like the earth, bearing all burdens unbendingly; with a mind like adamant, having an unbreakable will; with a mind like a mountain range, impenetrable to all miseries; with a mind like a servant, doing whatever is bidden; with a mind like a student, following all instructions; with a mind like a slave, willing to take on all tasks; with a mind like a nurse, not overwhelmed by afflictions; with a mind like a servant, taking up any task obediently; with a mind like a street cleaner, getting rid of pride and conceit; with a mind like a full moon, appearing at the proper times; with a mind like a good horse, avoiding all unruliness; with a mind like a vehicle, carrying a precious cargo; with a mind like an elephant, tame and docile; with a mind like a mountain, unshakable; with a mind like a dog, not getting angry; with a mind like an outcaste youth, free from arrogance and egotism; with a mind like a bull with its horns cut off, stripped of all haughtiness; with a mind like an apprentice, free from inflated ideas of your own worth; with a mind like a ship, coming and

going tirelessly; with a mind like a bridge, crossing over with the directions of spiritual benefactors; with a mind like a good son, looking up to the countenance of spiritual benefactors; with a mind like a prince, carrying out the directives of the spiritual king.

98. *Brahmacarya* usually refers to celibacy, but Jamgön Kongtrul is using it in its general meaning of pure conduct. In this case, pure conduct refers to following a qualified teacher. See Translator's Introduction above, pp. 67-68.

99. For comments on this verse see my Introduction. Also see the two translations of Nagarjuna's *bShes-pa'i spring-yig; Suhṛllekha,* Toh 4496: Nagarjuna, *Golden Zephyr,* 55-56; and Nagarjuna, *Nāgārjuna's Letter,* 94-95.

100. It seems that Kongtrul is paraphrasing from memory. The entire quote from the *Gaṇḍavyūha-sūtra* follows, from Cleary, *Flower Ornament,* 325:

Sustained by spiritual benefactors, bodhisattvas do not fall into bad ways; supported by spiritual benefactors, bodhisattvas do not fall away from the Mahāyāna; minded by spiritual benefactors, bodhisattvas do not overstep the precepts of bodhisattvas; guarded by spiritual benefactors, bodhisattvas do not come under the sway of bad influences; protected by spiritual benefactors, bodhisattvas do not deviate from the laws of bodhisattvas; aided by spiritual benefactors, bodhisattvas go beyond the stage of sentient beings; taught by spiritual benefactors, bodhisattvas do not drop into the fall of those who seek individual liberation alone; hidden by spiritual benefactors, bodhisattvas rise above the world; developed by spiritual benefactors, bodhisattvas are unstained by mundane things; followed by spiritual benefactors, bodhisattvas become heedful and alert in all their practices; roused by spiritual benefactors, bodhisattvas do not give up their undertakings; assisted by spiritual benefactors, bodhisattvas become invulnerable to active afflictions; based on the power of spiritual benefactors, bodhisattvas can not be crushed by any demons; in association with spiritual benefactors, bodhisattvas develop all the elements of enlightenment.

101. This refers to Kun Khyen Longchenpa. For a discussion of the benefits of following the wisdom teacher, see Longchenpa, *Kindly Bent to Ease Us,* 83.

102. In both editions of the Tibetan text—Peking Edition, p. 19.4, and IAIC Edition, p. 19.3—the word is spelled *'drongs,* which means to believe, confide in, to bear, to keep in mind, to stick in one's head. *'Drongs* is translated here not as "to believe," but instead as "uproot," which is a variant of *drangs.*

103. Kg rGyud, Toh 496. Given in Roerich, *Blue Annals,* as *Phyag-rdor dbang-bskur* (*Vajrapāṇyabhiṣeka-mahā-tantra*).

104. Guhyapati is another name for Vajrapani.

105. According to the Peking Edition, p. 19.15, the spelling is *bla-ma'i ba spu'i khung-bu gcig,* "a pore of hair." In the IAIC Edition, p. 21, *ba-spu'i* was unreadable.

106. Textual discrepancy: the Peking Edition, p. 19, reads *chos-sgrub,* "practitioner," while the IAIC Edition reads *chos-smra,* "dharma speaker." *Chos-smra* is probably correct, because a few lines later it appears in both editions.

107. In Poussin's French translation, book 4, v. 118, p. 240.

108. According to Khenpo Tsultrim Gyamtso, the bodhisattva is not considered just an Arya (Noble One), but is superior to an Arya.

109. Tg 'Dul-ba 4116: *'Dul-ba lung bla-ma'i bye-brag lung zu-ba'i 'grel-pa; Vinaya-agamottara-viśeṣāgama-praśnavṛtti*. Also see Sparham, *Tibetan Dhammapada*, 126, v. 8:

> Just as the clean kusha grass
> That wraps a rotten fish
> Will also start to rot,
> So too will those devoted to an evil person.

110. The Omniscient Longchenpa writes, in *Sems-nyid ngal-gso*, 371.5-6:

> Just as a vine [takes on the fragrance of] the sandalwood tree, and kusha grass growing in a dirty swamp [becomes impure], by following a sublime person, you yourself will become sublime; by following a bad person, you yourself will be come bad. Therefore, assiduously follow sublime beings and reject the harmful teacher.

111. For a discussion of the maras, see Guenther, *Jewel Ornament*, 199, note 11, where he explains them as follows: (1) *Skandhamāra—rūpa, vedanā, saṁjñā, saṃskārāḥ, vijñāna*; (2) *Kleśamāra—lobha* (attachment), *dveṣa* (aversion), and *moha* (ignorance); (3) *Mṛtyumāra—death māra*; (4) *Devaputramāra—god māra*. See also, Alex Wayman, *History of Religion*, for studies in mara and yama; Lessing and Wayman, *Buddhist Tantric Systems*; Anila Rinchen Palmo, trans., *Cutting Through Ego-clinging* (Montignac: Dzambhala, 1988), for Machig Labdron's instructions to her disciples on the maras in the context of *gcod* practice.

112. Khenpo Tsultrim Gyamtso said that for this text the sets of six, three, and eighteen maras are not relevant. The relevant list for this text is that of the four maras, listed below in the text. They are considered maras because they impede progress towards full liberation. He felt it important to emphasize that these maras are not ghosts, they are hindrances (*bar-chad*). Khenpo Tsultrim gave another example of a hindrance: If a student wants a short explanation on a particular subject and the lama gives a lengthy one, this might become a *bar-chad*, a mara. Or if the teacher likes to study and the student prefers to meditate, or vice versa, then the appropriate conditions are not present for the student to progress on the path to liberation. Therefore maras are obstacles, concepts, hindrances towards attaining the ultimate.

113. "Objects of engagement" refers to the objects engaged by the sense faculties: the eye consciousness engaging with form, the ear consciousness with sound, and so forth.

114. *rNam-rtog; vikalpa*. A sampling of the various translations follows: Guenther: "preconceived ideas"; for a discussion of this term see *Jewel Ornament*, 37, note 5, and 11, note 19. Tucci: "the process of thought"; see *The Religions of Tibet*, 87. Lessing and Wayman: "discursive thought"; see *Introduction to the Buddhist Tantric Systems*, 162. Hookham: "concepts, thoughts, preconceived ideas"; see *The Buddha Within*.

115. This means not being conditioned by *rnam-rtog* and agitated mind.

116. Faith is preliminary in the sense of preceding the accumulation of positive qualities.

117. Currently, many translators are translating *dad-pa* as "confidence," so as not to trigger negative associations many people have to the word "faith." I have chosen to translate *dad-pa* as faith, because when understood clearly, free of its negative associations of mindless following, faith is a more accurate term than confidence.

118. Here, in chapter nine, Kongtrul Rinpoche summarizes Gampopa's handling of this topic in his *Nor-bu thar-pa rin-po-che'i rgyan*, 22.9-26. I have translated the entire passage from Gampopa in order to give context to the discussion of faith. Gampopa, in the section, "the support is the excellent precious human body" (*rten-ni mi-lus rin-chen mchog*) (p. 14), discusses faith in the context of the explanation of the precious human existence. He states that the human body is precious because it is difficult to obtain and is very useful. But because it is easily destroyed, Gampopa encourages us to immediately use our body as a vehicle to escape from samsara. In this context, Gampopa states that if we wish to make the best use of our present human life we must have the three types of faith. He writes:

> For one who does so, faith is necessary. It is said that if one lacks faith the positive qualities will not arise in one's mind-stream. Therefore, as it has been said in the *Sutra of the Ten Noble Dharmas* ('*Phags-pa chos bcu-pa'i mdo*), "Positive qualities will not arise in people who are lacking faith; just as a seed burnt by fire [will not become] a green sprout."
>
> It has also been said in the *Buddha Avatamsaka Sutra* (*Sangs-rgyas phal-po che'i mdo; Buddhāvataṃsaka*), "Worldly people with little faith are unable to understand the enlightenment of the Buddha." Therefore, you should generate faith.
>
> Also, it has been said in *The Sutra of Vast Display* (*Phags-pa rgya-che rol-pa; Lalitavistara*), "Ananda, you should apply yourself to faith. This is the request of the Tathagata." [12b4-13a1]
>
> So, [concerning] faith, if it is asked, what is it like? If one classifies faith there are three kinds: faith which is trust, faith which is longing, and faith which is clear.
>
> So, trusting faith is born by relying on karma and its effect, the truth of suffering, and the truth of the origin of all suffering. Therefore, trust that the effect of virtuous activity is the arising of the happiness of the desire realm, and trust that the effect of unvirtuous activity is the arising of the suffering of the desire realm. Trust that the effect of unwavering activity is the arising of the happiness of the two higher realms. Trust in obtaining the five skandhas, which is called the truth of suffering, because of having engaged in (*spyad-pa*) karma and the defilements (*nyon-mongs*), which is called the origin of all suffering.
>
> Longing faith is recognizing unsurpassable enlightenment itself as something very special; then with devotion for the purpose of attaining it, training in the path.
>
> Clear faith is relying on the three excellent and rare objects, then giving rise to them. A clear mind is having respect and devotion for the

excellent rare objects [the three jewels]: the jewel of the Buddha who shows the path, the jewel of the dharma as being the path, and the jewel of the sangha as being the spiritual friends who accomplish the path.

Therefore as it has been said in the Abhidharma, (*Chos-mngon-pa*), "If asked, 'What is faith?', it is manifest trust in karma and result, [the four noble] truths, and the excellent rare ones [the three jewels]; it is longing, and a clear mind."

Also, it has been said in the *Precious Garland* (*Rin-chen phreng-ba; Ratnamālā*), "A person who does not pass over the dharma because of craving ('*dun*), anger (*zhe-sdang*), fear, and stupidity (*rmongs-pa*), that one is called 'one who has faith,' and is a supreme vessel for higher attainment."

As for that, "not passing over the dharma because of craving" means not giving up (*mi-gtong-ba*) the dharma from the perspective of attachment ('*dod-chags*). For example, someone might say, "If you give up the dharma, I will give you wonderful delightful things such as food, wealth, women, and a royal existence." Still, do not give up [the dharma].

"Not passing over the dharma because of anger" means not to give up the dharma from the perspective of hatred (*khong-khro-ba*). For example, someone has previously done harm to me and an opportunity now arises for me to do great harm [in return], still, do not give up the dharma [and retaliate].

"Not passing over the dharma because of fear" means not to give up the dharma from the perspective of terror. For example, someone might say, "If you do not give up (*mi-gtong*) the dharma I will request three hundred warriors to cut five ounces of flesh from your body." Still, do not give up the dharma.

"Not passing over the dharma because of stupidity" means to not give up the dharma from the perspective of not knowing. For example, if someone says, "Karma is not true, effect is not true, the three jewels are not true. What is the use of practicing the dharma? Leave the dharma!" Still do not give up the dharma.

Therefore, someone possessing these four aspects is called "one who has faith." By that, he or she is a supreme vessel for the excellent accomplishment. Therefore, if there are these [three kinds of] faith there are immeasurable benefits, such as the mind of the supreme person arises; [the eight] unfavorable conditions are abandoned; the senses (*dbang-po*) are sharp and clear; morality is unimpaired; afflictions are removed; mara's sphere of activity is passed beyond; the path of liberation is found; extensive virtues are accumulated; many Buddhas are seen, etc. The excellent qualities arising are incomprehensible by the mind.

Therefore, it is said in the *Precious Talala Sutra* (*dKon-mchog ta-la-la'i gzungs; Ratnolkā-nāma-dhāraṇi*): "When there is faith in the Victorious One and the Victorious One's dharma, and one has faith in the way of life of the heirs of the Buddhas, and faith in unsurpassable enlightenment, then the mind of the 'great person' arises." [14b]

Also, if there is faith, the Bhagavat Buddhas come near and teach one the dharma. Therefore, as it is said in the *Bodhisattva-piṭaka* (*Byang-chub sems-dpa'i sde-snod*): "Therefore, when the bodhisattva who resides in faith is known by the Bhagavat Buddhas as a vessel of the buddha-dharmas, then they draw near to that one, and perfectly teach the bodhisattva path."

In this way, what is called the precious human body is endowed with the two aspects of leisure and opportunity (*dal-'byor*), and the mind is endowed with the three aspects of faith; this is the person (*gang-zag*) who is the support (*rten*) for the accomplishment of unsurpassable enlightenment.

119. Toh 145, 847.

120. *Dang-ba* (clear) refers to a mind without any doubt, which is devoted to the three jewels and the lama.

121. This quotation and the following one are from *Nor-bu thar-pa rin-po-che'i rgyan*, 13b1-3.

122. The expanded meaning which is contained within the brackets comes from Gampopa. Kongtrul writes: *gSum-pa ni/ Bla-na-med-pa'i byang-chub thob-pa'i ched-du gus-pa dang-bcas te lam-la slob-pa'o//* (22.9-11). Gampopa writes: *'Dod-pa'i dad-pa ni/ Bla-na med-pa'i byang-chub de-nyid khyad-par-can du thon-nas/ de thob-pa'i ched-du gus-pa dang-ldan-pas lam-la slob-pa'o//* (23.12).

123. In Gampopa's *Nor-bu thar-pa rin-po-che'i rgyan* this same quote is cited and its source given as the *Rin-chen 'phreng-ba (Ratnāvali)*. It is probably a sutra citation from the *'Phreng-ba*. For Gampopa's commentary on this verse, see note 118.

124. A synonym of *'dun-pa*.

125. A synonym for bodhicitta.

126. "...and so on" refers back to Gampopa's writing. See note 118 above.

127. Same quote as in Gampopa. One minor textual discrepancy: Kongtrul has *rgyal-sras rnams-kyi*. Gampopa has *sangs-rgyas sras-kyi*.

128. Buton, in *The Jewelry of Scripture*, 73-74, also describes what should be done on the part of the master in regard to the preparation. Buton writes that the teacher should teach, having in mind the students, the aim, and the manner of conducting the teaching. The latter point contains the preparations, the teaching itself, and the conclusion. Buton discusses making arrangements with a slightly longer introduction than Kongtrul:

> [The teacher must] make the due arrangements, address a prayer to the three jewels, and, having banished the evil one [by means of the charm especially prescribed for this purpose], manifest great love with regard to all the hearers.

129. Literally, "a throne with feet." "Feet" refers to the eight lions on which the throne rests.

130. Buton, *Jewelry of Scripture*, 74-75, continues with a more extended quotation from the *Dam-chos pad-ma dkar-po (Saddharma-puṇḍarīka)*, as follows:

It is said in the *Saddharma-puṇḍarika*:

(1) The teacher, when he thinks that the time has come, is to enter the schoolhouse, and having closed the door and taken a review of the Doctrine, in all its parts, is to teach with a mind free from dismay. (2) The sage, always good-tempered and sitting at ease, preaches the doctrine after having erected a spacious seat in a clean and agreeable spot. (3) He dresses himself in a clean religious robe, well-dyed with exquisite colors, puts on the black mantle and the spacious skirt. (4) Then, on the seat, a footstool covered with diverse garments, he seats himself, and having well washed his feet, rises up, anoints head and face; (5) and there, sitting on the preacher's seat, to the people that have assembled and are full of attention, he is to deliver diverse sermons, for monks and for nuns; (6) for the devotees of the laity, male and female, and likewise for kings and princes. The teacher must always be free from envy and teach with a sweet voice and on diverse subjects. (7) He must reject all indolence and never be subjected to lassitude; become free from uneasiness, and meditate upon the power of love, [which he exercises] with regard to his hearers. (8) By day and by night is he to preach the highest of doctrines in the form of millions of diverse parables, to gladden and to gratify the hearers, but never to desire anything for himself [in return]. (9) Neither of food nor beverage, of garments, a couch, a seat, a religious robe, nor even of a remedy if he is ill, dare he think and accept such from his hearers. (10) Other must be his thoughts: "May I and all these living beings attain enlightenment; to teach the Doctrine in order to help mankind, this is the sole foundation of my happiness!"

The section in *Dam-chos pad-ma dkar-po* where this quotation originates can be found in Leon Hurvitz, *Scripture of the Lotus Blossom of the Fine Dharma* (New York: Columbia University Press, 1976), 214. He translates from the Chinese of Kumarajiva. This quote is from chapter 14, "Comfortable Conduct." This chapter is Buddha's response to Manjushri's question on how a bodhisattva should teach the *Lotus Sutra* during this dark spiritual age. For an alternative translation, see Bunn Kat, *The Threefold Lotus Sutra* (Tokyo: Kosei Publishing, 1988), 227-228.

A discussion on the preparations for teaching the dharma can also be found in Gampopa's *Nor-bu thar-pa rin-po-che'i rgyan*. This is contained within Gampopa's treatment of generosity, the first of the paramitas (pp. 186-202). The specific section on making arrangements can be found at p. 197.8. The discussion on eradicating mara is on p. 197.9. For an English translation, see Guenther, *Jewel Ornament*, 158.

131. For this section, "Annihilating mara" (10.1.1.2), Kongtrul quotes only a segment of the verse quoted by Buton from the *Sāgaramati-paripṛcchā-sūtra* (Kg mDo 152).

132. Guenther, *Jewel Ornament*, 159, translates the mantra:

"Peace, peace, appeaser of enemies, conqueror of Māra, you who wear a garland of skulls, you resplendent one, you who look around, are pure and immaculate and remove all stains; you who look everywhere, who bind all evil and are yourself free from the fetters of Māra. You who are wholly pure, let all devilish impediments vanish." Sāgaramati, when one repeats this mantra before the explanation starts and then expounds the dharma, the Mārakuladevatās in a radius of one hundred miles cannot come to annoy and obstruct you. After the recitation you should explain the dharma in a moderately loud voice.

For more information, see Guenther's note 6, p. 162. He says that this is "a paraphrase of the Tibetanized Sanskrit of the mantra." (Gampopa, *Nor-bu thar-pa rinpo-che'i rgyan*, 198.1.) Buton, *Jewelry of Scripture*, 75, also gives the mantra to dispel mara. The mantra and fuller quotation from Buton follows:

Śame! Śamavati! Śamita Śatruṃ! aṅkure! maṅkure! marajiti! karāḍe! keyūre! tejovati! ojasvini viśiṣṭanirmale! malāsane! okhare! khage! grase! grasane! omukhe! parṇāmukhe! varannkhe! All the bonds of the demons are removed, all the antagonists are vanquished, [we are] released from the chains of the Evil One and stamped with the seal of Buddha, and all the devils are annihilated. May all the works of Māra vanish by virtue of the perfect purity of the Immovable One! Such, O Sāgaramati, are the words that vanquish the Evil One and remove all defilement. He, that expounds the Doctrine, must duly recite them and then, having occupied the preacher's seat, let his thoughts full of love [which manifest themselves in the desire] to secure supreme Enlightenment extend over all the circle of hearers. He must think of himself as of a physician; of the doctrine as if it were a remedy; of those that are to study as of patients; and of Buddha, as of the Highest of living beings. Moreover, he has to consider that the rules of the Doctrine must be established so as to have a long existence. Now, if he teaches the Doctrine, having first uttered the mantra [which has been mentioned], the Evil One and his hosts will not dare to approach him, in order to divest him from teaching, within the reach of a hundred miles, and those who still chance to come near, will not be able to make any disturbance.

133. This is the distance at which you can hear a shout, times one hundred.

134. In regards to this section (10.1.1.3) "The master should purify his behavior," Buton makes a brief comment: "And, the teacher must be [morally] pure, of virtuous behavior, [outwardly] clean and neatly dressed."

135. "Excellent" (*phun-sum tshog*) refers to the complete qualities of the speech of the Buddha, which are listed as sixty. The following list was taken from the *Mahāvyutpatti* 444, 77-78:

mNyen-pa, soft, appealing; 'jam-pa, mild; yid-du 'ong-ba, pleasing to the mind; yid-la 'thad-pa, agreeable to the mind; dag-pa, pure; dri-ma med-pa, stainless; gsal-dbyangs, clear-sounding; snyan-'jebs-pa, pleasing; mnyan-par 'os-pa, worthy to be heard; mi-tshugs-pa, not harsh; snyan-pa, agreeable; dul-ba, refined, soft; mi-rtsub-pa, not rough; mi-brlang-ba, not harsh or abusive; rab-tu dul-ba, very soft; rna-bar snyan-pa, pleasing to the ear; lus sim-par byed-pa, causing happiness or refreshment to the body; sems sim-par byed-pa, giving satisfaction to the mind; snying dga'-bar byed-pa, making the heart joyful; dga'-ba dang bde-ba bskyed-pa, producing joy and happiness; yongs-su gdung-ba med-pa, without anguish; kun-tu shes-par *bya-ba,* making entirely intelligible; *rnam-par rig-par bya-ba,* making fully comprehensible; *rnam-par gsal-ba,* very clear; *dga'-bar byed-pa,* making cheerful; *mngon-par dga'-bar byed-pa,* causing great delight; *kun-shes-par byed-pa,* making fully to understand; *rnam-par rig-par bya-ba,* making to perceive the annexed instruction; *rigs-pa,* skillful; *'bel-ba,* coherent, consistent; *tshig zlos-pa'i skyon-med-pa,* not having the fault of repetition; *seng-ge'i sgra'i-shugs,* the power of a lion's roar; *glang-po-che'i sgra-skad,* a voice like the sound of an elephant; *'brug-gi sgra-skad,* a voice like the sound of thunder; *klu'i dbang-po'i sgra,* sound of the naga king; *dri-za'i glu-dbyangs,* the melodious song of the gandharva; *ka-la-ping ka'i dbyangs,* the melodious voice of the sparrow; *tshangs-pa'i sgra dbyangs bsgrags-pa,* uttering a melodious sound like that of Brahma; *shang-shang te'u sgra dbyangs bsgrags-pa,* uttering a melodious sound like that of a partridge; *lha'i dbang-po'i dbyangs-ltar snyan-po,* a voice pleasing like that of Indra's; *rnga'i sgra,* the sound of a large drum; *ma-khengs-pa,* not puffed up; *mi-dma'-ba,* not inferior; *sgra thams-cad kyi rjes-su zhugs-pa,* following every sound or voice; *tshig-zur chag-pa med-pa,* without corrupt words; *ma-tshang-ba-med-pa,* not deficient; *ma-zhum-pa,* not fearful; *mi-zhan-pa,* not feeble; *rab-tu dga'-ba,* very joyful; *khyab-pa,* encompassing; *chup-pa,* perceiving; *rgyun-chags-pa,* continual, flowing; *'bel-ba,* playful; *sgra thams-cad rdzogs-par-byed-pa,* accomplishment of all sounds; *dbang-po thams-cad tshim-par-byed-pa,* satisfying every sense; *ma-smad-pa,* not distressed; *mi-'gyur-ba,* unchanging; *ma-rtags-pa,* immovable; *'khor kun-tu-grags-pa,* resounding in every company; *rnam-pa thams-cad kyi mchog dang ldan-pa,* having the chief voice in all sorts of sounds.

136. This refers to meditation on the wisdom deities.

137. This section (10.1.2) is taken from Buton's *Jewelry of Scripture,* 83, the section entitled "The preparation [of the disciple]." Kongtrul and Buton each expound three points on the subject of the student's preparation. The three things Kongtrul states the disciple should do are offer a pure gift (10.1.2.1), attend to one's conduct (10.1.2.2), and meditatively cultivate joy in the favorable conditions you currently have (10.1.2.3). The three things delineated by Buton are think how to realize the dharma, attend to one's conduct, meditatively cultivate joy in the favorable conditions you currently have. The only difference is in point one, which Buton gives as, "[One must] first of all think how to realize [the aim of] the Doctrine, as it is said [in the Jatakas]: 'The realization, which follows study, must be regarded as most important.'"

138. Tg mDo LVIII,142b; Toh 4150.

139. A synonym of *bsnyen-bkur.*

140. This is the same quote as in Buton. Toh 47: *De-bzhin-gshegs-pa'i gsang-ba bsam-gyis mi-khyab-pa bstan-pa; Tathāgata-acintya-guhya-nirdeśa.* Kongtrul identifies it as the *gSang-ba bsam-gyis mi-khyab-pa,* Kg dKon I, 119a7-119b1.

141. Until this point, Kongtrul is quoting from Buton, *Jewelry of Scripture,* although Buton, p.84, contains one final line in the quotation: "...even during a hundred

aeons." Kongtrul ends this section with the one-line summary that follows this quote, but Buton continues:

And the *Sutra of the Vast Display* says: "Human birth and the appearance of a Buddha [in this world] are not easy to be met with, and so are likewise the attainment of faith, avoidance of the eight unfavorable states of existence, and the opportunity to study the doctrine. At present, the Buddha has appeared, and the favorable states of existence, faith, and the possibility to study the doctrine are all of them secured. Therefore, do away with all distraction. There may come a time when, for millions and millions of aeons, it will not be possible to hear [the word of] the Doctrine. Therefore, since you may obtain it now, give up all distractions."

Moreover, we read in the *Vyākhyāyukti* [*Principles of Elucidation*]: "The word of the Buddha, the opportunity to hear it, the desire [to study], wisdom, and the absence of impediments—these four are hard to be obtained. Therefore, listen to the word of the Buddha [when it is possible]."

And: "If a living being dies, will he [in his next birth] meet with the jewel of the doctrine or not, will he come to study the doctrine, and will there be one who explains it to him—no one can tell. Therefore, at present you must zealously listen to the words of the Teacher."

Again [in the *Saddharma-puṇḍarīka*]: "If one exists in the phenomenal world, one is inevitably reborn, but this new life usually passes away in vain, for the Perfect Word [that shows us the right way] is seldom to be heard here. It is rare as the flower of the Udumbara."

142. Section 10.2.1.1.1, "Wisdom as being learned," is taken directly from Buton, *Jewelry of Scripture*, 64-65. Kongtrul left out the list of twenty antidotes of the eleven faults of speech which are explained in the *rNam-bshad rigs-pa*. This is given by Buton at the end of the section beginning on p. 65, line 26. I will include this below at the end of the section.

143. The eight characteristics of the wisdom teacher are the three types of wisdom, the two types of kindness, and the three types of patience—all to be explained by Kongtrul in this section.

144. See Jamgön Kongtrul, *Shes-bya kun-khyab*, book 2, 204, for discussion of *tshig-don*. Also see the *Madhyāntavibhāga*, chapter 5, first of ten points; translated by Michelle Martin as *Distinguishing the Middle from the Extremes, Chapter Five: The Distinctive Path of the Mahayana* (Kathmandu: Modern Press, 1992).

145. *Mahāyāna-sūtrālaṃkāra*. See chapter 12, verses 10-13, of Sylvain Levi, trans., *Mahāyānasūtrālaṃkāra, exposé de la doctrine du Grand Véhicule selon le système Yogācāra* (Paris: Champion, 1907).

146. Generally, the three spheres refer to subject, object, and action. In the commentary to the *Mahāyāna-sūtrālaṃkāra* it states that the three spheres refer to how the Buddha teaches, the speech or voice, and the words taught.

147. Obermiller says that *brtan-mi-byed* is correct, instead of *bstan-mi-byed*, and translates points 5 and 6 as "impossibility to clear doubt and confirm the absence of such." See Buton, *Jewelry of Scripture*, 65 and 162, note 645.

148. Tg mDo LVIII, 33b5-6; Toh 4061. This is one of Vasubandhu's major texts and is his main hermeneutical treatise on how to interpret a sutra. See Nakamure, *Indian Buddhism*, 271.

149. Buton, *Jewelry of Scripture*, 65-67, continues with the list of twenty antidotes of the eleven faults of speech:

> Otherwise, as it is explained in the *rNam-bshad rigs-pa* [*Principles of Elucidation*], there are twenty aspects of dharma discourse which are the antidotes of the eleven defects in speech, as follows:
>
> (1) Teaching at due time. This is an antidote against that fault which consists in teaching to a person who, by his immoral conduct, is unworthy of being taught. This method is observed by teaching only after having become convinced that the hearer really wishes to study and is worthy to receive instruction. My own means of teaching and studying are defective as regards this first method; they are therefore without real value and do not attain their aim. [A note by Obermiller states that this is Buton's own comment].
>
> (2) Teaching accurately, by admitting no carelessness in speech. This method is directed against the defect of incompleteness.
>
> The following three methods are antidotes against the defect of broken, interrupted speech: (3) Teaching in regular order, by beginning with the communication of subjects which, as regards time, are to be mentioned first, namely charity etc., or of high, sublime matters. (4) Teaching in due connection, with a view to the sutra that is to be explained, and replying to the awkward questions of opponents. (5) Teaching with a regard for one's hearers by giving instruction in accordance with their questions, instructions in the form of one categorical answer etc.
>
> The methods which act against the defect of unintelligible speech are, likewise, three in number, as follows: (6) Causing delight to those that are devoted [to the Doctrine]. (7) Arousing the desire [to study] in those that first meet [with the Doctrine] and are hostile to it. (8) Giving satisfaction to those that are on the way toward apprehension, but are still full of doubt.
>
> The defect of speech that consists in disregard [for the Doctrine] has the two following antidotes: (9) Not speaking so as to gratify those that lead sinful lives and are therefore unworthy of being pleased. (10) Not [abusing] others who through this become depressed.
>
> An antidote against the defect of incorrect speech is: (11) Having recourse to logic in never being in conflict with modes of right cognition.
>
> That defect in speech which consists in communicating matters of profound meaning to a pupil of weak intellectual faculties [who is unable to understand them] is avoided by: (12) Gradual progress—from the preceding to the following.
>
> Then: (13) Precision—an antidote against the defect of distraction, by withholding from discourses on other subjects. (14) Dependence on the Doctrine—that is, being in harmony with the teaching of virtue. This is an antidote against the defect of [communicating] useless theories. (15) Accordance with the circle of adherents, whosoever they might be, an antidote against ill-suited speech.

The remaining five methods act against the defect of teaching, in being [at the same time] possessed of sinful thoughts. As to the latter, such may be of three kinds, namely, the consideration of oneself to be virtuous and trustworthy, the desire of being honored and praised, and [envy in regard to the merit of others]. The first of these has three antidotes: (16) A mind full of love; (17) A mind full of desire to help; and (18) A mind full of compassion, which manifest themselves in the desire for others to be happy, dispassionate, and free from suffering; otherwise, with regard to the virtuous, the vicious, and the indifferent, by words full of love etc. respectively, and in a third way, by wishing others to attain Nirvana, to obtain full knowledge of the path that leads to it, and to understand completely the meaning of that which is to be taught.

The antidote against sinful thoughts of the second kind is: (19) Not to look for profit, honor, and praise, in rejecting the desire of such. And of the third: (20) Not to be inclined to arrogance and deprecation of others, that is to abandon the desire of being regarded as trustworthy, and to become free from envy.

Of these twenty methods, each group of five, respectively, shows: how, for whose sake, in what form, and by what kind of teacher the Doctrine is to be communicated, or otherwise, the course of the teaching, its work, the qualities of the speech, and those of the speaker. To follow these twenty methods and to avoid the [eleven] defects in speech is to be skillful in the way of expressing oneself.

150. Section 10.2.1.1.1.3 is taken directly from Buton, *Jewelry of Scripture*, 67. Kongtrul did not reproduce the quotation from the *Daśacakra-kṣitigarbha* which ends the section in Buton. It will be reproduced below.

151. Knowing the ayatanas, dhatus, and vasanas, means that the teacher knows the capacity, personality, and habitual tendencies of the student, and therefore is capable of applying the teaching based upon the needs of that student.

152. Buton, *Jewelry of Scripture*, 67-68, continues:

It is said in the *Daśacakra-kṣitigarbha:* "A worldling, with feeble faculties and indolent, who is not keen upon [the study of] the two Vehicles, will never come to master the teaching of the Mahayana, for he is not worthy of it."

And further on: "In the same way, if the adherents of the Śrāvaka Vehicle, unworthy of the Great One, come to hear the teaching of the latter, they will become confused, adhere to nihilistic views and fall into evil births. For this reason you must teach the Doctrine only after having examined the faculties of the hearers."

Again: "It is not proper to preach Hinayanistic Doctrines to one that is worthy of the Great Vehicle."

And: "Speak not of matters sublime and of profound meaning to one that adheres to the Small Vehicle. As [all these passages] show, thorough knowledge of the pupil's behavior or character is needed."

153. This section (10.2.1.1.2) on the two types of kindnesses comes from Buton, *Jewelry of Scripture*, 68. Kongtrul does not include the entire section, which continues:

It is said in the *Sūtrālaṃkāra:* "The powerful ones, with a joyful heart, ever and anon give away their lives and property, which are hard to obtain and of no real value, for the sake of the suffering living beings, thus practicing the highest form of charity. How much more will they do so in regard of the high Doctrine, which administers help to all that lives, always and in every way, is easy to obtain, increases the more you grant of it, and never becomes exhausted."

Now, if the teaching has not such a character, a great sin will be committed, namely that of trading with the Doctrine. We read in the *Mañjuśrī-vikurvāṇa-parivarta:* "If the Doctrine is expounded, but commiseration with regard to the pupils is wanting, it will be an action of the evil one, and if a teacher, being himself greatly learned, conceals parts of the Doctrine for fear that others should come to know them, this will be likewise an action of the evil one."

The *Saṃdhinirmocana* says: "Those that teach the Highest Doctrine out of desire [of gain], having got their wishes fulfilled, take birth again and again. These infatuated beings, though they are in possession of the invaluable jewel of the Doctrine, roam about, as if they were beggars."

Kongtrul merely summarizes this material with the sentence which follows.

154. This section (10.2.1.1.3) is identical to Buton, *Jewelry of Scripture*, 69, up to this point. Buton continues:

It is said, likewise, that tolerance is needed with regard to the faults made by the pupils. This may be fulfilled if one is possessed of that supernatural insight through which one comes to know the amount of help that is to be administered to others. If [this insight] is wanting, one must abstain from teaching to those that are not devoted to the Doctrine and to those that wear insignia, and to the following five [categories of persons, the teaching to whom is prohibited by the Vinaya] etc. Such persons will be always opposed to a teaching that humiliates them and become full of passion and hatred. Consequently, the teaching and study of the Doctrine that has such an unfavorable result cannot be of help for the attainment of felicity and salvation.

After Kongtru's next sentence, "With these three abilities the wisdom teacher will be able to embrace the disciple," he returns to Buton's discussion of this point.

155. See Buton, 69, for same quote.

156. Tg mDo LVI,138b6-139a3. This section is drawn from Buton, *Jewelry of Scripture*, 70, except that Buton refers to fourteen doors: "In the *Abhidharma-samuccaya*, four-teen, or from another point of view, six doors of teaching are mentioned...." The following examples of these "six doors" are found in Jinaputra's *Abhidharma-samuccaya-bhāṣya* (Tg mDo LVII, 129b6-8; see Obermiller's notes 665-668, pp. 163-164):

For example: (1) The subject is the skandhas, dhatus, and ayatanas. (2) They are all characterized by impermanence, suffering, and non-self. (3) The cause of knowing them is guarding the doors of the senses. (4) Thorough knowing refers to the thirty-seven dharmas which are the factors of awakening. (5) The result is liberation. (6) Higher knowing is the knowledge or vision of liberation. This means experiencing the result of the knowing.

In the next sentence Kongtrul makes reference to twelve doors, before returning to Buton's text in the following section (10.2.1.2.1.2) beginning, "In some texts..."

157. Buton, *Jewelry of Scripture*, describes fourteen doors:

The fourteen doors of teaching are: (1) The door of abridged explanation. (2) The door of concentration of teaching upon one subject. (3) The door of taking recourse to minute details. (4) The door of [communicating the different degrees of perfection, each of which is respectively the foundation of] higher and still higher [virtues]. (5) The door of exclusion [of all that does not come under the category in question]. (6) The door of changing the meaning of [ordinary] words [into technical terms]. (7) The door of demonstrating matters worldly and unworldly [in regard to each other]. (8) The door of indicating the individual [to whom one intends to teach]. (9) The door of analysis of the stuff [by quadrilemmas, etc.]. (10) The door of the six modes. [Obermiller states that the six modes are: *de-kho-na'i don gyi tshul; 'thob-pa'i tshul; bshad-pa'i tshul; mtha'-gnyis spangs-pa'i tshul; bsam gyis mi-khyab-pa'i tshul; dgongs-pa'i tshul*]. (11) The door of [enlarging upon] the full apprehension of the Truth etc. (12) The door of showing the power [of each word taken separately to indicate an idea], and the impotence [if one word is omitted, of the others to render the contents intelligible]. (13) The door of repeated teaching. (14) The door of evident proofs.

158. This section, up to 10.2.1.2.2, is taken directly from Buton, *Jewelry of Scripture*, 71.

159. For a good text and glossary on rhetoric in Tibetan Buddhism, see Daniel Perdue, *Debate in Tibetan Buddhism* (Ithaca: Snow Lion, 1992).

160. This refers to the sources used.

161. The wisdom teacher must be able to state his view in various ways. (Khenpo Tsultrim Gyamtso)

162. These are the three inabilities of a teacher. (Khenpo Tsultrim Gyamtso)

163. When the Buddha's teaching is provisional it is called *dgongs-pa can*. This is a characteristic of Buddha's speech from the Abhidharma onwards. An intended meaning is not literal or obvious. For example, "kill him" means kill the self-clinging. If a student has a doubt whether it should be taken literally or not, it can be clarified by a teacher using scripture and reasoning. (Khenpo Tsultrim Gyamtso)

164. Kongtrul summarizes Buton's handling of this material in *Jewelry of Scripture*, 71-72. Buton's complete explanation is as follows:

We read in the *Vyākhyāyukti:*

> Those that communicate the meaning of the Sūtras must explain it [having in view] the aim, the contents in abridged form, the meaning of the words, the connection between the parts, the objections [which may be met with] and the reply given to such.

The two last points are to be viewed together, in order that one may know how to give a good reply.

Having first come to know the aim of the sūtras, he that is devoted to the study and observation [of the Doctrine] must indicate their aim. As such is to be understood from a brief indication of the contents, one must give such, that is, demonstrate the body of a discourse or an exegetical treatise—words and sense—or, otherwise, the subject matter condensed. The latter is in its turn apprehended through the knowledge of the [precise] meaning of each word. Therefore, on the basis of the four methods of elucidating the meaning of a word, one has to explain so as to remove all doubt, and after having taken into consideration all the questions and refutations. Otherwise, one may explain the meaning of words by taking recourse to synonyms, homonyms, or to one of the many meanings of a word, by changing ordinary words into technical terms, or by changing the word itself, by omitting, for instance, negative particles etc. Moreover the *Vyākhyāyukti* says:

> The meaning of the words may be apprehended in four ways, namely by means of (1) synonyms, (2) definition, (3) etymology, and (4) the varieties [of the character of ideas expressed by such and such word].

Synonyms are other names [given to the same object], the definition is [the indication of] the meaning in which the word is used, and the etymology, that of the reason for using the term [in the sense which is applied to it]. Some consider that the etymology of a word does not explain its meaning, but this is not correct, because, according to Aprashibha when a word is explained, this can be done in eight different ways.

The due connection is the accordance between the preceding and the following as concerns the meaning and the order [of the words]; by it we know [that our speech] is not contradictory to the order in which one word is to follow the other in regard of its meaning. The absence of contradiction with regard to logic and disagreement between the preceding and the following is to be known from the objections that are made, and the answers given in return; therefore, having [always] in view an opponent who attacks words and sense, one must explain so as to render the latter completely certain and incontrovertible.

165. This refers to embellishing an important section in the text. It is alright to bring in quotes from other sutras to make the meaning clear. For example, one verse from *Discriminating the Middle from the Extremes* (*dBus-mtha' rnam-'byed; Madhyānta-vibhāga*) deals with that which is temporary. You may add that it also points to the luminous nature of the mind; in this case you can cite material from

another text that deals with the luminous nature of the mind. Therefore, if a subject is not clearly explained in this text, then you may go to another text in which the subject is extensively addressed. (Khenpo Tsultrim Gyamtso)

166. For example, *Discriminating the Middle from the Extremes* contains three main divisions and six subdivisions. One lays these out without contradiction between them. (Khenpo Tsultrim Gyamtso)

167. There can be three levels to a text: (1) Main divisions (*spyi-sdom*); (2) subdivisions (*nang-gses*); (3) branch divisions (*yan-lag*). For example, *Discriminating the Middle from the Extremes* is divided into three main divisions:

> 1) The unsurpassable practice (*sgrub-pa bla-na-med-pa*)
> 2) The unsurpassable focus (*dmigs-pa bla-na-med-pa*)
> 3) The unsurpassable correct accomplishment (*yang-dag 'grub-pa bla-na-me-pa*)

Under unsurpassable practice there are six subdivisions (*nang-gses*):

> 1) Genuine practice (*dam-pa'i sgrub-pa*)
> 2) Practice of mental cultivation (*yid-byed sgrub-pa*)
> 3) Practice in accordance with dharma (*rjes-su mthun-chos sgrub-pa*)
> 4) Practice of giving up the two extremes (*mtha' gnyis spangs-pa'i sgrub pa*)
> 5) Practice with a special trait (*khyed-par-can sgrub-pa*)
> 6) Practice without a special trait (*khyed-par-med sgrub-pa*)

Under the six divisions there are numerous branches (*yan-lag*). Each is divided clearly and brought together without mixing up the meaning. They are separated into parts and combined clearly. Show the connections between them without mixing the parts together, and also show them separately. (Khenpo Tsultrim Gyamtso)

168. Excellent qualities 2-6 are based upon the first excellent quality. (Khenpo Tsultrim Gyamtso)

169. The "general overview" means that you do not give a word-by-word explanation, just the topics in general. One goes through and extracts the important meanings, giving an overview of the text by abstracting the meaning: a précis, of each chapter. (Khenpo Tsultrim Gyamtso)

170. These are technical terms relating to how one works with the Sanskrit text in order to analyze it. (Khenpo Tsultrim Gyamtso)

171. For example, in *Discriminating the Middle from the Extremes*, vipashyana is explained by the ten unmistaken aspects.

172. The explanation is done with a mind which has generated bodhicitta.

173. *Thun-mong-pa mngon-pa* is the Abhidharma which is common to both Hinayana and Mahayana. *Thun-mong ma-yin-pa mngon-brjod* is the Abhidharma specific to the Mahayana.

174. For a discussion on being unmistaken about letters, see Maitreya/Asanga, *Discriminating the Middle from the Extremes* (*dBus-mtha' rnam-'byed; Madhyāntavibhāga*), chapter 5, 14-15.

175. "...the way in which they are joined" refers to case endings, such as the form the genitive takes: *gi, gyi,* or *kyi.*

176. "Like that" refers to the connection of the terms by case endings mentioned above.

177. "These things" refers to cause and result, and the other items of the list.

178. Buton, *Jewelry of Scripture,* 73, also follows with a discussion on how to teach the dharma in three sections, which Kongtrul did not use. According to Buton, one must teach having in view the students, the aim, and the manner of conducting the teaching. Kongtrul, although drawing from Buton, reorganized the sections. Therefore, Kongtrul has already discussed the character of teaching as regards the aim in section 10.2.1.2.2.1; and for the procedure of teaching, preparations are discussed under section 10.1.1.1, the teaching itself is located in section 10.2.1, and the conclusion is located in section 10.3.1.

The following is Buton's discussion (*Jewelry of Scripture,* 73) on how to teach with the student in view:

> To the students [possessed of] acute, mediocre and weak intellectual faculties, one must, respectively, explain briefly, moderately, and in detail, just as we have three kinds of Sūtras—the extensive, the intermediate, and the brief. In accordance with the [spiritual] family to which the student belongs, one has to teach Mahāyāna or Hinayāna doctrines, and with regard to the different wishes of the pupils, that which proves most suitable. It is said in the *Samādhirāja:*
>
> If they entreat you to grant the gift of the Doctrine your first reply must be, 'I have not studied enough. You all are wise and greatly learned, how dare I speak in the presence of such illustrious persons?'—so art thou to say. Never speak at once, but only when you see that [the hearer] is worthy. But if you know that, teach, even if they do not pray you to do so.
>
> If you should perceive, among the hearers, many that are of immoral conduct, do not preach to them abstinence, but sing the praise of charity. If there be [others] with scant desire, but who live in pure morality, arouse [in yourself] thoughts full of love and speak of abstinence. If those with sinful desires be few, and the virtuous are great in number, then take thou the part [of the latter] and sing the praise of pure morality.

179. Textual correction: Khenpo Tsultrim Gyamtso made a correction in the Peking Edition, 29, line 6: adding *ma* to form *'gal ma-'brel gcod.* He also confirmed that *gcod* goes with both *'gal* and *ma-'brel.*

180. From Franklin Edgerton, *Buddhist Hybrid Sanskrit Dictionary* (Delhi: Motilal Banarsidass, 1985), 232. This is a name of a disciple of the Buddha, found in the *Mūla-sarvāstivāda-vinaya* and the *Mahāvyutpatti.*

181. This means that the time of death is unknown.

182. "...in accord with holding oneself to be wealthy" means that you can see that you are special, because being "wealthy" refers to the buddha-nature inherent within all sentient beings.

183. "Faults" here refers not just to drowsiness, but also to being distracted, excited, etc.

184. See *Jewelry of Scripture*, 77, where Buton speaks of thirteen, six, and three faults. Also see Patrul Rinpoche, *Kun-zang La-may Zhal-lung*, 13-20, for the three faults and six defects, and the five misapprehensions.

185. This is a well-known statement the Buddha makes throughout the sutras.

186. For a detailed explanation of the three faults compared to the three types of vessels, see Patrul Rinpoche, *The Words of My Perfect Teacher*, 10-12. Buton, *Jewelry of Scripture*, 79-80, gives an alternative illustration of the three faults of the student as follows:

> A vessel in which one intends to gather water when it rains may have three defects, which render it unable to exercise its function. It may (1) be turned downward or closed with a lid, the water having no entrance, (2) be dirty, so that the water, though it enters, will become polluted, and (3) may have a hole and through this be unable to retain the water. In the same way, the vessel that does not receive the rain of the doctrine, when such descends, may be defective in three ways: (1) The hearer may not listen at all, being distracted or plunged in apathy, and [the word of the doctrine] will not reach him. (2) If one does not listen with due attention [the words of the doctrine], though they reach one, are in danger of being perverted. (3) If one is forgetful, that which has been heard will not be retained in memory. "As an antidote against all this," says the Lord, "study thoroughly and be attentive."
>
> Otherwise, we may compare [those that do not study as it is prescribed] to patients who do not understand the directions of the physician, to those that understand them wrongly, and to those who, though they have understood them, waste the remedy that is given to them. Again, they are like patients that do not eat when they should do so, like those that eat what is unwholesome, and like those who, though they have eaten wholesome food, vomit it back again. Therefore, the teacher that knows the character [of his students] must, if they become distracted, speak so as to frighten them [in showing them the fatal consequences of their behavior] as follows: "The age of man that endures a hundred years is reduced to the half by night's sleep, and if we sleep by day, likewise, even this half will be diminished." And to such that are overpowered by sleep, he must, in order to arouse their attention, tell curious and amusing tales of the ass and the foal, the lion and the fox, the elder-man and the woman, the old woman and the thief, of Paraśurāma etc.

187. This quote from the *rNam-bshad rigs-pa* is taken from Buton, *Jewelry of Scripture*, 78. Buton also gives an alternative list of six defects.

188. This quote from the *rNam-bshad rigs-pa* is also taken from Buton, *Jewelry of Scripture*, 77-78. Buton says:

> [We know] thirteen, six, and three defects that are to be avoided. The *Vyākhyāyukti* mentions sixteen methods of study that act as antidotes against thirteen defects. The latter are as follows: (1) Disturbing the

teacher when he contemplates the subject to be expounded, and inde-
cent behavior [in general]. (2) Showing arrogance, being proud of [one's
own] high birth, etc. (3) Showing no real desire to study. (4) Becoming
oppressed at heart by disagreeing views. (5) Having no regard for the
teacher; (6) and thinking how to make some objection in order to refute
him, both out of disrespect. (7) Want of reverence in having no consideration for the merits of the Doctrine and of him that teaches it. (8) Showing contempt for the Doctrine and the teacher by considering the former
to be unconnected speech and, as regards the latter, by finding fault with
him, his morals, behavior, outward appearance, the way of expressing
himself etc. (9) Using abusive language. (10) Looking to profit and honour.
(11) Not listening duly, being distracted or plunged in apathy and sleepiness. (12) Not comprehending duly, by having incorrect views of the
meaning and the essence of the Doctrine. (13) Not paying due attention,
one's desire [to study] and efforts being too feeble.

Buton, 78, now continues by giving two sets of six defects of a student. Kongtrul only reproduces the second set:

The *Vyākhyāyukti* says: "Arrogance, want of faith, absence of desire [to
study], distraction, apathy, and lassitude, such may be the defects of the
student."

Otherwise [we distinguish]: (1) The defects of one's acts, (2) absence
of faith, (3) disrespect, (4) inappropriate thoughts, (5) discord, and
(6) the defects in apprehending.

Next Buton, 78, comments upon the latter list of six faults (which is the list
found in Kongtrul, unglossed):

As concerns the defects in one's actions, such may be corporeal—im-
moral behavior; oral and corporeal—not making the due efforts with
both body and speech; and mental—want of desire to study. The defects
that consist in inappropriate thoughts are to seek brawls and to think
how to escape a controversy. The defects [arising from] discord are five
in number, absence of reverence for the Doctrine by not taking it to be
the path that leads to salvation; and for the word of it, considering such
to be unconnected speech, etc.; disregard for the teacher, by finding fault
with him, his conduct and the manner of teaching; contempt for [the
teacher's] descent; and, last of all, self-deprecation, in thinking oneself
unable to understand the meaning of the doctrine and to act according
to the latter.

The defects in apprehending are likewise five: apprehending wrongly,
getting no clear conception of the meaning, misunderstanding the words,
disregarding the grammatical forms, and getting no full apprehension
[of the matter].

189. This includes things such as sticking one's legs out in the direction of the
lama, etc. (Khenpo Tsultrim Gyamtso)

190. *bSam-pa* refers to negative intention (*mi-bsam-pa*). This is confirmed by the
quotation from the *rNams-bshad rigs-pa* above. *Mi* is missing from the text, p. 30,
9 lines from the bottom. (Khenpo Tsultrim Gyamtso)

191. From Cleary, *Flower Ornament*, 326-327:

> Think of yourself as sick, and think of spiritual benefactors as physicians; think of their instructions as medicines, and think of the practices as getting rid of disease. Think of yourself as a traveler, and think of spiritual benefactors as guides; think of their instructions as the road, and think of the practices as going to the land of your destination. Think of yourself as crossing over to the other shore, and think of spiritual benefactors as boatmen; think of their instructions as a ford, and think of the practices as a boat. Think of yourself as a farmer, and think of spiritual benefactors as water spirits; think of their instructions as rain, and think of the practices as the ripening of the crops. Think of yourself as a pauper, and think of spiritual benefactors as the givers of wealth; think of their instructions as wealth, and think of the practices as getting rid of poverty. Think of yourself as an apprentice, and think of spiritual benefactors as mentors; think of their instructions as arts, and think of the practices as accomplishments. Think of yourself as fearless, and think of spiritual benefactors as heroic warriors; think of their instructions as attack, and think of the practices as vanquishing enemies. Think of yourself as a merchant, and think of spiritual benefactors as ship captains; think of their instructions as treasure, and think of their practices as obtaining treasures. Think of yourself as a good son, and think of spiritual benefactors as parents; think of their instructions as the family business. Think of yourself as a prince, and think of spiritual benefactors as the chief ministers of a spiritual king; think of their instructions as the precepts of kingship, and think of the practices as putting on the turban of truth adorned with the crest of knowledge and overseeing the capital of the spiritual sovereign.

192. Buton and Kongtrul use different schemata. Buton first divides the discussion into an explanation of the various topics in regard to the teacher, then an explanation of the various topics in regard to the student. Kongtrul discusses both the teacher and the student together under each topic. Therefore, Kongtrul is now combining and summarizing material found in two different sections of Buton's work. In regard to the teacher having the six perfections Buton, *Jewelry of Scripture*, 76, writes:

> The chief foundations of teaching must be six in number, corresponding to the six transcendental virtues, as follows: (1) Delivering the words and meaning according to one's own conception [charity]; (2) suppressing the sinful acts of the three media [morality]; (3) enduring heat, cold, and other odds [patience]; (4) perseverance in teaching [energy]; (5) concentration of the mind upon the subject of the latter [concentration]; (6) analysis in regard to the words and sense, as to their contradiction or right connection, etc. [analytic wisdom].
>
> The teacher Haribhadra says [the harmony with the six transcendental virtues is attained by]: (1) Granting the gift of the Doctrine etc. [charity]. (2) becoming free from thoughts that characterize a Hinayanist [morality]; (3) enduring harsh words from all those with whom one chances to meet [patience]; (4) arousing the desire to study [energy]; (5) bringing

about the concentration of mind [to a degree] which cannot be attained if one is a follower of other vehicles [concentration]; (6) clothing those that strive for Supreme Enlightenment in the armor of non-perception of the reality of separate entities (highest wisdom).

In regard to the student, Buton, 85, later writes:

[The study itself] must be in harmony with the six transcendental virtues. [One must]: (1) Consecrate the three media to the service of the Doctrine [charity]; (2) suppress sinful inclinations and remove all the defects [that hinder one to become] a worthy receptacle of the Doctrine [morality]; (3) endure odds [patience]; (4) be zealous in study [energy]; (5) concentrate the mind on words and sense [concentration]; (6) [as concerns the climax of wisdom, distinguish]: The highest degree, the attainment of transcendental knowledge; the intermediate, apprehension, preservation in memory, and analysis, in following the word; and the lowest, the five immeasurable feelings.

193. This is a general prayer which is used in numerous texts. (Khenpo Tsultrim Gyamtso)

194. This is a common dedication prayer:

Sod-nams 'di-yi thams-cas gzigs-pa nyid
Thob-nas nyes-pa'i dgra-rnams pham-byas shing
sKye rga na 'chi'i rba klong 'khrugs-pa yi
bSrid-pa'i mtsho las 'gro-ba sgrol-bar shog.

By this merit may we become omniscient;
From this attainment, after defeating all enemies that are our faults
Through the endless storm of birth, old age, sickness, and death,
May we liberate all beings from the ocean of existence.

195. Tg dBu-ma 3871.

196. Buton, *Jewelry of Scripture*, 85, lists three things to be done by the student, without commenting on them.

197. Mindfulness (*dran-pa; smṛti*). Vigilance (*shes-bzhin; saṃprajanya*). See discussions in: Batchelor, *Bodhisattva's Way of Life*, chapters 4-5, pp. 29-59; Guenther, *Jewel Ornament*, 228, note 35. Namgyal, *Mahāmudrā*, 22, offers this on *dran-pa*:

On the nature of memory the *Abhidharma-samuccaya* states: 'What is memory (*dran-pa*)? Memory is not forgetting things one has familiarized oneself with; its function is to effect an undistracted concentration.' Memory means not being distracted from a familiar mental image. The mind sustains the image vividly without lapse.

Quite often *dran-pa* is translated as "mindfulness." Namgyal, 424, explains in his notes that,

Although in this case the term 'memory' is used, its definition is applicable to the popular 'mindfulness.' The latter is preferred by most teachers and scholars, since it indicates a continued mental focus on any chosen object (either concrete, abstract, or formless) and on the precepts as well as the enlightened qualities.

Vigilance (*shes-bzhin*) is also defined by Namgyal, 22-23:

> With regard to vigilance the commentary on the *Madhyānta-vibhāga* says: 'Vigilance may be achieved [during meditation] by not forgetting the object of concentration while remaining fully attentive to any emerging distraction such as dullness, sensual incitement, or thought. With such a stream of awareness one remains on guard, forever watching and discerning any distraction upon its arising.'

198. Kg 'Dul-ba 3: *'Dul-ba rnam-par-'byed-pa; Vinaya-vibhaṅga.*

199. After receiving these instructions the student can guide herself through these meditations without needing further instructions from the wisdom teacher. "Dam-ngag" (*gdams-ngag*) are the instructions on how to meditate on the above four points, and "dependent on another wisdom teacher"(*rjes-su bstan-pa gzhan*) refers to increasing the understanding and meditation on these four topics. Meditation on these four topics are, then, not dependent on a wisdom teacher, because if you have become skilled in it you can do it on your own. For instance, once you have the outline and the subdivisions of the five skandhas you receive instructions on how to meditate on this. Upon becoming very skilled you can practice on your own. (Khenpo Tsultrim Gyamtso)

200. The six super-knowledges are: (1) Divine sight (*lha'i spyan*); (2) divine hearing (*lha'i nyan*); (3) knowledge of minds of others (*pha-rol gyi sems shes-pa*); (4) recollection of past lives (*sngon-gyi-nas rjes-su-dran-pa shes-pa*); (5) ability to perform miracles (*rdzu-'phrul gyi bya-ba shes-pa*); (6) knowledge of the exhaustion of defilements (*zag-pa zad-pa shes-pa*).

201. Toh 69: *Lhag-pa'i bsam-pa bskul-ba; Adhyāśaya-sañcodana.*

202. This refers to moral discipline.

203. This refers to the five hindrances (*grib-pa lnga*): Sense desire (*'dod-pa la 'dun-pa*), ill-will (*gnod-sems*), sloth and torpor (*rmugs-pa; gnyid*), excitedness and sense of guilt (*rgod-pa; 'gyod-pa*), and doubt (*the-tshom*).

204. Buton, *Jewelry of Scripture*, 85-86, also concludes his instructions for the student by emphasizing the need to combine study with practice. He states:

> In order that study and analysis might have an effective result, he that has studied and gives himself up to analysis, must live in pure morality and practice profound meditation. Accordingly, pure morals are needed in order to act as a support [for one who is to realize the aim of the Doctrine]. It is said in the *Samādhirāja:* "If he that has become well versed in numerous works on the Doctrine is proud of his knowledge and does not preserve his morals, he will not be able to save others by his great learning, and, morally impure, he is doomed to hell."
> [Accordingly] extensive study must always be connected with pure morals and analysis of the meaning and profound meditation. It is said in a passage of scripture concerning the monks who have got a firm stand in the principles of the Doctrine: By study and analysis only, without the practice of meditation, one is unable to get a firm stand in the Doctrine. Likewise is this impossible if one merely practices meditation

and does not take recourse to study and investigation. But if both parts [study on one side and analysis and meditation on the other] are resorted to and accepted as a foundation, one gets a firm stand in the Doctrine.

205. This refers to approaching any sacred place.

206. This may refer to the seventeen faults of speaking, which Buton quotes from the *Sutra That Arouses Superior Intention* (*Lhag-pa'i bsam-pa bskul-ba; Adhyāśaya-sañcodana*). Buton, *Jewelry of Scripture*, 87-90, states:

It is said in the *Adhyāśaya-sañcodana-sūtra*:

1) Proud of one's great learning, one is full of disregard [toward others], indulges in dispute and controversy, is forgetful and has no clear understanding. Such are the defects of he who takes delight in inane oratory.

2) One is far from having deep thoughts, one's outward appearance and mind lose their serenity as one is [alternatively] subjected to great arrogance and humiliation. Such are the defects of he who takes delight in inane oratory.

3) The worldling loses all consideration for the highest Doctrine, is harsh and has no thoughts of love, and is far from [possessing] śamatha and vipaśyana. Such are the defects of he who takes delight in inane oratory.

4) He is always irreverent in regards to the gurus, and, finding pleasure in obscene tales, pays attention to that which is worthless, and becomes destitute of high wisdom. Such are the defects of he who takes delight in inane oratory.

5) He is not esteemed by the gods and the spirits, nor has he any desire to obtain [such esteem], and, as to correct knowledge, he possesses none. Such are the defects of he who takes delight in inane oratory.

6) He is always reproved by the wise to whom his nature is perfectly clear; his life passes away in vain. Such are the defects of he who takes delight in inane oratory.

7) He is wavering like grass agitated [by the wind], is always full of doubt, and never may call a firm conviction his own. Such are the defects of he who takes delight in inane oratory.

8) Like an actor on the stage that speaks of the heroism of others, he has no prowess of his own. Such are the defects of he who takes delight in inane oratory.

9) He becomes fraudulent and easily loses hope, and again and again he enters upon dispute and controversy, and draws far from the noble dharma of the saint. Such are the defects of he who takes delight in inane oratory.

10) Feeble in strength, one rejoices to praise, and destitute of right knowledge, trembles when abused, one's mind is fickle like a monkey. Such are the defects of he who takes delight in inane oratory.

11) As one's mind is not possessed of correct knowledge, one commits errors or depends on others, and [finally] falls prey to the passions. Such are the defects of he who takes delight in inane oratory.

12) One's visual sense is deluded and so is the auditory, the olfactory sense errs and so does the gustatory, the tactile sense and the intellect are likewise erring. Such are the defects of he who takes delight in inane oratory.

13) One's mind being always in the power of auditory sensation, one is intoxicated by [well-sounding] words and acquires no true knowledge, thinks incorrectly and enters upon evil paths. Such are the defects of he who takes delight in inane oratory.

Having described [all these defects, the sūtra continues]:

14) Having for a long time found pleasures in fine words, one does not obtain real satisfaction, for it is better to ponder over [the meaning of] one word, through which one may obtain infinite joy.

15) The bark of the sugar cane [by itself] has no value, for that which gives pleasure, its sweet juice, is contained within. If one eats only the bark, one is not able to taste the exquisite juice of sugar.

16) The [mere] words [by themselves] are like the bark, and the meaning contained in them like the sweet juice. Therefore, having ceased to find pleasure in [the mere sound of] fine words, ponder over the meaning and always be attentive.

All these methods [of studying and preaching the Doctrine], Buton with the large mouth who has studied much, but has neither realized that which he has learned nor accumulated the factors [for attaining salvation], has written down. May he [nevertheless] by [the force of] previous virtues, after his death, which will soon take place, partake of Maitreya's religious feast in the regions of Tuṣita. Finished is the investigation of the methods of study and teaching, the first chapter of the *History of Buddhism,* entitled *The Jewelry of Scripture.*

207. "…and so forth" refers to wisdom. These are the three higher trainings and refer to practicing the dharma.

208. This quote is also found in Buton, *Jewelry of Scripture,* 86.

Appendix I: Outline of Kongtrul's Chapter on the Teacher-Student Relationship

Compiled by the Translator

1. How to seek the wisdom teacher
1.1 The dharma is the source of all benefit
1.2 Have faith and engage in the teaching
1.3 Attaining full enlightenment depends upon approaching, follow
ing, and respecting the wisdom teacher

2. The justification for following a wisdom teacher
2.1 Justification by way of scriptural authority
2.2 Justification by way of reason
2.3 Justification by means of example

3. Categories and characteristics of the master who should be followed
3.1 General explanation
3.1.1 General categories
3.1.2 General characteristics
3.2 Specific explanation
3.2.1 Specific categories
3.2.2 Individual characteristics
3.2.2.1 The pratimoksha master
3.2.2.2 The master of the bodhisattva vow
3.2.2.3 The mantra master

4. The way in which one enters into and goes astray—which follows
from the characteristics of the master

5. The characteristics of the student who follows
5.1 Those who should follow
5.1.1 The suitable vessel of the pratimoksha vow
5.1.2 The suitable vessel of the bodhisattva vow
5.1.3 The suitable vessel of the mantrayana
5.2 The explanation of the things to be abandoned along with their subsidiaries

6. How to follow
6.1 At first, examine the relationship
6.2 Then follow
6.2.1 Attitude
6.2.2 Application: the manner of honoring the wisdom teacher
6.2.2.1 Giving material things and honoring the wisdom teacher
6.2.2.2 Offering your services
6.2.2.3 Follow in terms of practice

7. The necessity of following the wisdom teacher in that way
7.1 Establish the necessity by proof
7.2 The advantages as explained in the scriptures

8. Avoiding contrary, harmful companions
8.1 Obstructions of a harmful teacher
8.2 The obstructions of mara

9. Creating faith as a favorable condition

10. The way that the teacher should explain and the student should listen to the holy dharma
10.1 What should be done as preparation
10.1.1 What should be done on the part of the master in regard to preparation
10.1.1.1 Making arrangements
10.1.1.2 Annihilating mara
10.1.1.3 The master should purify his behavior
10.1.2 What should be done by the student in regard to preparation
10.1.2.1 Offering a pure gift
10.1.2.2 Follow with respectful conduct
10.1.2.3 Meditatively cultivate joy in the favorable conditions you have accumulated
10.2 The main subject matter
10.2.1 The master explains well
10.2.1.1 The characteristics of explaining
10.2.1.1.1 Wisdom related to being knowledgeable
10.2.1.1.1.1 Being knowledgeable in the subject
10.2.1.1.1.2 Being knowledgeable in teaching
10.2.1.1.1.3 Being knowledgeable in conduct
10.2.1.1.2 Attitude of loving kindness

10.2.1.1.3 Possessed with patient practice
10.2.1.2 The method of explanation based upon whatever the object
10.2.1.2.1 The explanation in general
10.2.1.2.1.1 Explain the dharma utilizing six doors
10.2.1.2.1.2 Explain the dharma utilizing three doors
10.2.1.2.1.3 Explain the dharma utilizing two doors
10.2.1.2.1.4 Chimpa claims that explaining the dharma is to:
10.2.1.2.1.3.1 Teach the meaning
10.2.1.2.1.3.2 Explain the text
10.2.1.2.1.3.3 Make it certain
10.2.1.2.2 The explanation divided into particulars
10.2.1.2.2.1 The purpose of the teaching
10.2.1.2.2.2 The synopsis
10.2.1.2.2.2.1 Synopsis of the words
10.2.1.2.2.2.2 The individual synopsis
10.2.1.2.2.3 The literal meaning
10.2.1.2.2.4 The connections
10.2.1.2.2.4.1 The connection of the words
10.2.1.2.2.4.2 The connection of the meaning
10.2.1.2.2.5 Objections and responses
10.2.1.3 How to teach the dharma
10.2.2 The way in which the student listens with devotion
10.2.2.1 Remove the three faults
10.2.2.2 Remove the six stains
10.2.2.3 Listen with the proper frame of mind
10.2.3 Both should be endowed with the six perfections
10.3 What should be done afterwards
10.3.1 What should be done by the teacher
10.3.1.1 Ask for forgiveness for faults
10.3.1.2 Dedicate virtue to enlightenment
10.3.1.3 The extensive offering, which is objectless
10.3.2 What should be done by the student
10.3.2.1 Offer a gift which is an offering of thanks
10.3.2.2 Dedicate virtue to enlightenment.
10.3.2.3 Rely on the continuity of mindfulness and vigilance
10.4 Mentioning the advantages of explaining, listening, and so forth
10.4.1 General advantages
10.4.2 Specific advantages
10.4.2.1 Advantages of listening to the dharma
10.4.2.2 Advantages of explaining the dharma
10.4.2.3 Advantages of grasping the meaning of the dharma
10.4.2.4 Advantages of participating in listening and explaining
10.4.2.5 Putting the dharma which is comprehended into practice
10.4.2.6 Advantages of intermingling listening to teachings and then practicing

Appendix II: Tibetan and Sanskrit Works Cited in Kongtrul's Text

Abhidharmakosha
Chos-mngon-pa'i mdzod
Abhidharmakośa
Vasubandhu

Alternating Praises
sPel-mar bstod-pa
Matricheta and Dignaga

The Blazing Gem: The Wisdom Mind of the Five Hundred Thousand
    Tantras
rGyud 'bum-lnga'i dgongs-pa rin-chen 'bar-ba
Scripture

The Bodhisattva's Way of Life
Byang-chub sems-dpa'i spyod-pa la 'jug-pa
Bodhisattva-caryāvatāra
Shantideva

Buddha-Avatamsaka Sutra
Sangs-rgyas phal-po-che'i mdo
Buddhāvataṃsaka Sūtra
Scripture

Buddhaguhya's Gradual Path
Sangs-rgyas gsang-ba'i lam-rim
Buddhaguhya

Chakrasamvara Tantra
dPal bde-mchog 'byung-ba shes-bya-ba'i rgyud-kyi rgyal-po chen po
Śri-mahāsaṃbarodaya-tantrarāja
Scripture

The Changeless Nature
Theg pa chen po'i rgyud bla ma'i bstan bcos
Mahāyānottaratantra-śāstra
Maitreya/Asanga

The Collection of High Utterances
Ched-du brjod-pa'i tshom
Udānavarga
Scripture

Compendium
sDud-pa
Ratnaguṇa-saṃcayagāthā

Compendium Tantra
bsDus-pa'i rgyud (full title: *mChog gi dang-po'i sangs-rgyas las phyung-ba*
    rgyud kyi rgyal-po dpal dus-kyi-'khor-lo)
Paramādi-buddhoddhṛta-Śri-kālacakra-nāma-tantrarāja
Scripture

Compendium of Knowledge
Chos-mngon-pa kun-btus
Abhidharma-samuccaya
Asanga

Commentary to the Compendium of Knowledge
Chos mngon-pa kun-las-btus-pa'i bshad-pa
Abhidharma-samuccaya-bhāṣya
Asanga

The Commentary on the Bodhisattva
Byang-chub sems-dpa'i 'grel-pa
Pundarika

Consecration Tantra
Rab-tu gnas-pa mdor-bsdus-pa'i rgyud
Supratiṣṭha-tantra-saṃgraha
Scripture

Discriminating the Middle from the Extremes
dBus-mtha' rnam-'byed
Madhyānta-vibhāga
Maitreya/Asanga

Dombipa's Ten Verses on the Essentials of the Sphere of Wisdom Mind
Gur-gyi dgongs-pa Dom-bi-pa'i de-nyid bcu
Dombipa

Door Entering into the Dharma
Chos-la 'jug-pa'i sgo
Sönam Tsemo

Entering into the Conduct of the Bodhisattva
'Byang-chub sems-dpa'i spyod-pa-la 'jug-pa
Bodhisattva-caryāvatāra
Shantideva

The Essence of Mahamudra
Phyag-chen thig-le
Scripture

The Fifty Stanzas on Guru Devotion
bLa-ma nga-bcu-pa
Ashvaghosha

The Five Stages
Rim-pa lnga-pa
Pañcakrama
Nagarjuna

The Four Hundred
bsTan-bcos bzhi-brgya-pa zhes-bya-ba'i tshig le'ur byas-pa
Catuḥśataka-śāstra-kārikā
Aryadeva

The General Tantra
sPyi-rgyud
Scripture

The Great Commentary to the Root Sutra
mDo-rtsa'i 'grel-chen
Dharmamrita

The Guhyasamaja-tantra
gSang-ba dus-pa
Guhyasamāja-tantra
Scripture

Jataka Tales
sKyes-rab
Jātakamālā
Aryashura

Kalachakra Root Tantra
Dus-'khor rtsa-rgyud
Kālacakra-mūlatantra
Scripture

A Letter to a Friend
bShes-pa'i spring-yig
Suhṛllekha
Nagarjuna

The Life Story of Gyalpo Mi
rGyal-po mi'i rnam-thar

The Life Story of Paljung
dPal-byung-gi rnam-thar
Śrīsaṃbhava
Scripture

The Life Story of Upasika Acala
dGe-bsnyen-ma mi-g.yo-ba
Scripture

The Lotus Sutra
Dam-chos pad-ma dkar-po
Saddharma-puṇḍarika
Scripture

Magical Display
rGyud-kyi rgyal-po chen-po sgyu-'phrul dra-ba'i rgya-cher-bshad-pa
Māyājāla-mahātantra-rājaṭīkā-ākhya
Scripture

The Noble Eight Thousand Verse Perfection of Wisdom Sutra
'Phags-pa brgyad-stong-pa
Aṣṭasāhasrikā-prajñāpāramitā
Scripture

The Oral Instructions of My Excellent Lama
sNying-thig sngon-'gro'i khrid-yig kun-bzang bla-ma'i zhal-lung
Patrul Rinpoche

The Ornament of the Mahayana Sutras
mDo-sde rgyan
Mahāyāna-sūtrālaṃkāra
Maitreya/Asanga

An Ornament to Precious Liberation
Dam-chos yid-bzhin nor-bu thar-pa rin-po-che'i rgyan
Gampopa

Precious Garland
Rin-chen phreng-ba
Ratnamālā
Nagarjuna

Precious Talala Sutra
dKon-mchog ta-la-la'i gzungs zhes-bya-ba theg-pa chen-po'i mdo
Ratnolkā-nāma-dhāraṇī-mahāyāna-sūtra
Scripture

Principles of Elucidation
rNam-bshad rigs-pa
Vyākhyāyukti
Vasubandhu

Resting in the Nature of Mind
Sems-nyid ngal-gso
Kun Khyen Longchenpa

Scripture on Discernment
'Dul-ba rnam-par-'byed-pa
Vinaya-vibhaṅga
Scripture

Secret Teachings of the Tathagatas
De-bzhin gshegs-pa'i gsang-ba bstan-pa
Tathāgata-acintya-guhya-nirdeśa
Scripture

The Stages of the Bodhisattva
Byang-chub sems-dpa'i sa
Bodhisattva-bhūmi
Asanga

Sutra Arranged Like a Tree
sDong-po bkod-pa'i mdo
Gaṇḍavyūha-sūtra
Scripture

Sutra That Arouses Superior Intention
Lhag-pa'i bsam-pa bskul-ba
Adhyāśaya-sañcodana
Scripture

Sutra of the Meeting of the Father and the Son
Yab-sras mjal-ba'i mdo
Pitā-putra-samāgamana-sūtra
Scripture

Sutra of Vast Display
Phags-pa rgya-che rol-pa
Lalitavistara
Scripture

Sutra Requested by Sagaramati the Naga King
bLo-'gro rgya-mtshos zhus-pa'i mdo
Sāgaramati-paripṛcchā-sūtra
Scripture

Sutra Requested By Subahu
Lag-bzangs kyis zhus-pa'i mdo
Subahu-paripṛccha-sūtra
Scripture

Sutra of the Ten Noble Dharmas
Chos-bcu-pa'i mdo
Daśadharmaka-sūtra
Scripture

Sutra of the True Dharma of Clear Recollection
mDo dran-pa nyer-bzhag
Saddharma-smṛtyupasthāna
Scripture

Sutra on the Inconceivable Secret
De-bzhin-gshegs-pa'i gsang-ba bsam-gyis mi-khyab-pa bstan-pa
Tathāgata-acintya-guhya-nirdeśa
Scripture

Tattvasarasamgraha
De-kho-na-nyid kyi snying-po bsdus-pa
Tattva-sāra-saṃgraha
Scripture

The Three Hundred Verses
Sum-brgya-pa
Shakyaprabha

The Ultimate Service
Don-dam-pa'i bsnyen-pa
Śrī-Paramārthasevā
Pundarika

Vajra Essence Ornament
rDo-rje snying-po rgyan
Vajrahṛdayālaṃkāra
Scripture

Vajra Garland
rNal-'byor chen-po'i rgyud dpal rdo-rje phreng-ba mngon-par brjod-pa rgyud
    thams-cad-kyi snying-po gsang-ba rnam-par phye-ba
Vajra-mālā-abhidhāna-mahāyogatantra-sarva-tantra-hṛdaya-rahasya-
    vibhaṅga
Scripture

Vajrapani Empowerment Tantra
Lag-na rdo-rje dbang-bskur-ba'i rgyud
Vajrapāṇi-abhiṣeka-mahātantra
Scripture

Vinaya Scripture
'Dul-ba lung bla-ma'i bye-brag lung zu-ba'i 'grel-pa
Vinayāgamottara-viśeṣāgama-praśnavṛtti
Scripture

Bibliography

Ashvaghosha. "Fifty Stanzas of Guru Devotion." In *The Mahāmudrā: Eliminating the Darkness of Ignorance*, by The Ninth Karmapa Wang-Ch'ug Dor-je. Dharamsala: Library of Tibetan Works and Archives, 1989.

Atiśa. *A Lamp for the Path and Commentary.* Translated by Richard Sherburne, S.J. London: George Allen & Unwin, 1983.

Beyer, Stephan. *The Classical Tibetan Language.* Albany: State University of New York Press, 1992.

——. *The Cult of Tara: Magic and Ritual in Tibet.* Berkeley: University of California Press, 1978.

Chang, Garma C.C., trans. *The Hundred Thousand Songs of Milarepa.* 2 vols. Boulder: Shambhala, 1977.

——. *A Treasury of Mahayana Sutras.* University Park: Pennsylvania State University Press, 1983.

Chokyi Nyima Rinpoche. *The Union of Mahamudra and Dzogchen.* Hong Kong: Rangjung Yeshe Publications, 1989.

Cleary, Thomas, trans. *The Flower Ornament Scripture.* Vol. 3. Boston: Shambhala, 1987.

Conze, Edward. *Buddhist Studies: 1934-1972.* San Francisco: Wheelwright Press, 1967.

——. *Buddhist Thought in India.* Ann Arbor: The University of Michigan Press, 1973.

——. *Buddhist Wisdom Books: The Diamond and the Heart Sutra.* London: Unwin Paperbacks, 1988.

——. *Large Sutra on Perfect Wisdom.* Delhi: Motilal Banarsidass, 1990.

——. *The Perfection of Wisdom in Eight Thousand Lines*. San Francisco: Four Seasons Foundations, 1973.

Dalai Lama, The Third. *Essence of Refined Gold*. Translated by Glenn H. Mullin. Ithaca: Snow Lion, 1985.

Das, Sarat Chandra. *A Tibetan-English Dictionary*. Kyoto: Rinsen Book Company, 1983.

Dilgo Khyentse. *The Excellent Path to Enlightenment*. Ithaca: Snow Lion, 1996.

——. *The Heart Treasure of the Enlightened Ones*. Translated by the Padmakara Translation Group. Boston: Shambhala, 1992.

——. *The Wishfufilling Jewel: The Practice of Guru Yoga According to the Longchen Nyingthig Tradition*. Translated by Könchog Tenzin. Boston: Shambhala, 1988.

Douglas, Nik and Meryl White, eds. *Karmapa: The Black Hat Lama of Tibet*. London: Luzac & Company, 1976.

Dowman, Keith. *Masters of Mahamudra*. Albany: State University of New York Press, 1985.

——. *Sky Dancer: The Secret Life and Songs of the Lady Yeshe Tsogyel*. London: Routledge and Kegan Paul, 1984.

Dudjom Rinpoche. *Perfect Conduct: Ascertaining the Three Vows*. Boston: Wisdom Publications, 1996.

Edgerton, Franklin. *Buddhist Hybrid Sanskrit Grammar and Dictionary*. 2 vols. Delhi: Motilal Banarsidass, 1985.

Evans-Wentz, W.Y., ed. *Tibet's Great Yogi, Milarepa*. London: Oxford University Press, 1969.

Gampopa (mNyam-med dwags-po rin-po-che). *Dam-chos yid-bzhin nor-bu tharpa rin-po-che'i rgyan dang zhal-gdams rin-po-che phreng-ba, The Jewel Ornament of Liberation: The Precious Garland of the Supreme Path by Gampopa*. Rumtek, Sikkim: The Students' Welfare Union of Karma Shri Nalanda Institute, 1991.

——. *The Jewel Ornament of Liberation*. Translated by Herbert Guenther. Boulder: Prajna Press, 1981.

dGe-'dun Chos-'phel, trans. from Pali to Tibetan. *Dhammapada*. Translated into English by Dharma Publishing Staff. Berkeley: Dharma Publishing, 1985.

Govinda, Lama Anagarika. *Creative Meditation and Multi-Dimensional Consciousness*. Wheaton: The Theosophical Publishing House, 1976.

——. *Foundations of Tibetan Mysticism*. York Beach: Samuel Weiser, Inc. 1982.

Guenther, Herbert V. *The Life and Teaching of Naropa*. Boston: Shambhala, 1963.

——. *Tibetan Buddhism in Western Perspective*. Emeryville: Dharma Publishing, 1977.

Holmes, Ken, ed. *Dzalendara and Sakarchupa*. Translated by Katia Holmes. Scotland: Kagyu Samye, 1981.

Hopkins, Jeffrey. *Meditation on Emptiness*. London: Wisdom Publications, 1983.

——. *The Precious Garland and The Song of the Four Mindfulnesses*. New York: Harper & Row, 1975.

Hookham, S.K. *The Buddha Within*. Albany: State University of New York Press, 1991.

Hurvitz, Leon. *Scripture of the Lotus Blossom of the Fine Dharma*. New York: Columbia University Press, 1976.

Jamgön Kongtrul Lodrö Thayé. *Buddhist Ethics*. Translated by the International Translation Committee. Ithaca: Snow Lion, 1998.

——. *The Great Path of Awakening: A Commentary on the Mahayana Teaching of the Seven Points of Mind Training*. Translated by Ken McLeod. Boston: Shambhala, 1987.

——. *Jamgon Kongtrul's Retreat Manual*. Translated and introduced by Ngawang Zangpo. Ithaca: Snow Lion, 1994.

——. *Kongtrul's Encyclopaedia of Indo-Tibetan Culture*. Parts 1-3. Edited by Dr. Lokesh Chandra. New Delhi: International Academy of Indian Culture, 1970.

——. Kong-sprul Yon-tan rGya-mtsho. *Shes-bya Kun-khyab*. Lhasa: Mi-rigs dPe-skrun-khang, 1982.

——. *Myriad Worlds*. Translated by the International Translation Committee of Kunkhyab Chöling. Ithaca: Snow Lion, 1995.

——. *The Torch of Certainty*. Translated by Judith Hanson. Boston: Shambhala Publications, 1977.

Kalu Rinpoche. *The Dharma: That Illuminates All Beings Impartially Like the Light of the Sun and the Moon*. Albany: State University of New York Press, 1986.

——.*The Gem Ornament of Manifold Oral Instructions: Which Benefits Each and Everyone Appropriately*. San Francisco: KDK Publications, 1986.

Karma Thinley. *The History of the Sixteen Karmapas of Tibet*. Boulder: Prajna Press, 1980.

Karmapa Wang-Ch'ug Dor-je, The Ninth. *The Mahāmudrā: Eliminating the Darkness of Ignorance*. Translated and edited by Alexander Berzin. Dharamsala: Library of Tibetan Works and Archives, 1989.

Kat, Bunn. *The Threefold Lotus Sutra*. Tokyo: Kosei Publishing Co., 1988.

Lama Tharchin. *A Commentary on the Dudjom Tersar Ngondro*. Corralitos: Vajrayana Foundation, 1994.

Lessing, F.D. and Alex Wayman. *Introduction to the Buddhist Tantric Systems*. Delhi: Motilal Banarsidass, 1983. Previously titled *mKhas grub rje's Fundamentals of the Buddhist Tantras*. The Hague: Mouton, 1968.

Lhalungpa, Lobsang, trans. *The Life of Milarepa*. Boston & London: Shambhala, 1985.

Lipman, Kennard. *You Are the Eyes of the World.* Novato: Lotsawa, 1973.

Longchenpa. *Kindly Bent to Ease Us, Part 1.* Translated by Herbert V. Guenther. Berkeley: Dharma Publishing, 1975.

———. *Sems-nyid ngal-gso.* In *Ngal gso skor gsum, Rang grol skor gsum, and sNgags kyi spyi don: Structured Presentations of Nyingmapa Dzogchen Theory and Practice by Kun-khyen Klong-chen-pa dri-med-'od-zer.* Reproduced from a set of prints from the *A-'dzom 'brug-pa chos-sgar* blocks by the Ven. Dodrup Chen Rinpoche, vol. 1. Gangtok, India: 1973.

Maitreya/Asanga. *The Changeless Nature: Mahayana Uttara Tantra Shastra.* Translated by Ken and Katia Holmes. Scotland: KDDI, 1985.

———. *Distinguishing the Middle from the Extremes, Chapter Five: The Distinctive Path of the Mahayana.* Translated by Michele Martin. Kathmandu: Modern Press, 1992.

McLeod, Kenneth I., trans. *The Chariot for Travelling the Path to Freedom: The Life Story of Kalu Rinpoche.* San Francisco: Kagyu Dharma, 1985.

Mipham. *Calm and Clear.* Translated by Tarthang Tulku. Berkeley: Dharma Publishing, 1973.

Nagarjuna. *Golden Zephyr: Instructions from a Spiritual Friend.* Translated by Leslie Kawamura. Berkeley: Dharma Publishing, 1975.

———. *Nagarjuna's Letter to a Friend.* Translated by Geshe Lobsang Tharchin and Artemis Engle. Dharamsala: Library of Tibetan Works and Archives.

Nālandā Translation Committee, ed. and trans. *The Life of Marpa.* Boston: Shambhala, 1982.

———. *The Rain of Wisdom.* Boston: Shambhala, 1980.

Namgyal, Takpo Tashi. *Mahāmudrā: The Quintessence of Mind and Meditation.* Boston: Shambhala, 1986.

Obermiller, E., trans. *The History of Buddhism in India and Tibet by Bu-ston.* Delhi: Sri Satguru Publications, 1986.

———. *The Jewelry of Scripture of Bu-ston.* Delhi: Sri Satguru Publications, 1987.

Palmo, Anila Rinchen, trans. *Cutting Through Ego-Clinging.* Montignac: Dzambhala, 1988.

Patrul Rinpoche (rDza dpal sprul). *sNying-thig sngon-'gro'i khrid-yig Kun-bzang bla-ma'i zhal-lung.* Sichuan, China: Si-khron mi-rigs dpe-skrun-khang [Sichuan Ethnic Nationality Publications], 1988.

———. *Kun-zang La-may Zhal-lung.* Part 1. Transcribed by Pal-trul O-rgyan 'jigs-med chos-kyi dbang-po Rin-po-che. Translated and edited by Sonam T. Kazi. Upper Montclair, NJ: Diamond-Lotus Publishing, 1989.

———. *The Words of My Perfect Teacher.* San Francisco: Harper Collins, 1994.

Perdue, Daniel. *Debate in Tibetan Buddhism*. Ithaca: Snow Lion, 1992.

——. *Debate in Tibetan Buddhist Education*. Dharamsala: Library of Tibetan Works and Archives, 1976.

Reynolds, John. *The Golden Letters*. Ithaca: Snow Lion, 1996.

Ricard, Matthieu. *The Life of Shabkar: The Autobiography of a Tibetan Yogin*. Albany: State University of New York Press, 1994.

Robinson, Richard H. *The Buddhist Religion*. Belmont: Wadsworth Publishing Company, 1982.

Robinson, James B. *Buddha's Lions: The Lives of the Eighty-four Siddhas*. Berkeley: Dharma Publishing, 1979.

Roerich, George N., ed. *The Blue Annals*. 2 parts. Delhi: Motilal Banarsidass, 1979.

Shantideva. *A Guide to the Bodhisattva's Way of Life*. Translated by Stephen Batchelor. Dharamsala: Library of Tibetan Works and Archives, 1992.

Snellgrove, David. *The Hevajra Tantra: A Critical Study*. Part 1. London: Oxford University Press, 1959.

——. *Indo-Tibetan Buddhism*. 2 vols. Boston: Shambhala, 1987.

Snellgrove, David, and Hugh Richardson. *A Cultural History of Tibet*. Boston: Shambhala, 1986.

Sparham, Gareth. *The Tibetan Dhammapada: Sayings of the Buddha*. London: Wisdom Publications, 1986.

Stcherbatsky, Th. *Buddhist Logic*. 2 vols. New York: Dover Publications, 1930.

Surya Das. *The Snow Lion's Turquoise Mane*. San Francisco: Harper San Francisco, 1992.

Tai Situpa, The Twelfth Khentin. *Tilopa: Some Glimpses of His Life*. Eskdalemuir: Dzalendara Publishing, 1988.

Taranatha. *Taranatha's History of Buddhism in India*. Edited by Debiprasad Chattopadhyaya. Delhi: Motilal Banarsidass, 1990.

Tatz, Mark, trans. *Asanga's Chapter on Ethics: With the Commentary by Tsong-kha-pa*. Lewiston: Edwin Mellen Press, 1986.

Thinley Norbu. *Magic Dance: The Display of the Self-Nature of the Five Wisdom Dakinis*. New York: Jewel Publishing House, 1985.

——. *Small Golden Key to the Treasure of the Various Essential Necessities of General and Extraordinary Buddhist Dharma*. Boston: Shambhala, 1993.

——. *White Sail: Crossing the Waves of Ocean Mind to the Serene Continent of the Triple Gems*. Boston: Shambhala, 1992.

Thrangu Rinpoche. *Buddha Nature*. Translated by Erik Pema Kunsang. Kathmandu: Rangjung Yeshe Publications, 1988.

Tobgyal, Orgyen. *The Life and Teaching of Chokgyur Lingpa*. Kathmandu: Rangjung Yeshe Publications, 1988.

Trungpa, Chogyam. *The Life of Marpa the Translator*. Boston: Shambhala Publications, 1986.

——, ed. *The Rain of Wisdom*. Boulder: Shambhala, 1980.

Tsultrim Gyamtso Rimpoche. *Progressive Stages of Meditation on Emptiness*. Translated by Shenpen Hookham. Oxford: Longchen Foundation, 1988.

Tulku Thondup Rinpoche. *Buddhist Civilization in Tibet*. London: Routledge & Kegan Paul, 1987.

——. *Masters of Meditation and Miracles*. Boston: Shambhala, 1996.

Tulku Urgyen Rinpoche. *Rainbow Painting*. Boudhanath, Nepal: Rangjung Yeshe Publications, 1995.

Wayman, Alex. *The Buddhist Tantras*. London: Routledge & Kegan Paul, 1973.

——. *The Ethics of Tibet: Bodhisattva Section of Tsong-Kha-pa's Lam Rim Chen Mo*. Albany: State University of New York Press, 1991.

——. *Yoga of the Guhyasamājatantra*. Delhi: Motilal Banarsidass, 1977.

Willis, Janice D., trans. *On Knowing Reality: The Tattvārtha Chapter of Asanga's Bodhisattvabhūmi*. Columbia University Press: New York, 1979.

Yeshe Tsogyal. *Life and Liberation of Padmasambhava, Parts 1-2*. Dharma Publishing: Berkeley, 1978.